COUNTIES FERMANAGH & TYRONE

A

TOPOGRAPHICAL DICTIONARY

OF THE PARISHES, VILLAGES AND TOWNS
OF THESE COUNTIES IN THE 1830s

ILLUSTRATED WITH
CONTEMPORARY MAPS AND ENGRAVINGS

BY SAMUEL LEWIS

PREFACE

BY BRIAN M. WALKER

BELFAST

PUBLISHED BY FRIAR'S BUSH PRESS

2004

THIS SELECTED EDITION
PUBLISHED 2004
BY FRIAR'S BUSH PRESS
160 BALLYLESSON ROAD
BELFAST, BT8 8JU
NORTHERN IRELAND

FIRST PUBLISHED 1837
BY S. LEWIS & CO.
87 ALDERSGATE STREET, LONDON

COPYRIGHT OF THIS SELECTION AND ADDITION OF ILLUSTRATIONS IS RESERVED

ISBN 0-946872-64-3

TEXT COPIED BY IRISH TIMES (IRELAND.COM)

PRINTED BY DATAPLUS PRINT & DESIGN
13 HILL STREET, DUNMURRY, BT17 OAD

PREFACE

This volume brings together three important contemporary sources of information about life and society in Counties Fermanagh and Tyrone in the 1830's. The text is taken from the monumental two-volumed topographical dictionary of Ireland, published by Samuel Lewis in 1837. His work covered all of Ireland in alphabetical order in a grand total of 1405 double columned pages. Maps of the main towns have been photographed from the first edition Ordnance Survey maps, which were published in the mid 1830's, and are integrated into the text. A considerable number of engravings, mostly from the 1830's, has also been included. In the case of all three components of this book-the topographical text, the maps and the engravings, the period of the 1830's witnessed new heights in the availability and worth of such sources. Brought together here in this particular form, the material presents a special view of these parishes, villages and towns in the period before the great changes of Victorian Ireland. It gives a compelling record of agriculture, industry, population, buildings and antiquities over one hundred and sixty years ago.

Samuel Lewis, publisher

Our knowledge about the life of Samuel Lewis is fairly limited. We do know, however, that during the 1830's and 1840's he ran a publishing business in London, first at 87 Aldersgate Street and secondly at 13 Finsbury Place South. He died in 1865. More is known about the outcome of his publishing efforts, in particular the very successful series of topographical dictionaries for which he was responsible. His 4 volumed topographical dictionary for England appeared in 1831 (7th edition 1849) to be followed a year later by a similar two volumed work for Wales (4th edition 1849). In 1837 he produced a two volumed dictionary for Ireland (2nd edition 1842), accompanied by an atlas of the counties of Ireland. Finally, he published a three volumed topographical dictionary for Scotland in 1846.[1]

Production of the Irish dictionary involved a vast entreprenurial enterprise.[2] Starting in early 1833, agents were dispatched to all parts of Ireland to gather information for the work and also to obtain advance subscribers. The dictionary was priced at two guineas per volume while the atlas was also available for two guineas. As was explained in the preface to the first volume, compared to England and Wales, there was less available for Ireland in the form of county histories and other such work, so it was important to gain extensive personal information. His principal sources of information were local landowners and clergy. When the dictionary appeared finally in 1837, the list of subscribers (including many of his informants) ran to a total of nearly 10,000 names, including large numbers in both these counties.

The publication of the Irish dictionary led to considerable controversy, caused not by the content of the volumes but by objections from some of those listed as subscribers to being included on the list. A number of legal cases ensued over questions of liability for payment for the two books. There seems to have been relatively little debate over the accuracy of the contents. The 1842 revised edition made some corrections but also updated the figures in accordance with the 1841 census and replaced educational material with extra material on the railways. The entries reprinted here are from the first edition and so relate to the 1830's.

This dictionary by Lewis gives a unique coverage of life in Ireland, parish by parish and town by town. No-one before had produced such an extensive survey. At the same time as the appearance of these volumes by Lewis an enterprise was underway to record Irish society and economy as part of the Ordnance Survey (O.S.) with the writing of memoirs to accompany the production of the first O.S. maps for Ireland. This project collapsed finally in 1840, however, after only the northern counties had been investigated, and just one volume was published for the parish of Templemore in County Londonderry. Only in the last decade of the twentieth century have the memoirs been published.[3] These volumes by Lewis are very valuable for us today not just because he gathered important personal information at local level but also because he availed of much of the statistical and factual information which was now becoming available for Ireland, often through parliamentary papers and reports. In particular, he used the 1831 census report, new educational data and O.S. acreage figures.

At the same time, we must be aware of some of the perspectives and weaknesses of the material. A man of his time, Lewis approached his work from the standpoint of a society run by the gentry. The parishes are those of the Church of Ireland which was the established church. We must appreciate that some of his accounts of Irish pre history and archaeology would be questioned by historians and archaeologists today. His information on these matters reflects the state of knowledge about them at the time, which changed considerably in the course of the nineteenth century, thanks to the work of people such as John O'Donovan. For example his references to 'druidical altars', and some of his accounts of the origins of the early people of Ireland would not now be accepted. Those interested in the composition of placenames should check Lewis's interpretation with modern works on the subject.[4] It should also be noted that Lewis gives distances in Irish miles (10 Irish miles equal a little over 12 miles British). Spellings of names have been left as found in the original text.

Maps and map makers

Run by officers of the Royal Engineers, and starting in the 1820's, a complete mapping survey of the whole country was carried out under the auspices of the Ordnance Survey of Ireland, based at Phoenix Park in Dublin.[5] This led to the appearance in 1833 of the first six inches to the mile maps for County Londonderry, to be followed by similar maps for all the Irish counties over the next nine years. The first maps for County Tyrone were published in 1834 while those for County Fermanagh appeared in 1835. This surveying project was a vast undertaking which involved considerable expenditure and manpower. The result was a very extensive cartographic record for Ireland, which had no equivalent in the world at the time.

In this volume plans of the main towns in the two counties have been copied from the original 6 inch O.S. maps. For sake of greater clarity the town maps have been magnified by 40 per cent. Map publication dates have been recorded, but it should be noted that the actual surveying could have been done in the previous one or two years. We have also included a map of each of the two counties from Lewis's atlas. An advantage of this map is that it gives the location of the parishes, and, while it does not show the parish boundaries, it can be helpful to give people some idea of which parish their area is located in. The maps in the atlas were based on drawings reduced from the Ordnance Survey and other surveys.

Artists and engravers

The period from the early 1820's to the early 1840's witnessed an upsurge in the appearance of topographical views of Ireland, partly due to technological advances, such as the advent of line engraving on steel in the early 1820's. The bulk of the illustrations in this book come from the 1830's, although some are as late as 1847. The publication of the weekly *Dublin Penny Journal*, 1832–5, with its many wood engravings, was an important new departure in the level of illustrated material available at a low cost. The journal carried topographical articles and illustrations on many parts of Ireland. Besides the *Dublin Penny Journal*, there now appeared a large number of illustrated books, covering special areas or all of the country. Well known artists, such as George Petrie (who worked for the Ordnance Survey in the 1830's), were employed to provide drawings to be engraved for these works.

Of special interest in this activity is the work of a number of northern artists. Views by the Belfast born Andrew Nicholl (1804–86) appeared frequently, both in the *Dublin Penny Journal* and in various published tours and guides. James Howard Burgess (c.1817–90) of Belfast was a skilled topographical artist who provided 25 views for S.C. Hall's *Ireland: its scenery, character, &c.* (London, 1846).(6) The *Irish Penny Journal*, which ran only for the year 1840, contained work by Burgess and other artists. We have included here illustrations of Devenish and Enniskillen by Burgess which seem to have been published as individual prints in 1837.

In recent times engravings such as these have often been used to illustrate texts, but usually there has been little attempt to name the artist and engraver involved or to accurately date the picture. In this volume, however, an effort has been made to identify both the artist and engraver responsible for a particular piece of work. This has not been possible in every case and where the full information has not been given this is because it is not available. The title of the book, and the date and place of publication, have been given with each print so that we can establish a date for the particular view.

Brian M. Walker **Belfast, 2004**

References

(1) See Frederick Boase, (ed.) *Modern English biography*, vol. 2 (London, 1965), p. 417.

(2) See Tim Cadogan's introduction to *Lewis's Cork* (Cork, 1998). Extracts of parts of Co. Londonderry have been published by the enterprising Ballinascreen Historical Society. *Lewis's Loughinsolin*, foreword by Seamus Heaney, (Draperstown, 1999).

(3) Angelique Day and Patrick McWilliams, *Ordnance survey memoirs of Ireland*, vols 1–40 (Belfast, 1990–8).

(4) See Patrick McKay, *A dictionary of Ulster place-names* (Belfast, 1999); Gregory Toner (ed.), *Place-names of northern Ireland; vol. 5, Co. Derry; the Moyola Valley* (Belfast, 1996).

(5) See J.H. Andrews, *A paper landscape: the ordnance survey in nineteenth century Ireland* (Oxford, 1993; second edition, Dublin, 2002).

(6) See John Hewitt, *Art in Ulster* (Belfast, 1977). Bio. notes by Theo Snoody.

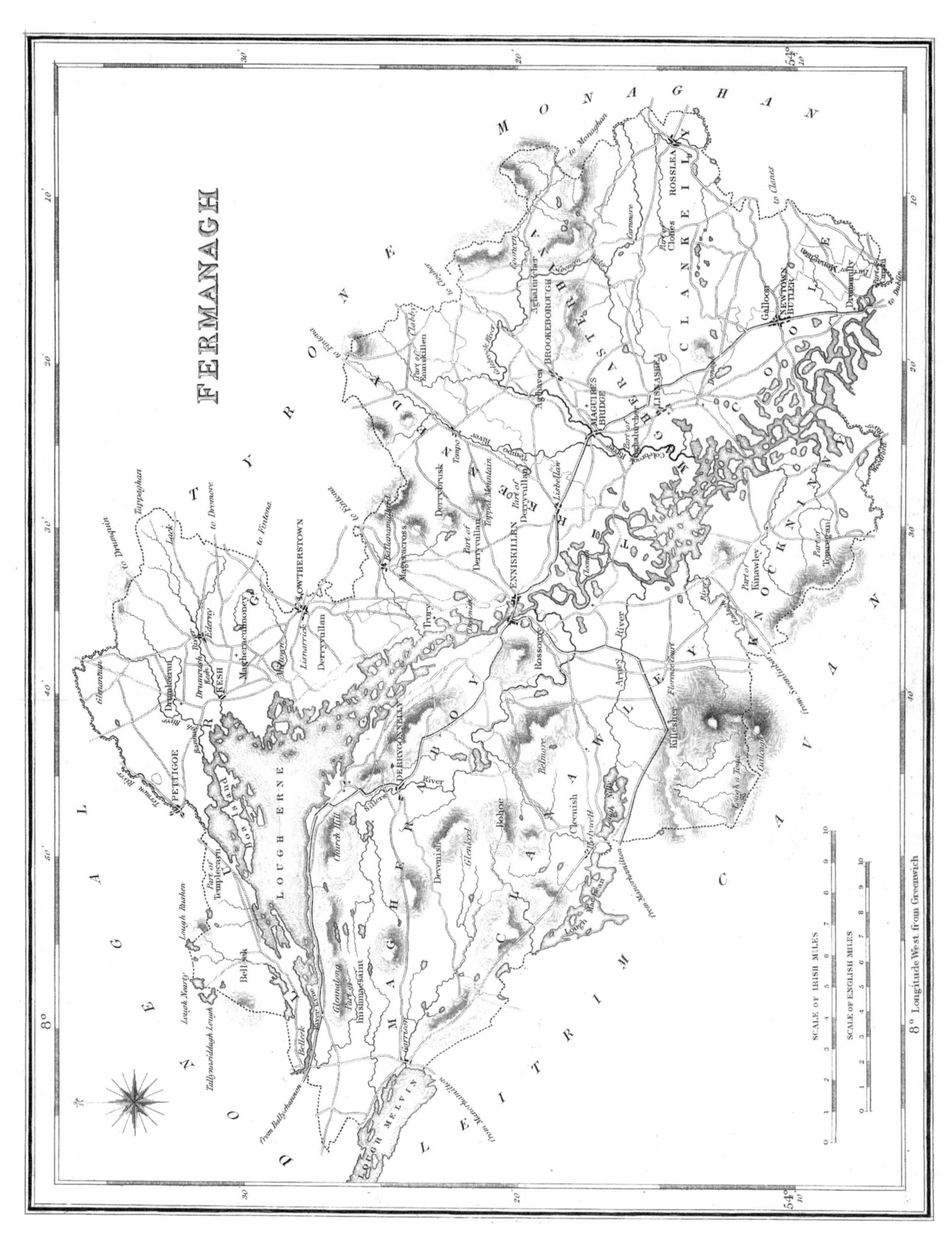

Fermanagh. Drawn by R. Creighton and engraved by I. Dower. From Lewis's Atlas, *(London, 1837).*

COUNTY FERMANAGH

A

TOPOGRAPHICAL DICTIONARY

FERMANAGH, an inland county, of the province of ULSTER, bounded on the east by Monaghan and, on the north by Donegal, on the west by Donegal and Leitrim, and on the south by Cavan. It extends from 54° 7′ to 54° 40′ (N. Lat.), and from 7° 1′ to 8° 5′ (W. Lon.); and comprises an area, according to the Ordnance survey, of 456,538½ acres, of which 320,599 are cultivated land, 46,755 are under water, and the remainder are unprofitable bog and mountain. The population, in 1821, amounted to 130,997; and in 1831, to 149,555.

The Erdini, according to some authorities, were the inhabitants of this district in the time of Ptolemy; but Whitaker considers it to have been part of the territory of the Nagnatae. By the ancient Irish it was called Feor Magh Eanagh, or "the Country of the Lakes," and Magh Uire, or "the Country of the Waters:" it was also called Ernai or Ernagh, and the inhabitants who lived round Lough Erne, Ernains and Erenochs, a name supposed to be derived from the Erdini. It was divided into two great portions, one called Targoll, the ancient seat of the Facmonii, and of the Macmanii, or the MacManuses; the other named Rosgoll, occupied by the Guarii or Guirii, from whom the MacGuires, or Maguires, derive their origin. This family was so powerful that the greater part of the county was for several centuries known by the name of MacGuire's country. It was made shire ground in the 11th of Elizabeth, by the name which it still retains. The unsettled state of the district at this period may be inferred from the anecdote told of its chieftain, when the lord-deputy sent to inform him that he was about to send a sheriff into his territory; Maguire's answer was, "that her majesty's officer would be received, but at the same time he desired to know his eric, the fine to be imposed on his murderer, in order that, if he happened to be slain by any of his followers, the amount might be levied on the offender's chattels."

It was one of the six counties which escheated to the Crown by the flight of the Earls of Tyrone and Tyrconnel, on an imputed conspiracy, and which were included in the celebrated scheme of James I. for the improvement of the north of Ireland, under the name of the Plantation of Ulster. According to the arrangements therein made, the county is supposed to have consisted of 1070 tates of 30 acres each, besides 46 islands, great and small: of these, 212 tates, containing about 6360 acres, were assigned to the church, and the remainder disposed of among the English and Scotch settlers, who, from their undertaking to fulfil the conditions of the plantation, were called Undertakers. A portion, consisting of 390 tates, was assigned to the head of the MacGuire family; and the rest of the native inhabitants were here, as in the other five counties, removed to waste lands in Munster or Connaught. The principal settlers were Sir James Belford, Sir Stephen Butler, Sir Wm. Cole, Sir John Hume, Malcolm Hamilton, John Archdall, George Hume, and John Dunbar, who were Scotchmen; John Sedborrow, Thomas Flowerdew, Edward Hatton, Sir Hugh Wirrall, George Ridgwaic, Sir Gerrard Lowther, Edw. Sibthorp, Henry Flower, Sir Edw. Blenerhasset, and Thomas Blenerhasset, Englishmen; besides whom, Sir John Davis, Capt. Harrison, Sir Henry Folliott, and Captains Gore and Atkinson, acquired large tracts in the allotments set apart for such natives as were suffered to reside. Of these, Con MacShane O'Neal, and Brian MacGuire were the only persons of sufficient consequence to be noted in the report to the English government on the state of the plantation in 1619.

In the war of 1688, this county became famous by the gallant stand made by its inhabitants, under the name of the Enniskillen men, in favour of King William, during which period they not only maintained themselves in the town of Enniskillen, thus preserving this important pass between Ulster and Connaught, in spite of all the attempts made to obtain possession of it, but made incursions into the neighbouring counties, from which they carried off many prisoners and much booty, and paralysed the operations of a large portion of the Irish army before Derry, from an apprehension of an attack from this quarter. After the relief of this city, they joined the army of William in Ulster, and from their gallant demeanour and knowledge of the country rendered him good service, and made the name of the Enniskilleners respected among their English friends and dreaded by the Irish enemy. The military spirit thus drawn forth has been maintained ever since, so that not only do the sons of the native farmers frequently prefer a soldier's life abroad to that of an agriculturist at home, but young men from other counties anxious to enlist travel thither to the recruiting parties which are always ready to receive them.

According to the ecclesiastical arrangements the county is partly in the diocese of Kilmore, but chiefly in that of Clogher. For the purposes of civil jurisdiction it is divided into the baronies of Clonkelly, Coole, Glenawly, Knockninny, Lurg, Magheraboy, Magherastephana, and Tyrkennedy; it contains the borough, market and county town of Enniskillen, the market and post-towns of Irvinestown (formerly Lowtherstown), Lisnaskea, and Brookborough; the market-town of Maguires-bridge (which has a penny post); and the post-towns of Florence-Court, Kesh, Tempo, Church Hill, Newtown-Butler, Belleek, and Lisbellaw, together with the villages of Ballinamallard, Ederney, and Holywell. Prior to the Union it sent four members to the Irish parliament, viz., two knights of the shire, and two burgesses for the borough of Enniskillen; and since that period it has returned three representatives to the Imperial parliament, the number for the borough having been then reduced to one, and so continued under the Reform act. The elections take place in the county town. The county constituency, as registered at the close of the January sessions, 1836, consists of 220 freeholders of £50, 246 of £20, and 1120 of £10; one leaseholder of £50, 24 of £20, and 36 of £10; two rent-chargers of £50, and 11 of £20;

Lower Lough Erne. Drawn by T. Creswick and engraved by R. Wallis. From S.C. Hall, Ireland: its scenery, character&c. *vol. iii (London, 1846).*

making a total of 1660 registered electors. The county is included in the North-west circuit. The assizes and general quarter sessions of the peace are held at Enniskillen, where the county gaol and courthouse are situated: quarter sessions are also holden at Newtown-Butler, where there are a sessions-house and bridewell. The number of persons charged with criminal offences, and committed for trial in 1836, was 409.

The local government is vested in a lord-lieutenant, 14 deputy-lieutenants, and 64 other magistrates, together with the usual county officers, including a coroner. The constabulary police consists of an inspector, paymaster, stipendiary magistrate, 4 officers, 21 constables, 90 sub-constables, and 5 horses, quartered in 20 stations; the expense of their maintenance is defrayed in equal proportions by Grand Jury presentments and by Government. The district lunatic asylum is at Armagh, the county infirmary is at Enniskillen, and there are dispensaries at Church Hill, Rosslea, Kesh, Brookbo rough, Maguires-bridge, Lisnaskea, Irvinestown, Newtown-Butler, Holywell, Ballinamallard, Belleek, and Lisbellaw. The amount of Grand Jury presentments for 1835 was £16,346.8.1$^3/_4$, of which £3098.19.9$^1/_2$ was for the roads, bridges, &c., of the county at large; £4380.11.1$^1/_4$ for the roads, bridges, &c., being the baronial charge; £6566.11.6$^1/_2$ for public buildings, charities, officers' salaries, and incidents; and £2300.5.8$^1/_2$ for the police. In the military arrangements the county is included in the northern district, and contains barracks for artillery and infantry at Enniskillen, affording accommodation for 14 officers and 547 non-commissioned officers and men, with 98 horses.

The surface is very uneven, and presents great varieties both of soil and aspect. On the eastern verge of the county the land is elevated and sterile, and on the western still more so: indeed, with the exception of small portions in the north and south, the county may be said to consist of hills environed by mountains, and having its centre depressed into a great natural basin or reservoir, serving as a receptacle for the numerous rivers and streams from the higher grounds, whose accumulated waters form one of the noblest lakes in Ireland. Of these mountains the most elevated is Cuilcagh, which, though generally considered as belonging to Leitrim and Cavan, has its lofty eastern extremity, 2188 feet high, altogether in Fermanagh. The Slievebaught or Slabby mountain, which forms the boundary towards Monaghan and, extends far westward into this county, and, in like manner, that of Barnesmore in Donegal penetrates southward into it. The most conspicuous of the mountains which are wholly within the county is Belmore, 1312 feet high, between the Shannon and the Erne. Tosset, or Topped mountain, of inferior elevation, commands a range of prospects, which for grandeur, variety, and extent is not surpassed by any other in the north of Ireland. Turaw mountain, rising boldly from the waters of Lough Erne, forms a beautiful and striking feature of its scenery. The other mountains of remarkable elevation are Glenkeel near Derrygonnelly, 1223 feet; North Shean, 1135; Tappahan on the borders of Tyrone, 1110; and Carnmore near Rosslea, 1034 feet.

But the grand distinguishing characteristic of the county is Lough Erne, which extends forty miles from north-west to south-east, forming in reality two lakes, embayed by mountains and connected by a deep and winding strait, on an island in the centre of which stands the county town of Enniskillen. Of the two lakes, the northern or lower, between Belleek and Enniskillen, is the larger, being upwards of 20 miles in length, and 7$^1/_2$ in its greatest breadth; the southern or upper, between the latter town and Belturbet, is 12 miles long by 4$^1/_2$ broad. Both are studded with numerous islands, which in some parts of the upper lake are clustered so closely together as to present the appearance rather of a flooded country than of a spacious lake. It is a popular opinion that the number of these islands equals that of the days in the year; but accurate investigation has ascertained that there are 109 in the lower lake, and 90 in the upper.

The largest is Bo or Cow island, near the northern extremity of the upper lake; it takes its name from being mostly under pasture. Ennismacsaint, also in the upper lake, is noted for a burying-ground, which is held in great veneration; Devenish island, in the same lake, near Enniskillen, is particularly remarkable for its ancient round tower and other relics of antiquity, all of which are described in the article on the parish of that name. The other more remarkable islands in this division are Eagle, Innisnakill, and Gully, all richly wooded; Cor and Ferney, mostly under pasture, and Herring island, said to derive its name from the quantities of fresh-water herring found near its shores. Innismore, the largest island in the upper lake, forms part of the two nearest parishes on the main land. Belleisle has long been celebrated for its natural beauties, which were much heightened by the judicious improvements they received when it was the residence of the Earl of Rosse: it is connected with the main land by an elegant bridge. Near it is Lady Rosse's island, so called from the improvements bestowed on it by that lady. Knockninny was used as a deer-park by the nobleman just named. In descending the lake from Belturbet, the first two miles present the appearance of a large river winding through the county without any striking features to arrest attention; but as the lake widens, a succession of rich and picturesque views opens upon the eye. The banks on each side, as well as the islands that present themselves in rapid succession, are clothed with stately timber, which rises boldly from the water's edge, occasionally interrupted by sweeps of low marsh overgrown with rushes and enlivened by herons and other aquatic fowl. After narrowing in to the strait of Enniskillen, and expanding again into a still wider sheet of water in the lower lake, it is finally contracted into a river which quits the county at the village of Belleek in a magnificent fall. The

Devenish Island. Drawn by J.Franklin and engraved by Mary Williams. From S.C. Hall, Ireland: its scenery, character&c. *vol. iii (London, 1846).*

lakes called Lough Melvin, Lough Macnean, and Lough Kane, which form part of the boundary between Fermanagh and Leitrim, may be considered as partly belonging to the former county.

The soil in some parts is a rich loam upon a substratum of limestone, or calcareous gravel; in others, a light friable soil on slaty gravel; and again in others, a heavy soil mixed with stones, beneath which is blue and yellow clay on a substratum of basalt, here called whinstone; but throughout almost every part, the soil is wet and cold, obstinately retaining the surface water unless counteracted by constant draining. The size of farms varies from 3 acres to 500; those of large size are mostly near the mountains, and occupied in grazing young cattle. Considerable tracts of land are let in bulk, and the holders of them are generally middlemen, who sublet in small portions: proprietors of this description are called Terney begs, or "Little Lords." The manure, which is seldom used for any crop except potatoes, is generally a compost of stable dung, lime, and bog mould; the scourings of ditches are sometimes used as a substitute for lime. Marl is in high repute; it is of a dusky white colour, mostly found at the bottom of bogs; near Florence-Court and in some other places it shews itself in large ridges resting upon gravel, whence issue numerous springs impregnated with vitriolic acid: in the vicinity of these springs the marl is found in various curious shapes, cylindrical, spherical, oblong, and curved, highly indurated, and of a dirty red colour, but when exposed to the action of a winter's atmosphere, and used either in top-dressing or as a compost, it retains its efficacy for two or three successive seasons. The staple crops are oats and potatoes, with some wheat; flax, barley, turnips, clover, and vetches are occasionally planted; the culture of barley is every year extending, but that of all the others is chiefly confined to the gentry and wealthy farmers. In the mountain districts, much of the land is cultivated with the spade or the old heavy wooden plough; in other parts, the use of the improved iron plough and light angular harrow is universal, as well as that of all other new and improved implements. The old car with solid wooden wheels has given way to the light cart with spoke-wheels, and the slide-car is rarely used, except in the most mountainous districts to bring turf down the precipitous roads.

These mountain farms are chiefly appropriated to the rearing of young cattle, great numbers of which are annually purchased in Leitrim, Sligo, and Donegal, at a year old, and kept by the mountain farmer for one or two years, when they are sold to the graziers of the adjoining counties; great numbers of milch cows are kept, and large quantities of butter made, which is mostly salted in firkins, and bought up in the neighbouring markets, chiefly for the merchants of Belfast and Newry. Perhaps less attention is paid to the breed of cattle in this than in any other county in Ireland; almost every sort of stock known in the kingdom is to be found here in a day's journey, but so crossed as to defy the possibility of distinguishing the original breeds; that best adapted to the soil and climate is the long-horned Roscommon. Sheep are numerous in some districts; they are generally a small mountain breed, and mostly kept for the purpose of furnishing wool for domestic clothing, but many of the gentry have very excellent stocks, being for the most part a cross between the Leicester and Sligo breed. Pigs, though found in all parts, are by no means so numerous as in the adjoining county of Monaghan; indeed in many instances the food which should be given to the pig is carefully saved for the cow. Goats are so numerous as to be highly detrimental to the hedges, which are everywhere stunted by the browsing of this animal. The horses are bad, being neither of the hack nor waggon kind; larger than the poney and smaller than the galloway: but great numbers of a very superior description are brought into the county by dealers for the use of the gentry. The fences for the most part are dry stone walls, or sods, except in the lower and level districts, where white thorn and other quicksets have been planted; these, wherever properly protected, thrive remarkably well. Draining is sometimes practised, mostly by open trenches; irrigation rarely or never.

Every part of the county appears to produce forest timber spontaneously, particularly ash and beech; to such an extent does the former grow, as to be called the weed of the country; and towards the northern part and in some other districts, excellent ash and beech are to be seen growing to a large size as hedgerow timber. At Crum and Castle Caldwell there are excellent and extensive woods of oak, beech, and ash, and much full-grown ornamental timber and young plantations around Florence-Court and Castle Coole; indeed, plantations are more or less connected with the residence of almost every gentleman, and they are yearly increasing. The fuel universally used is turf, cut from the numerous bogs scattered over every part of the county, from the lowest levels to the sides, and even to the summits of the mountains. Coal is sometimes brought to Enniskillen, but the expense of conveyance limits its use to the more wealthy part of the community.

In a geological point of view this county is highly interesting: the great central limestone district of Ireland terminates in it, and the western coal and iron formation commences; here the granite of Donegal forms a junction with the basaltic range, which, with little intermission, extends to the coast of Antrim; here also the Escars (that extraordinary chain of low hills, which extends from Lough Neagh to the remotest part of Galway and Mayo,) seem to form a nucleus, whence they radiate in every direction; so that within a very limited space are found almost every kind of rounded nodule, from the jasper and agate down to the softest clay slate. Generally speaking, the rock of the county is either secondary limestone, abounding with organic remains (particularly encrinites), or quartose sandstone, in some districts equal in closeness of grain, uniformity of structure, and durability to any in the British islands. Limestone of several kinds is found in the islands of Lough Erne, and in other places on the mainland; the quarries of the latter are extensively worked. Near Florence-Court is brown marble beautifully veined; it receives a fine polish, and when worked into ornaments presents a surface which, for mellowness of tint and variety of veins, is not excelled even by the celebrated marble of Iona. In the parish of Killasher are large beds of marble, having a perpendicular face of 53 feet in height, projecting boldly from the neighbouring cliffs; it is of a grey colour, often beautifully clouded, but it has never been worked for ornamental purposes.

Near the foot of Cuilcagh are vast deposits of ironstone, veins of which can also be traced in the bed of the neighbouring streams: numerous mines were opened, and the ore extensively wrought as long as the forest afforded fuel; but when this source failed, the works were abandoned, and time furnaces and mills have gone to decay. In this mountain and in the Tosset are thin seams of coal, which appear to form the verge of the great Leitrim and Roscommon field, the indications and strata of the base of Cuilcagh, exactly corresponding with those of the Iron mountain in the county of Leitrim; some slight excavations have been made by the peasantry, but no effort on an extended scale has been attempted to search for this valuable fossil. In the hills of Glengarron are also indications of coal; but the great quantity of turbary in every part affords so many facilities for procuring turf at a cheap rate, as to prevent any effort towards the working of the collieries. When the canal between Loughs Neagh and Erne is finished, and the navigation opened to Ballyshannon, there is every reason to hope that the mineral treasures of Fermanagh will prove a new source of national wealth and prosperity.

Fermanagh may be said to be almost exclusively an agricultural county: the only staple manufacture is that of linen, which in some districts is briskly carried on; the cloth for the most part is 7/8ths; a stronger kind, principally for domestic use, is made from the refuse and tow. Flax-spinning is general throughout the county; scarcely a house is without a wheel and reel. The yarn is carried to the market-towns, and bought lip in large quantities for the manufactures of the more northern counties. Wool-spinning prevails in the mountain districts, and excellent flannels and blankets are made: druggets, with linen warps of a very superior quality, are also manufactured; likewise a very useful stuff, principally for domestic wear.

The fish most common in Lough Erne are salmon, perch, pike, bream, trout, and eels. It is said that perch first appeared in this lake about the year 1760, and that they were seen in all the other lakes in Ireland and in the Shannon at the same period. There are some large eel-weirs

Monea Castle. Engraved by Branston. From The Irish Penny Journal, *vol.1, 1841.*

at Enniskillen, where great quantities of that fish are caught: they come from the sea when young, and are intercepted in their return; those which are not sold fresh, or sent to Dublin, are cured in barrels containing about eight dozen each, and sold at Belturbet. There is also an eel-weir near the falls of Belleek; but this town is more remarkable for its salmon fishery, considered, in conjunction with that at Ballyshannon, a little lower down the river, to be one of the most productive in Ireland. Large flights of wild geese and swans occasionally visit Lough Erne towards the close of the year, the appearance of which is considered to prognosticate a severe winter.

The only river of any consequence is the Erne, which, entering the county a short distance from Belturbet, flows into Lough Erne at its southern extremity, and, after passimig Belleek at its northern extremity, discharges itself into Donegal bay at Ballyshannon; all the other rivers empty themselves into Lough Erne. The Finn is navigable for boats as far as Cumber bridge on the confines of Monaghan; the Pettigo and the Omna rise near Lough Derg, in Donegal, and after uniting their streams fall into the lake a mile south of the town of Pettigo: the Scillies rises near Churchhill, and takes a southern direction to the lake. There are upwards of fifty smaller streams, all contributing to augment the waters of the great central reservoir. The Ulster canal, intended to unite Lough Neagh and Lough Erne, will enter this county from Monaghan, not far from Clones; thence proceeding towards Belturbet, it is to fall into Lough Erne. The roads are numerous, but for the most part badly laid out; many of them are flooded during winter, exceedingly inconvenient, and kept in indifferent repair.

The number of Danish raths in all parts is very great, but none of them are peculiarly singular in their construction. Tumuli also occur, surrounded with circles of upright stones; when opened, urns and stone coffins have been found in them. At Wattle bridge, three miles from Newtown-Butler, on the banks of the Finn, are the remains of a Druidical temple. There are but few remains of monastic institutions: those of Devenish and Gola are the only structures in which traces of the original buildings can be discovered: the abbeys of Ennismacsaint, Cleenish, Kilskerry, and Rossory have been converted into parish churches: those of Ariodmuilt, Derough, Domnachmore, Inniscasin, Inniseo, Innisrocha, and Loughuva are now known only by name. About a mile from Pettigo stand the ruins of Castle MacGrath, the residence of the first Protestant bishop of Clogher, from whom the building took its name. Lisgool, a castle on the bank of the Rale opposite to Enniskillen, also suffered during the civil war of 1641, being burnt by the Irish. The ruins of Callahill castle are near Florence-Court. Castle Hume, which was the seat of Lord Loftus, is now a pile of ruins. Enniskillen, which was little more than a fort in Elizabeth's time, has since completely changed its character; the castle is in ruins, and its defences and outworks have been gradually converted by the progress of civilization into peaceful and substantial dwelling-houses. The modern residences of the nobility and gentry are noticed in the articles on the parishes in which they are respectively situated.

The peasantry are a fine race, much superior in appearance to those of any of the other northern districts: they are tall, well formed, and robust: their countenances display the bloom of health, and they possess that uninterrupted flow of spirits which is the constant attendant on regular living and active, yet not over-strained, industry. Whether from habit or a natural propensity, the people do not rise until a late hour in the morning, and the cows are not milked until noon. The cottiers who dwell in the more retired and mountainous parts are poor, and their cabins are wretched huts, with a wattled door and a straw mat on the inside; many of the herdsmen, who are able to give their daughters a marriage portion of £20 and a feather bed, live in these cabins. The lower classes have no confidence in physicians: when one is called in, the patient despairs of life; hence a dislike is entertained for the whole medical profession. Yet, notwithstanding the reluctance to spend money upon medicine, considerable sums are lavished on the wake which precedes interment. The English language is universally spoken, and most of the children are educated in the parochial and national schools.

Mineral springs are very numerous: Rutty gives a list of twenty, partly chalybeate, partly sulphureous. Of the former are those of Aghalun, Coolauran, Drumcroe, Killinshanvally, Largy, and Tullyveel; of the latter, Aghnahinch, Ashwood, Derryinch, Derrylester, Killasher, Lisbleak (two springs), Meham (two springs), Owen Brewn, and Pettigo: the water of the last-named is more strongly impregnated with the mineral than even the celebrated spring at Swanlinbar. A spring at Maguires-bridge, and two at Drumgoon, are sulphureous, with a prevailing admixture of an alkali. Four miles north-west of Enniskillen, near Ballycassidy, are some natural caves called the Daughton: the entrance is by a large arch, 25 feet high, the roof being composed of various pieces of rock in regular order; the passage leads to a second vault of the same form, but not so high, and thence it is continued by narrow windings to a brook, which, passing through unknown recesses, discharges itself at the first entrance. At Belcou, a small distance west of Enniskillen, is a celebrated well, called Davagh Phadric, reputed the best cold bath in Ireland, and in great esteem for nervous and paralytic disorders: it discharges a large stream which turns two mills at the short distance of 150 yards from its mouth. This county gave the title of Viscount to the Verney family, now extinct.

AGHALURCHER a parish, partly in the barony of CLOGHER, county of TYRONE, but chiefly in that of MAGHERASTEPHENA, county of FERMANAGH, and province of ULSTER, on the mail coach road from Cavan to Enniskillen; containing, with the towns of Maguire's-bridge and Lisnaskea, 15,218 inhabitants. This parish is situated on Lough Erne, and is 17 miles in length (extending from the island of Cordillar, near Crumcastle, to Ballaghlough, within two miles of Clogher), and 5 miles in breadth. It comprises, according to the Ordnance survey, 47,015$^3/_4$ statute acres (including 3157$^1/_4$ covered with water), of which 4708$^1/_4$ are in, and 42,307$^1/_2$ in Fermanagh, and of which also, about one-fourth are pasturable mountain and bog. The system of agriculture is greatly improved, and the crops and stock are generally productive and of good quality; the peasantry, in addition to their agricultural pursuits, are employed in spinning and weaving, and are generally industrious and in comfortable circumstances. Limestone and limestone gravel abound, and there are some good quarries of freestone and of mill-stone. Slushill quarry is considered one of the best in the North of Ireland, and produces freestone of excellent quality. The only river of note is Maguire's river, which runs nearly the whole length of the parish; it is navigable, and abounds with pike, perch, trout, and eels. There are two bridges over this river, one at Maguire's-bridge (which is a flourishing market-town), and one at Ballindanaford, between that place and Lough Erne, a substantial structure of seven large arches, on the great line of road. Lough Erne, in which are seven islands included within this parish, abounds with salmon, pike, eels, perch, and bream; it is navigable from Belleek, and affords a facility of supplying the barracks of Belturbet with turf from this place.

The principal seats are Cole-Brooke, the residence of Sir A. B. Brooke, Bart.; Drumgoon, of R. Graham, Esq.; Curragh, of Capt. Chartres; Nutfield, of Lady Brooke; Shebrag, of H. Gresson, Esq.; and Holybrook, of H. Leslie, Esq. The living is a rectory and vicarage, in the diocese of Clogher, and in the patronage of the Provost and Fellows of Trinity College, Dublin: the tithes amount to £831. The church, a plain building at Coletrain, for the erection of which the late Board of First Fruits, in 1762, gave £200, was, by an act of the 7th of Geo. III. (1767), constituted the parish church: the Ecclesiastical Commissioners have lately granted £142 for its repair. There is also a chapel of ease at Lisnaskea. The glebe-house, with a glebe comprising 518 statute acres, of which two-thirds are arable land, and one-third moor and bog, is situated within a mile and a half from the church; there is also another glebe, which is from 5 to 6 miles distant from either the church or chapel. The R. C. parish is co-extensive with that of the Established Church; there are two chapels, one at Maguire's-bridge, and the other called the Moate Chapel, near Lisnaskea. There are also places of worship for Presbyterians and Primitive Wesleyan Methodists at Maguire's-bridge; the former is in connection with the Synod of Ulster, and of the third class. There are seven public schools, affording instruction to about 440 boys and 200 girls; also six Sunday schools, and ten private schools, in which latter are about 300 boys and 160 girls. Within two miles of Lisnaskea are the venerable ruins of the ancient church of Aghalurcher, said to have been built towards the close of the 9th century, and dedicated to St. Ronan. There are some remains of an old castle on the townland of Aheter, within a mile of Five-mile-town, on the Cole-Brooke estate, in which the insurgents are said to have sustained a siege in the last rebellion of the Maguires. There are two old castles in Largy deer-park; and one in the town of Brookboro', in the parish of Aghaveagh, all of which belonged to the Maguire family; and on Naan, an island in Lough Erne, are the remains of a very extensive castle, which in remote times was a formidable strong hold, surrounded on all sides by water of the lake more than a mile in breadth. There are numerous sulphureous and chalybeate springs in the parish. – See MAGUIRE'S-BRIDGE and LISNASKEA.

AUGHAVEA, or AGHAVEAGH, a parish, in the barony of MAGHERASTEPHENA, county of FERMANAGH, and province of ULSTER, on the road from Lisnaskea to Five-mile-town; containing, with the post-town of Brookborough, 6281 inhabitants. It comprises, according to the Ordnance survey, 17,142 statute acres, of which 10,096 are applotted under the tithe act. About $17^1/_2$ acres are water, and nearly one-fourth of the land is bog or mountain, the former affording good fuel, and the latter pasturage for cattle; there is no wasteland but what may occur from neglect or from a bad system of cultivation. The greater portion of the land is under tillage, and the system of agriculture is improving. There are some excellent quarries of freestone, which is raised for building and for other uses. The principal seats are Nutfield, the residence of Lady Brook; Abbey Lodge, of J. Macartney, Esq.; Greenhill, of Major Irvine; Whitepark, of A. Bailey, Esq. and Gola, of Major Dundas. The living is a rectory and vicarage, in the diocese of Clogher, and in the patronage of the Bishop; the tithes amount to £300; there are 14 townlands in the parish, the tithes of which are annexed to the old abbey of Lisdoune, in the possession of the Leonard family, and are not included in the applotment under the tithe act. The church is a plain edifice, erected by aid of a gift of £200 and a loan of £300 from the late Board of First Fruits, in 1813 and divine service is also performed every Sunday in the school-house at Brookborough. The glebe-house is a handsome modern building; the glebe comprises 43 acres. In the R. C. divisions the parish forms part of the union or district of Aughalurcher, and has a chapel. There is a place of worship for Wesleyan Methodists at Brookborough, where is the parochial school, supported under the patronage of Sir A. H. Brooke, Bart. There are also five other schools in the parish. – See BROOKBOROUGH

BALLYNAMALLARD, a village, in the parish of MAGHERACROSS, barony of TYRKENNEDY, county of FERMANAGH, and province of ULSTER, $5^1/_4$ miles (N. by E.) from Enniskillen, on the road to Omagh; containing 72 houses and 323 inhabitants. It is a constabulary police station; and has fairs on Feb. 12th, Aug. 5th, and Nov. 28th, of which only the first is kept and is a good fair for horses. There is a penny post to Enniskillen and Omagh. The parish church is in the village; and there are also places of worship for Wesleyan and Primitive Methodists, and a dispensary. – See MAGHERACROSS.

BELCOE, a village, in the parish of BOHOE, barony of GLENAWLEY, county of FERMANAGH, and province of ULSTER, 9 miles (W. S. W.) from Enniskillen: the population is returned with the parish. It is situated near Lough Macnean, on the confines of the county of Cavan, and has fairs on April 5th, June 5th, Aug. 5th, Oct. 6th, and Nov. 26th. Here is a noted well, called Darugh Phadric. – See BOHOE.

BELLEEK, a parish, in the barony of LURG, county of FERMANAGH, and province of ULSTER, 3 miles (E.) from Ballyshannon; containing 2702 inhabitants, of which number, 260 are in the village. This place is situated on Lough Erne, and on the road from Enniskillen to Ballyshannon, and was erected into a parish in 1792, by disuniting 36 townlands from the parish of Templecarn; it comprises, according to the Ordnance survey, $12.848^1/_2$ statute acres, of which 9706 are applotted, under the tithe act, and 2576 are water. The land is principally heathy mountain, but that which is under tillage is of very superior quality; the state of agriculture, though very backward, is gradually improving; there is a large tract of bog, and abundance of limestone. The seats are Castle Caldwell, the residence of J. C. Bloomfield, Esq., and Maghramena, of W. Johnston, Esq. The village contains 47 houses, and has a penny post to Ballyshannon and Enniskillen. It is a station of the constabulary police; fairs are held on Feb. 3rd, March 17th, May 17th, June 20th, and Oct. 10th, and petty sessions every alternate Thursday. The living is a rectory and vicarage, in the diocese of Clogher, and in the patronage of the Bishop: the tithes amount to £110. The church, a neat plain edifice, was erected in 1790, and the Ecclesiastical Commissioners have recently granted £267.9.2 for its repair. The glebe-house is a handsome residence: the glebe comprises 660 statute, acres. In the R. C. divisions the parish forms part of the union or district of Templecairn or Pettigo; the chapel is a spacious and well-built edifice, with a slated roof. There are schools at Belleek and Tullynabehogue, partly supported by the rector; and at Castle Caldwell is a school supported by Mrs. Bloomfield. In these schools are about 60 boys and 80 girls; and there are also three pay schools, in which are about 180 boys and 70 girls, and a Sunday school. There are some ruins of the old church; on the shore of Lough Keenaghan are those of an abbey; and there are remains of several Danish forts in the parish.

BOHOE, a parish, partly in the barony of MAGHERABOY, but chiefly in that of CLANAWLEY, county of FERMANAGH, and province of ULSTER, $5^1/_2$ miles (W.)

from Enniskillen; containing 2581 inhabitants. It is situated on the road from Enniskillen to Sligo, and comprises, according to the Ordnance survey, 15,058½ statute acres, of which 6151¼ are in the barony of Magheraboy, and 8907¼ in that of Clanawley. The living is a rectory and vicarage, in the diocese of Clogher, and in the patronage of the Bishop: the tithes amount to £120. The church, a plain edifice, was erected by aid of a gift of £200 from the late Board of First Fruits, in 1777, and the Ecclesiastical Commissioners have recently granted £157.10 for its repair. There is no glebe-house; the glebe comprises 142 acres. In the R. C. divisions the parish forms part of the union or district of Devenish or Derrygonelly, and also part of that of Innismacsaint; the chapel, an indifferent building, belongs to the union of Devenish. The parochial school is supported by an annual donation from the incumbent, aided by subscription; and affords instruction to about 50 boys and 30 girls; and there are four pay schools, in which are about 150 boys and 70 girls. The mountain of Belmore, in this parish, has an elevation of 1312, and that of Glenkeel 1223, feet above the level of the sea.

BOW, or BOA, ISLAND, partly in the parish of TEMPLECARNE, and partly in that of DRUMKEERAN, barony of LURG, county of FERMANAGH, and province of ULSTER, 2 miles (S.) from Pettigo; containing 382 inhabitants. This island, situated in the upper portion of the lower Lough Erne, comprises, according to the Ordnance survey, 1342 statute acres, of which nearly 787 are in Drumkeeran, and the remainder in the parish of Templecarne. The land is good, and the island is divided into a number of small farms varying from two to forty acres. There is a fine quarry of freestone. In the townland of Caldragh is a burial-ground.

BROOKBOROUGH, a post-town, in the parish of AUGHAVEA, barony of MAGHERASTEPHENA, county of FERMANAGH, and province OF ULSTER, 13 miles (E.) from Enniskillen, and 75½ miles (N.W.) from Dublin; containing 83 houses and 480 inhabitants. This town is situated on the road from Lisnaskea to Five-mile-town, and is a chief constabulary police station. Fairs are held on the third Tuesday of every month, for the sale of cattle, sheep, and pigs, and of butter, cloth and yarn; premiums are given every fair day to the largest purchasers by a committee who have the management of the fairs. A manorial court is held occasionally, at which small debts are recoverable; and petty sessions are held every alternate Tuesday. Divine worship, according to the form of the Established Church, is performed in a parochial school-house every Sunday evening; and there is a place of worship for Wesleyan Methodists.

CHURCH-HILL, a post-town, in the parish of INNISMACSAINT, barony of MAGHERABOY, county of FERMANAGH, and province of ULSTER, 9 miles (N. W.) from Enniskillen, and 89½ miles (N. W.) from Dublin: the population is returned with the parish. This place is situated near the mail coach road from Dublin to Ballyshannon, and has a sub-post-office to the latter place and Enniskillen. Fairs are held on the 14th of May, 30th of August, and 30th of November. There is a place of worship for Wesleyan Methodists; and a dispensary.

CLEENISH, a parish, partly in the baronies of MAGHERASTEPHANA and TYRKENNEDY, but chiefly in the barony of CLANAWLEY, county of FERMANAGH, and province of ULSTER; containing, with the post-town of Lisbellaw (which see), 10,557 inhabitants. This place derived its name, originally Cluan Innis, from an island in Lough Erue, where was a monastery, of which St. Synell was abbot about the middle of the 6th century, and with whom St. Fintan resided for more than 18 years. The parish, which is situated on the shores of Lough Erne, and on the road from Dublin to Enniskillen, comprises, according to the Ordnance survey, 36,531 statute acres (including islands), of which 9961/4 are in the barony of Magherastephana, 48981/4 in that of Tyrkennedy, and 30, small loughs. In Upper Lough Erne are several islands, of which those of Bellisle, Killygowan, and several smaller ones, arc within the limits of this parish. There is little wood, except on gentlemen's demesnes, and there are several bogs and a large tract of mountain. The land is of good quality, and the system of agriculture is improving; a large portion is in meadow and pasture, and that which is under tillage produces good crops. Limestone and freestone are abundant and are quarried for agricultural and for building purposes; and in the mountainous parts of the parish good flags are obtained. The gentlemen's seats are Fairwood Park, the residence of J. Denham, Esq.; Skea, of G. Hassard, Esq.; Garden Hill, of W. Hassard, Esq.; Bellisle, of the Rev. J. G. Porter; Snow Hill, of J. D. Johnstone, Esq.; Russian, of Capt. Jones; Ballanaleck, of A. Nixon, Esq.; Lisbofin House, of C. Fausset, Esq. Corrard House, the property of Sir A. B. King, Bart.; and Cliniharnon Cottage, the residence of the Rev. J. O'Reilly, commanding fine lake and mountain views. Near it is a holy well, overspread by the branches of a large thorn. Fairs are held at Holywell and Lisbellaw, for cattle and pigs. A manorial court is held on the estate of Gen. Archdall: and petty sessions are held at Shanmullagh and Lisbellaw every fortnight.

The living is a rectory and vicarage, in the diocese of Clogher, and in the patronage of the Provost and Fellows of Trinity College, Dublin: the tithes amount to £568.15.4. The church is a neat edifice, built in 1818 by aid of a gift of £900 from the late Board of First Fruits, and is surrounded by plantations. There are also chapels of ease at Lisbellaw and Mullaghdan, both neat buildings, to the latter of which the Ecelesiastical Commissioners have recently made a grant of £134.9.11 for repairs. The glebe-house is a good residence, built in 1825; the glebe comprises 840 statute acres. In the R. C. division is the parish forms part of the union or district of Enniskillen, and is partly a parish of itself; there are four chapels, one of which, at Lisbellaw, belongs to the union of

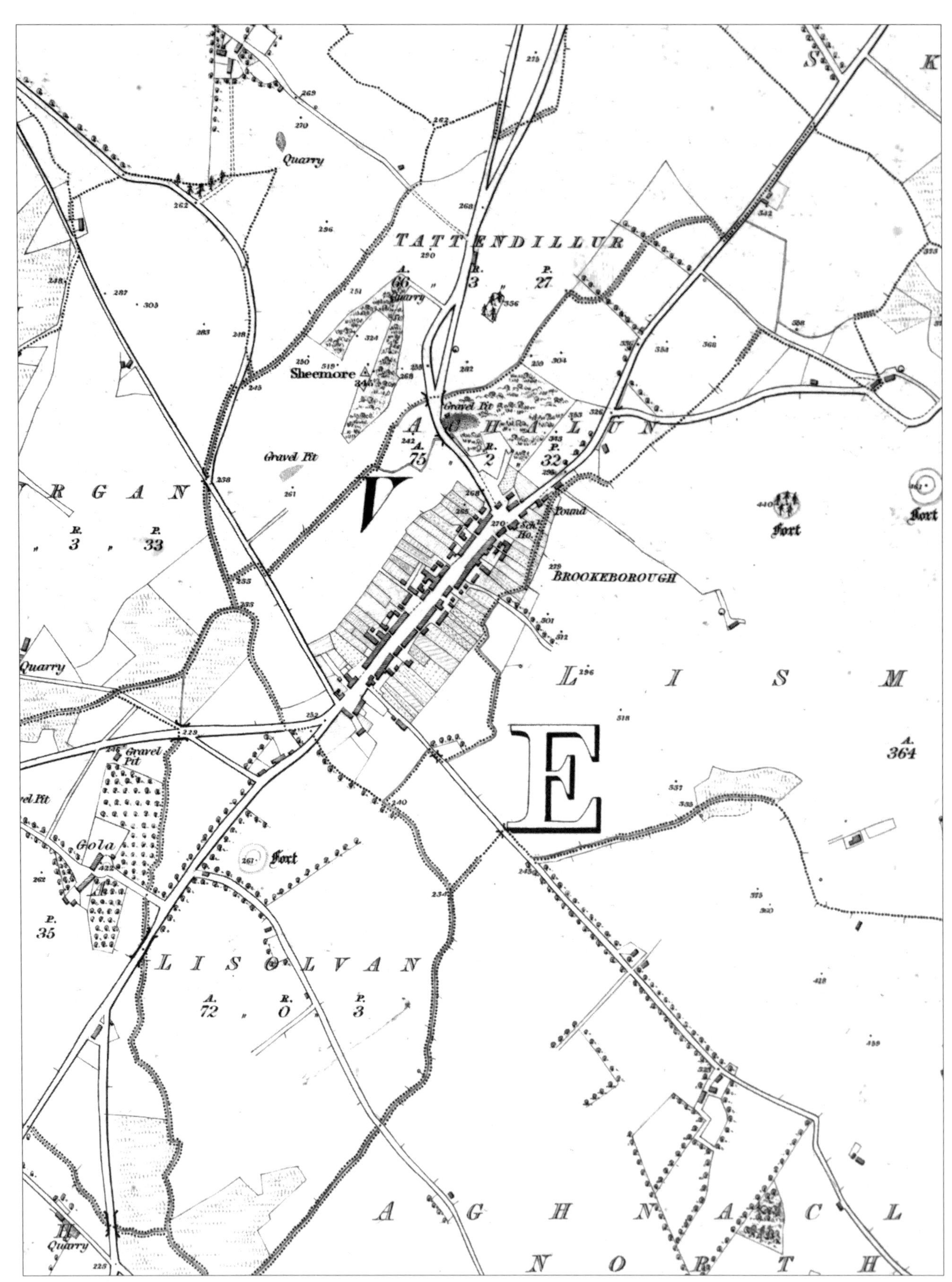

Brookeborough. Part of 6 inch O.S. map of Co.Fermanagh, sheet 28, published 1835 (reproduced at 140%).

Enniskillen, and the other three to this parish; the latter are situated respectively at Mullaghdan, Mullymeisker, and Holywell, and are all neat edifices; that at Holywell was built in 1829, at an expense of £400. There are two places of worship for Presbyterians of the Seceding Synod, one of the second class at Lisbellaw, and the other at Corrard. There is also at Lisbellaw a place of worship for Wesleyan Methodists. There are two schools aided by subscription, and a national school at Mullymeisker, in which together about 200 boys and 130 girls are instructed. There are also 16 pay schools, in which are about 560 boys and 300 girls, and seven Sunday schools. Several mineral springs exist in different parts of the parish, but they are not used medicinally.

DERRYBRUSK, a parish, partly in the barony of MAGHERASTEPHENA, but chiefly in that of TYRKENNEDY, county of FERMANAGH, and province of ULSTER, 4 miles (N. E.) from Enniskillen; containing 1329 inhabitants. It comprises, according to the Ordnance survey, 4656$^1/_4$ statute acres, of which 4373$^1/_4$ are in the barony of Tyrkennedy; 241$^1/_2$ are water, and 2298 are applotted under the tithe act. Adjoining Lough Erne a monastery for Dominican friars was founded, and dedicated to the Blessed Virgin, by MacManus, lord of the place, of which there are still some remains, also traces of the village of Gola, in which it was situated. Derrybrusk House is the seat of J. Deering, Esq. The living is a rectory and vicarage, in the diocese of Glogher, and in the patronage of the Bishop: the tithes amount to £77.10.9$^1/_4$; the glebe comprises 40 acres. There has been no church from time immemorial in this parish; the Protestant inhabitants of the central and southern portions attend the churches of the neighbouring parishes, and divine service is performed in a school-house once on the first Sunday in every month. There is a school at Ballyreague, in which are about 50 children.

DERRYGONNELLY, a market-town, partly in the parish of DEVENISH, and partly in that of INNISMACSAINT, barony of MAGHERABOY, county of FERMANAGH, and province of ULSTER, 7 miles (N. W.) from Enniskillen, on the road to Sligo; the population is returned with the respective parishes. This town, which is the property of Gen. Archdall, consists of one main street of newly built houses, and a market-house: it has a penny post to Enniskillen. The market is on Saturday; and fairs are held on the 24th of each month for general farming stock. A constabulary police force is stationed here, and petty sessions are held every alternate week: a manorial court also is occasionally held. It contains a R. C. chapel dependent on that of Devenish, which union or district is also called Derrygonnelly, and a place of worship for Wesleyan Methodists. Near the town are the ruins of an old church, originally a chapel of ease to the parochial church, built by the Dunbar family.

DERRYVULLEN, a parish, partly in the barony of TYRKENNEDY, but chiefly in that of LURG, county of FERMANAGH, and province of ULSTER, on the road from Enniskillen to Kesh; containing, with the post-town of Irvinestown, 10,646 inhabitants. This parish comprises, according to the Ordnance survey (including islands and detached portions), 23,645$^3/_4$ statute acres, of which 15,070$^3/_4$ are in the barony of Lurg, 2576$^1/_4$ acres are in Lower Lough Erne, and 571 in small loughs. It is in six detached parts, which are severally on the roads from Enniskillen to Pettigoe, Lisnaskea, Tempo, Ballynamallard, and Irvinestown, and from Maguire's-bridge to Florence-Court: this last portion includes part of Eanismore island, half of which is in this parish and the remainder in Cleenish. The land is of middling quality, and the state of agriculture improving; the arable land is estimated to comprise 12,000 acres, and there are 500 acres of bog. The gentlemen's seats are Castle Archdall, the residence of Gen. Archdall; Rosfad, of J. Richardson, Esq.; Doraville, of Capt. H. Irvine; and Riverstown, of C. Archdall, Esq. The living is a rectory and vicarage, in the diocese of Clogher, and in the patronage of the Provost and Fellows of Trinity College, Dublin: the tithes amount to £606.8.9$^3/_4$. There is a glebe-house, with a glebe of 600 acres. The church is at Irvinestown (which see), and there is a chapel of ease on the road from Enniskillen to Lisnaskea. In the R. C. divisions the parish is partly in the union or district of Enniskillen, and partly the head of a district, called Whitehill; it contains three plain chapels at Lisson, Whitehill, and Lissaroe. The Primitive and Wesleyan Methodists have each a place of worship. The parochial school-house was given by the Earl of Belmore; there are also eight other schools, in which about 460 boys and 300 girls are educated; about 270 boys and 140 girls are taught in nine private schools, and there are five Sunday schools.

DEVENISH, a parish, in the barony of MAGHERABOY, county of FERMANAGH, and province of ULSTER, 2$^1/_2$ miles (N. W.) from Enniskillen; containing 8219 inhabitants. This parish takes its name, signifying "Ox Island," from the island of Devenish in Lough Erne; and comprises, according to the Ordnance survey (including a detached portion and islands), 32,243$^1/_4$ statute acres, of which 1436$^1/_4$ are in Lower Lough Erne, 193$^3/_4$ in Lough Melvin, and 312$^3/_4$ in small lakes. More than half may be considered good arable land, and the remainder pasture and mountain; the system of agriculture improves very slowly. The river Scillies, rising in the mountains near Churchhill, intersects the parish, and proceeding in a southward direction falls into Lough Erne, near Enniskillen; and several inconsiderable lakes are scattered over the parish. Over the Scillies are three bridges, each of three arches, and there is also a bridge over an arm of Lough Erne. The surface is very uneven, and in the centre is a chain of mountains of great breadth, extending four miles, and frequently interspersed with patches of arable and meadow land,the greater part affording pasture only in dry seasons. In that part of the parish near Enniskillen there is a scarcity of bog, but in other parts there is sufficient to supply the inhabitants with fuel. There are excellent quarries

Island of Devenish. From The Dublin Penny Journal, *vol. 1, 1833.*

of limestone, and on the shore of Lough Erne is some of superior quality, which is quarried for manufacturing into chimney-pieces and for building, and for the conveyance of which the lake affords every facility. The village of Monea is wholly within the parish, and there are two others, Derrygonnelly and Garrison, of which the former is partly in Innismacsaint, in which also is situated an isolated portion of this parish, constituting the farm of Aughamuldoney.

Of the gentlemen's seats, the principal are Ely Lodge, the property of the Marquess of Ely, situated on a picturesque island in Lough Erne, connected with the mainland by a bridge, and commanding an interesting view of wood and water in beautiful combination; Graan, the seat of A. Nixon, Esq.; Castletown, of J. Brien, Esq.; and Hall Craig, the property of J. Weir, Esq., an ancient and spacious mansion beautifully situated on the banks of the Scillies. The manufacture of linen is carried on by most of the farmers, who engage weavers to work at their own looms, and many of the women are employed in spinning flax. The river Scillies abounds with pike, bream, and perch, and salmon is occasionally taken in it; and in Lough Melvin, near the western boundary of the parish, is found the Gillaroo trout. Lough Erne is navigable from Belturhet to Belleek, a distance of 40 miles; and the river Scillies is also partly navigable but is very little used. Fairs are held at Monea on Feb. 7th, Whit-Monday, July 7th, Aug. 26th. Oct. 13th, and Nov. 12th, for cattle of all kinds, yarn, and turner's ware; fairs are also held at Garrison and Derrygonnelly.

The living is a rectory and vicarage, in the diocese of Clogher, constituting the corps of the prebend of Devenish in the cathedral of Clogher, and in the patronage of the Bishop: the tithes amount to £295.7.8$^{1}/_{4}$. The glebe-house was erected in 1820, by aid of a loan of £843 from the late Board of First Fruits: the glebe comprises 400 acres. The parish church, for the repair of which the Ecclesiastical Commissioners have recently granted £205.10.10, is an ancient edifice without any remarkable architectural features, situated in the village of Monea. There is a chapel of ease at Garrison, erected by aid of a gift of £900 from the late Board of First Fruits, in 1828: it is served by a curate, and divine service is also performed in a farm-house on the mountains. In the R. C. divisions the parish is the head of a union or district, called also Derrygonnelly, and comprising also parts of the parishes of Innismacsaint and Bohoe; there are three chapels, one at Monea, one at Derrygonnelly, and one at Garrison, all plain structures. There are places of worship for Wesleyan Methodists, at Derrygonnelly and at Springfield, in each of which divine service is performed on alternate Sundays. Schools are supported by the rector at Monea and Levelly; a school for children of both sexes is supported at Moyglass, by the Marquess of Ely; one at Derrygonnelly, and another at Monea, by Mrs. Brien, of Castletown; and there is a school under the National Board at Knocknashannon, altogether affording gratuitous instruction to 450 children: there are two pay schools, in which are about 50 boys and 50 girls.

The island of Devenish appears to have derived its early importance from the foundation of a religious establishment, in honour of St. Mary, by St. Laserian, called also Molaisse and now Molush, who died in 563, and was succeeded by St. Natalis, son of Ængus, King of Connaught. This establishment was plundered by the Danes in 822, 834, and 961, and appears to have been refounded in 1130, and to have continued till the dissolution. The island, though not in itself very remarkable for picturesque beauty, forms a portion of the most interesting scenery in Lough Erne; it comprises about 70 or 80 Irish acres, and the land is so fertile as to require little or no manure; when viewed from the water, it presents an outline of oval form, but whether from neglect, or from the great value of the land, it is entirely destitute of timber. Of its ancient religious establishments there are some interesting remains: the lower church, dedicated to St. Molush, is 76 feet long and 21 feet wide, with a large aisle on the north; and near it is an ancient building, 30 feet long and 18 feet wide, with a roof entirely of hewn stone, called St. Molush's house. Near the summit of the hill are the remains of the abbey, of which the ruined church is 94 feet long and 24 feet wide, with a large aisle northward; near the centre is an arch of black marble, resting on four pillars and supporting a belfry tower, with a grand winding staircase leading to the summit, which commands an extensive prospect over the lake and the surrounding country.

Within the abbey is a stone, bearing the inscription, in old Saxon characters, "Matheus O'Dubagan hoc opus fecit, Bartholomeo O'Flannagan Priori de Daminis. A. D. 1449." About 100 paces from the abbey is St. Nicholas' well to which great numbers formerly resorted. Near the church of the abbey is an ancient round tower in excellent preservation: it is 82 feet high and 49 in circumference, and formed of stones accurately hewn to the external and internal curve, and cemented with mortar in quantity so small that the joints of the stones are almost imperceptible; it is covered with a conical roof of hewn stones in diminishing series; under the cornice which encircles it at the top, and which is divided into four equal compartments, each containing a sculptured subject, are four windows facing the cardinal points, above each of which is a carved human head; below there are other windows at different distances, and about seven feet from the base is the entrance doorway, about four feet high. This beautiful monument of antiquity, which was beginning to show symptoms of partial dilapidation, was thoroughly repaired in 1835. There are some remains of an old castle at Monea, and of' an ancient family residence at Tullycalter; several Danish forts are scattered over the parish; and in the bogs have been found querns or handmills for grinding corn, the stones of which were about two feet in diameter. – See DERRYGONNELLY and GARRISON.

DRUMKEERAN, or DRUMCHEERAN, a parish, in the barony of LURG, county of FERMANAGH, and province of ULSTER, 1/4 of a mile (N.) from Kesh, on the road from Enniskillen, by Pettigo, to Donegal; containing 8522 inhabitants. This parish is bounded on the south-west by Lough Erne, and on the southeast by the river Ederny, which falls into the lough a little below the town of Kesh. It comprises, including islands, according to the Ordnance survey, 27,159 statute acres, of which 3498 are part of Lower Lough Erne; the land generally is of inferior quality and principally in pasture; but the system of agriculture is improving: there is no waste land, but a large extent of bog, which partly supplies the town of Enniskillen with fuel. There is abundance of limestone for agricultural purposes, and some good quarries of freestone for building. The gentlemen's seats are Clonelly, the residence of F. W. Barton, Esq., and Drumrush, of the Rev. J. Delap. The living is a rectory and vicarage, in the diocese of Clogher, and in the patronage of the Bishop: the tithes amount to £415. The glebe-house is a large and handsome residence; the glebe comprises 270 acres. The church, a plain building with a tower, was formerly a chapel belonging to Vaughan's endowed school, the governors of which presented it to the parishioners, on the separation of Drumkeeran from the parish of Magheraculmony: the Ecclesiastical Commissioners have lately granted £105 for its repair. In the R. C. divisions the parish is the head of a union or district, called Blackbog, comprising also parts of the parishes of Magheraculmony and Templecarne, and con taining three chapels, situated respectively at Edendycrummin, Blackbog, and Banna. There is a place of worship for Presbyterians, in connection with the Synod of Ulster, of the third class; also two places of worship for Wesleyan Methodists. The late George Vaughan, Esq., bequeathed, in 1758, an estate now producing £1000 per ann., for the foundation and endowment of a school for boarding, clothing, and educating Protestant children, under the direction of 13 trustees: there are 60 boys and 24 girls at present in the school, who, when of age, are apprenticed with a fee to the master, and a premium is given to each on the expiration of his indenture, on producing a certificate of good conduct. There is also a parochial school: a large school-house has been built in the Elizabethan style by the Rev. Mr. West, who as a landlord has done much for the improVement of husbandry; and about 450 children are taught in nine private schools. There are several raths, and some chalybeate and sulphureous springs, one of which issues from a rock in the centre of the river.

DRUMMULLY, a parish, partly in the barony of DARTRY, county of MONAGHAN, but chiefly in that of COOLE, county of FERMANAGH, and province of ULSTER, 4 miles (W. by S.) from Clones, on the road from Dublin to Enniskillen; containing 667 inhabitants. According to the Ordnance survey it comprises 7639 statute acres, including part of Drumkrin; of these, 2520 are in Monaghan and 5119

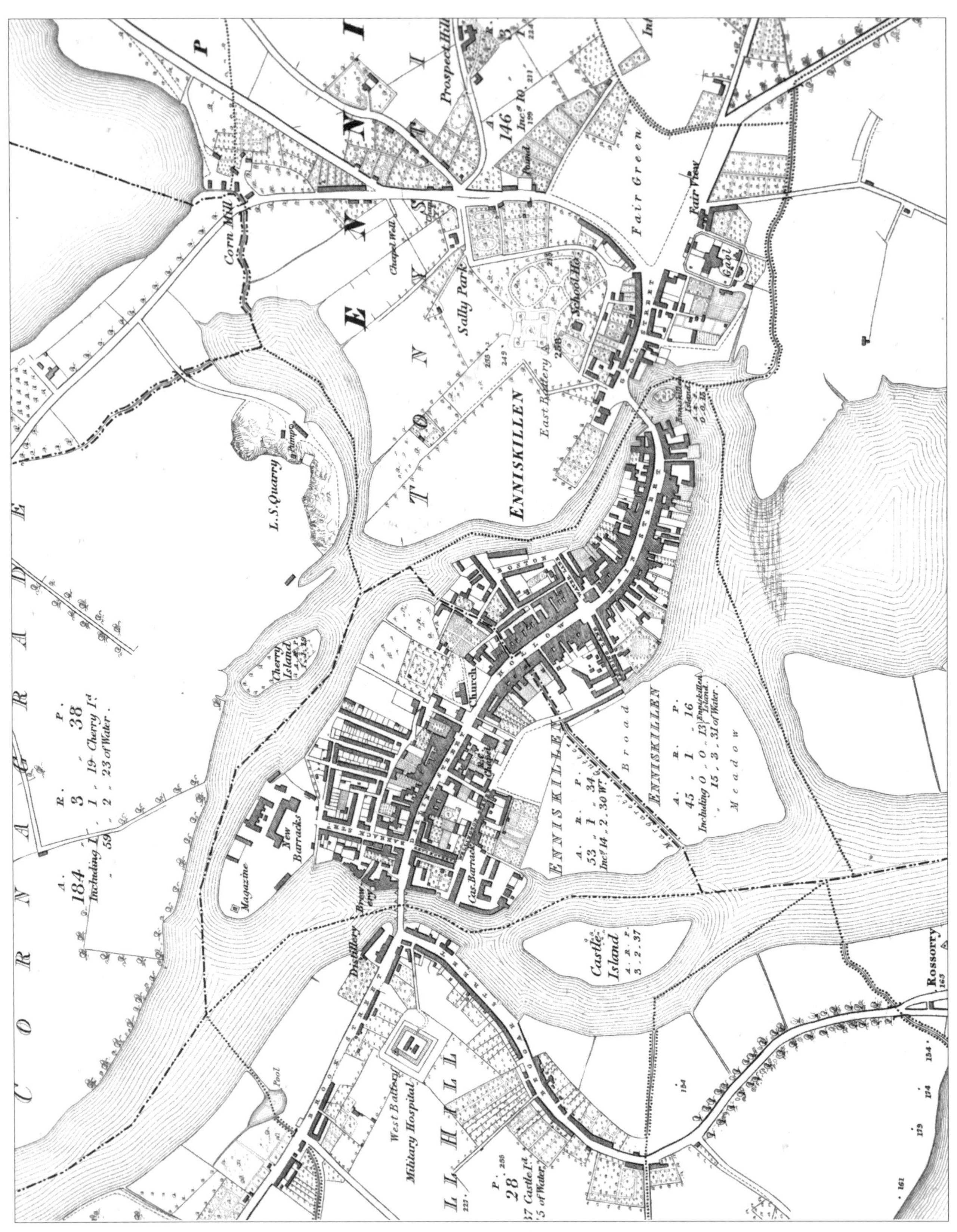

Enniskillen. Part of 6 inch O.S. map of Co.Fermanagh, sheet 22, published 1835 (reproduced at 140%).

in Fermanagh. The soil is generally good, and there is no waste land, but abundance of bog and limestone; about 600 acres are under water. Among the seats are Cara, the residence of J. Hassard, Esq.; Lake View, of D. Smith, Esq.; and Farm Hill, of C. Crowe, Esq. The living is a rectory and vicarage, in the diocese of Clogher and patronage of the Bishop; on the demise of the incumbent of Currin, a considerable part of Drumkrin, which is now held with that parish, will be united to Drummully. The tithes amount to £19, and the glebe comprises 154 acres. The church is a small building. In the R. C. divisions it is the head of a district, including Drummully, Drumkrin, and Galloon, and has two chapels in the last-named parish: about 60 children are educated in a public and 100 in a private school.

EDERNEY, a village, in the parish of MAGHERACULMONY, barony of LURG, county of FERMANAGH, and province of ULSTER, 2 miles (N.) from Kish, on the road from Enniskillen to Derry; containing 32 houses and 132 inhabitants. It is the property of the Rev. Mr. West, who is about to erect a market-house and some good dwelling-houses. Fairs are held on March 1st, May 16th, July 18th, Oct. 6th, Nov. 28th, and the 17th of every other month.

ENNISKILLEN, a borough and market-town, and a parish, partly in the barony of MAGHERABOY, but chiefly in that of TYRKENNEDY, county of FERMANAGH, (of which it is the chief town), and province of ULSTER, 21½ miles (S. E.) from Ballyshannon, and 80½ (N. N. W.) from Dublin; containing 14,563 inhabitants, of which number, 13,777 are in the parish of Enniskillen, and the remainder in that part of the town which extends into the parish of Rossory; the borough and town contain 6796 inhabitants. This place, which takes its name from the island in Lough Erne, in which it is situated, and was formerly called Inniskillen, was, previously to the time of Jas. I., merely a stronghold of Maguire, chieftain of Fermanagh, who had a castle here, which was taken by the English forces under Sir Richard Bingham, in 1594; but no sooner had that general retired, leaving in it a royal garrison, than it was besieged by the forces of O'Donnel and his confederates. A detachment sent to its assistance by the lord-deputy was totally defeated, and the garrison, after holding out to the last extremity, being compelled to surrender, were inhumanly slaughtered by the assailants, who pleaded the like cruelty on the part of Bingham, when he took the town, as a justification of their revenge. The town, though it holds a conspicuous place in Irish history and is now the capital of the county, is of no great antiquity. The island being considered an important spot for the establishment of a military force, a royal fort was erected there about the commencement of the 17th century; and the advantage of its situation for a town induced Jas. I., in 1612, to make a grant of one-third of it to William Cole, Esq., ancestor of the Earl of Enniskillen, on condition of his building a town upon it, settling in it twenty British families to be incorporated as burgesses, some of whose descendants still hold burgage tenements; and assigning convenient places for a church and churchyard, a market-house, public school, 30 acres for a common, and a site for a prison to be built for the custody of prisoners and malefactors within the limits of the county of Fermanagh. This last condition seems to imply that it was intended to make this the assize town and capital of the county from the very date of its foundation.

On the breaking out of the war in 1641, the town was defended by its founder and governor, then Sir William Cole, who despatched the first intelligence of that event to the English government; and so active were the inhabitants in opposing the enemy, that they not only repulsed the insurgents with great loss, but also made themselves masters of the castle of Maguire. While the Earl of Ormonde acted in concert with the royalists, this town opposed the parliamentarian interest and firmly resisted every attack made upon it by the forces of that party; but it was finally compelled to surrender to Sir Charles Coote. During the war of the revolution the inhabitants firmly adhered to the cause of Wm. III., whom they proclaimed king; they chose Gustavus Hamilton as their governor, and bravely defended the town, which became a refuge for the Protestants of the north-west, from all assaults of the adverse party; and from the embarrassment they caused to James's forces during the siege of Londonderry, the Protestants assembled in the town soon became celebrated as the "Enniskillen men." Lord Galmoy was sent with a detachment of James's army to reduce them, and for this purpose invested Crom castle, their frontier garrison, situated on Lough Erne; after an unsuccessful stratagem to produce intimidation, by ordering two painted tin cannons to be drawn by eight horses towards the fort, the garrison, being reinforced from Enniskillen, made a vigorous sally upon the besiegers, drove them from the trenches, and returned in triumph with considerable booty and the mock cannon which had with so much apparent difficulty been drawn up and planted against them.

So successful and formidable were the frequent excursions of this band, that the ruling party in Dublin actually expected them speedily at their gates; and at length a plan was formed for attacking the town at once by three different armies. For this purpose, Macarthy, an experienced officer, who had been recently created a peer, encamped at Belturbet with 7000 men; Sarsfield, another general equally distinguished, led an army from Connaught; while Fitz-James, Duke of Berwick, prepared to attack it from the north. The Enniskilleners, aware of the movements of the Connaught army only, marched out of the town with great rapidity, surprised the camp and routed the forces with much slaughter. On the approach of the Duke of Berwick, some companies sent from the town to seize a post which they might have defended against his numbers, ventured beyond the prescribed bounds and were cut to pieces; but on the approach of Hamilton, the governor of the town, the

Enniskillen, 1837. Drawn by J.H. Burgess and engraved by Branston.

Duke of Berwick retired with his forces. Macarthy, at the head of an army which had already defeated Lord Inchiquin in Munster, marched towards Enniskillen and invested Cromcastle; a detachment under an officer named Berry was sent to the relief of the castle, but finding it necessary to retreat before a very superior force, which had been detached by the enemy to intercept him, he was pursued and a skirmish followed, in which the townsmen were victorious. The arrival of the main bodies respectively under the command of Macarthy and Wolsley, the latter, one of Col. Kirk's officers, brought on a general engagement near Newtown-Butler and Lisnaskea, from both which places the battle has taken its name. The inferiority of the Enniskilleners in numbers was counterbalanced by superior resolution and energy; they defeated and pursued the assailants, granting quarter to none but officers; about 2000 were killed in the engagement, and of 500, who plunged into the lake, only one escaped drowning; about the same number of officers were taken prisoners, among whom was their general Macarthy.

The town is situated on an island in the narrowest part of Lough Erne, or rather in a strait several miles in length; which connects the great northern and southern expanses of the lake, and in which are numerous inlets. It is remarkable for its respectable and thriving appearance, and for the advantages it possesses in the navigation of the lake and the facility afforded for excursions among the rich and beautiful scenery for which it is distinguished; it has increased considerably of late, and is still improving. The principal street takes an irregular course across the island, from the bridge which connects it with the main land, on the east, to that which crosses the opposite channel on the west, which two bridges form the only outlets. Several smaller streets diverge from the main street; and contiguous to the eastern bridge, in the townland of Toneystick, and parish of Enniskillen, is a suburb in which is an old redoubt, called the East Fort; and beyond the western bridge is another suburb, in the parish of Rossory, in which is the West Fort. The total number of houses is 1036, of which 375 are slated and the remainder thatched. Here are barracks for artillery and infantry, and a constabulary police station. Among the buildings that have recently been erected, is a range of respectable houses, called Brook-place, built by Mr. Richard Kirkpatrick, on the mail coach road to Ballyshannon; a very neat house, called Brook View Lodge, pleasantly situated on the side of a hill commanding an extensive view of Lough

Enniskillen Castle. Drawn by R. O'C. Newenham and engraved by J.D.Harding. From R. O'C. Newenham, Picturesque views of the antiquities of Ireland, *vol. 1, (London, 1830).*

Erne and the surrounding country; and a number of respectable houses, called Willoughby-place, which, when completed, will add much to the beauty of the town.

The chief trade is in timber, coal, and slates, imported from Ballyshannon to Belleek, at the lower extremity of the lough, 18 miles distant, and brought by water to the town. The manufacture of leather is carried on upon a limited scale, and there are two distilleries and a brewery A considerable trade is also carried on in corn, of which great quantities are sold, partly for the supply of the town and of the distilleries here and at Belturbet, and partly for exportation to Sligo and Strabane; this is also the chief retail market for a very large surrounding district. The patent granted to William Cole, in 1612, authorised the holding of a market on Thursdays, and a fair on Lammas-day, with tolls; and in 1813 a patent was granted to the Earl of Enniskillen for holding fairs on the 10th of each month, except March, May, and August. Besides the general market on Thursdays, a butter market is held on Tuesdays. A butter and grain market have been built on land belonging to the Earl, at an expense of upwards of £900; there is another market-house under the town-hall, also a pig market; and convenient shambles have been erected at an expense of £750, which was advanced by the Earl to the corporation. A linen-hall was built a few years since at an expense exceeding £400, but has never been used as a hall, and is lent gratuitously to the conductor of a private school.

By the charter of Jas. I., granted in 1613, the corporation consists of a provost, 14 burgesses, and all the inhabitants of the island as a commonalty. The provost is elected by the free burgesses on Midsummer-day, and is sworn into office on the 29th of Sept.; he is a justice of the peace for the borough, and also usually for the county. The government is vested in the provost and free burgesses, who elect members of their own body, admit freemen, appoint officers, and manage the property of the corporation. The borough court, held every Thursday, has jurisdiction to the amount of £3.6.8 late currency, and proceeds by attachment. The same charter conferred upon the entire corporation the privilege of sending two members to the Irish parliament, which they continued to do till the Union, since which time they have returned one to the Imperial parliament. By the act of the 2nd of Wm. IV., cap. 88, the right of election is vested in the resident burgesses and £10 householders, amounting, in 1836, to a constituency of 220, of whom 211 were £10 householders, and nine resident burgesses; the provost is the returning officer. The electoral boundaries comprehend an area of 156 statute acres. The assizes for the county and quarter sessions of the peace are held in the county court-house, which is a plain building near the eastern bridge. The county gaol, built about 20 years since, is near the town, on the Dublin road: it is on the radiating plan, with the governor's house in the centre, and will contain 120 prisoners; the number of cells is 36, of which four are for females; and there are five day-rooms, seven airing-yards, a treadmill, hospital, and school. The prisoners are regularly employed in breaking stones for repairing the roads: the expense of maintenance, &c., for 1835, was £1334.8.1.

The parish comprises, according to the Ordnance survey (including islands), 26,440½ statute acres, of which 26,387 are in the barony of Tyrkennedy, and 681¾ are water. The residences of the nobility and gentry are numerous, among which are Ely Lodge, that of the Marquess of Ely; Florence Court, of the Earl of Enniskillen; Castle Coole, of the Earl of Belmore; Rosfad, of J. Richardson, Esq.; Rockfield, of J. Irvine, Esq., D.L.; Castle Archdall, of Gen. Mervyn Archdall; Riverstown, of C. Archdall, Esq.; Prospect, of J. Nixon, Esq., Gran, of A. Nixon, Esq.; Levaghy, of Jason Hassard, Esq.; Dunbar, of T. Nixon, Esq.; Crocknacrieve, of Col. T. Stewart; Cork Hill, of the Rev. A. H. Irvine; and Bellview, of G. Knox, Esq. On the border of Lough Erne stands Bellisle, the beautiful and romantic seat of the late Earl of Rosse, now in the possession of the Rev. J. Grey Porter; it is in a dilapidated state, but is about to be rebuilt, together with the bridge leading to its extensive demesne. The living is a rectory and vicarage, in the diocese of Clogher, forming the corps of the precentorship of the cathedral, in the patronage of the Provost and Fellows of Trinity College, Dublin: the tithes amount to £550; and the glebe, consisting of 315 acres, with the glebe-house, is valued at £293.4.6 per annum, making the income of the precentor £843.4.6. The church is a plain building, erected in 1637; and there is a chapel of ease at Tempo. Divine service is also performed in the school at Derryhean. In the R. C. divisions the parish is the head of a union or district, including the town of Enniskillen, the parish of Rossory, and parts of Derryvullen, Cleenish, and Derrybrusk; there is a very large chapel in the town, in which are also a meeting-house for Presbyterians in connection with the Synod of Ulster, of the third class, and places of worship for Wesleyan and Primitive Methodists. About 670 children are educated in nine public schools, and about 900 in 25 private schools, exclusive of those taught in eight Sunday schools.

The royal school of Enniskillen was founded by Chas. I., in 1626, and endowed with lands near the town, which, according to a survey made in 1795, comprise 3360 statute acres. The school-house in the town being too small, about 1777, the Rev. Mark Noble, who was then headmaster, and had the absolute disposal of the school funds, built a spacious house for it at Portora, in the vicinity, capable of accommodating 70 boarders. The school contains about 65 children; the head-master has a salary of £500 per annum, late currency, besides the payments from the pupils and the house and grounds, which include 33 acres; the first classical assistant has £250, and the second £100 per annum. Four scholarships of £20 per annum each are conferred by the Commissioners of Education on those scholars who are most distinguished for proficiency in study and propriety of conduct, and are held during their stay at the school; and the Rev. Burke bequeathed three sums of £110, late currency, for the use of three of the pupils on their entering Trinity College, Dublin. The Commissioners of Education appropriate £400 per annum of the funds of this school to the endowment of five king's scholarships of £50 each, and five of £30 each in Trinity College, Dublin, to be held for five years by scholars elected by the board of Trinity College, out of those who have been three years at least in either of the royal schools of Enniskillen, Armagh, or Dungannon. The charitable institutions are a mendicity society, a dispensary, and a county infirmary, which is a large building on an eminence outside the town, on the Dublin road. Enniskillen is the birthplace of Lord Plunket, and gives the titles of Earl and Viscount to the family of Cole, by which it was founded.

GALLOON, a parish, partly in the baronies of KNOCKNINNY and CLONKELLY, but chiefly in that of COOLE, county of FERMANAGH, and province of ULSTER, 5½ miles (S. S. E.) from Lisnaskea, on Lough Erne, and on the road from Cavan to Enniskillen; containing 10,506 inhabitants, now including the ecclesiastical district of Currin. The parish, according to the Ordnance survey, comprises (including islands) 25,287 statute acres, of which 432½ are in the barony of Knockninny, 9341¼ in that of Clonkelly, and 15,513¼ in that of Coole; about two-thirds are good arable and pasture land, 1455½ are in Upper Lough Erne, 1072 in small lakes, and of the remainder a very large portion is bog, which is easily reclaimable. The system of agriculture is in a very unimproved state; limestone is abundant, and freestone of good quality is procured for building and other purposes. The only seat of importance is Crom Castle, the residence of the Earl of Erne, about three miles from Newtown-Butler, a handsome mansion recently erected, in which is still preserved the armour worn by McCarthy Moore at the battle of Kilgarret. The lake affords considerable facility of water conveyance, and it is in contemplation to open the port of Ballyshannon by the river Erne; there is a large flour-mill at Roosky, in this parish. The living is a rectory, in the diocese of Clogher, and the corps of the chancellorship of the cathedral of Clogher, in the patronage of the Bishop: the tithes amount to £410, and the gross annual value of the benefice, including glebe, is £540. There is no glebe-house; the glebe comprises 128 Irish acres. The old church was burnt by an accidental fire in 1819, and the present spacious cruciform edifice was erected in 1821, by aid of a grant of £2000 from the late Board of First Fruits. In the R. C. divisions the parish is the head of a union or district comprising also four townlands of the parish of Drummully; there are two chapels, situated at Newtown-Butler and Donagh; the former erected in 1830, at an expense of £400, and latter in 1826, at an expense of £500. There are also places of worship for Wesleyan and Primitive Wesleyan Methodists; the latter is a fine new building, one-half of the expense of which was contributed by J. Butler Danvers, Esq. About 670 children are taught in five national and four other public schools; and there are six private schools, in which are about 540 children, and ten Sunday schools. There are several raths in the parish; and at Mulnagone is a chalybeate spa, strongly impregnated with sulphur, which has been found efficacious in chronic diseases. There are some ruins of old churches on the island of Galloon and also at Donagh. – See NEWTOWNBUTLER.

GARRISON, a village, partly in the parish of INNISMACSAINT, and partly in that of DEVENISH, barony of MAGHERABOY, county of FERMANAGH, and province of ULSTER, 7 miles (W.) from Churchhill, on the road from Ballyshannon to Manorhamilton; containing 69 inhabitants. Here are a chapel of ease to the parish church of Devenish, a R. C. chapel, and a school. It is a constabulary police station, and fairs are held on May 21st, July 19th, Oct. 21st. and Dec. 21st, besides which fairs have lately been established every alternate month.

INNISMACSAINT, or CHURCHHILL, a parish, partly in the barony of TYRHUGH, county of DONEGAL, but chiefly in that of MAGHERABOY, county of FERMANAGH, and province of ULSTER; containing, with the post-town of Churchhill, the market-town of Derrygonnelly, and part of the post-town of Ballyshannon, (each of which is separately described), 14,801 inhabitants. The name Innismacsaint is derived from an island in Lough Erne, about half a mile from the shore, where a celebrated abbey was founded by St. Nenn, or Nennid, early in the sixth century. This afterwards became the parish church until, in the reign of Queen Anne, one was built at Drumenagh; part of the ancient building still exists. According to the Ordnance survey the parish comprises 52,994$^1/_4$ statute acres, of which 9505 are water, including a considerable portion of Lough Erne and part of Lough Melvin: of these, 45,867$^1/_4$, including several small islands, are in the county of Fermanagh, and 7127 in Donegal. About two thirds of it are arable and pasture, and the remainder waste and bog: 23,616 acres are applotted under the tithe act. Agriculture is in a backward state, especially in the Fermanagh part of the parish. There is a

Tully Castle. Drawn by J.H. Burgess and engraved by Branston. From The Irish Penny Journal, *vol. 1, 1840.*

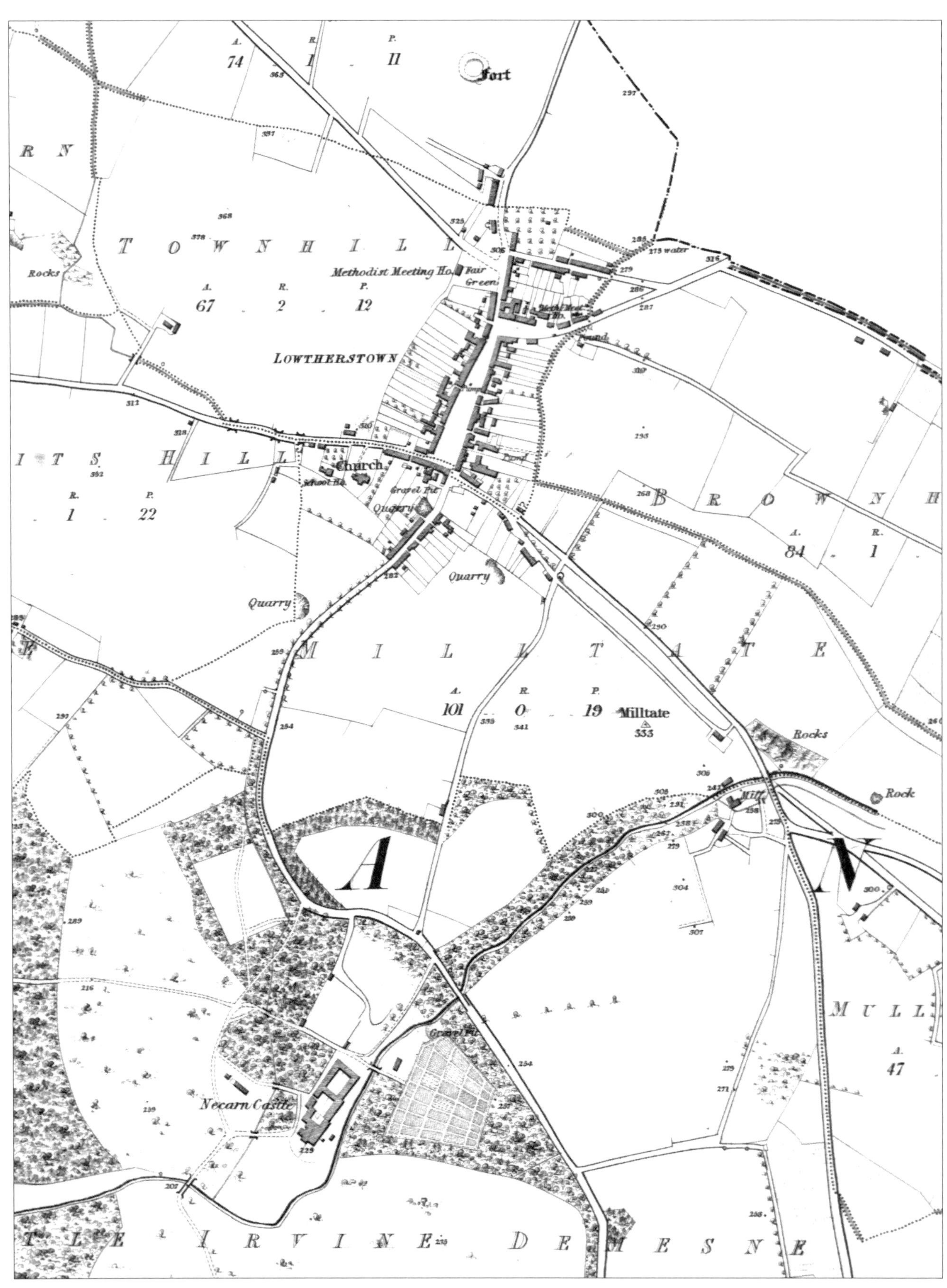

Irvinestown or Lowtherstown. Part of O.S. map of Co. Fermanagh, sheet 11, published 1835 (reproduced at 140%).

great quantity of bog, particularly on the Wyault mountains, where there is a basaltic dyke. Coal appears in several places in thin layers, and there are quarries of good sandstone used for building. The mountain of Glennalong rises 793, and Shean North 1133, feet above the level of the sea. Lough Erne affords a navigable communication with Enniskillen, Belturbet, and Ballyshannon.

The living is a rectory and vicarage, in the diocese of Clogher, and in the patronage of the Marquess of Ely: the tithes amount to £500. The glebe-house at Benmore, the residence of the Rev. H. Hamilton, was built by a loan of £1000 and a gift of £100 from the late Board of First Fruits, in 1829; it is situated on a glebe of 540 acres. The church is a handsome building with a tower, erected in 1831 by a loan of £1385 from the same Board, and the Ecclesiastical Commissioners have recently granted £101 for its repair. There are also chapels of ease or district churches at Slavin and Finner. In the R. C. divisions parts of this parish are united to Bohoe and Devenish, and the remainder forms the union or district of Bundoran. There are plain chapels at Roscor, Knockaraven, Bundoran, and Carrickbeg. At Churchhill is a meeting-house for Wesleyan Methodists, and at Cosbystown one for Primitive Methodists. The parochial school was built by a bequest of £200 from the late Rev. J. Nixon, and is aided by an annual subscription of £5 from the rector; there is a school at the rector's gate-house, where girls are taught needlework by his family; a girls' school is supported by the Marchioness of Ely; and a school has been recently erected at Fasso, by the Marquess of Ely, who is proprietor of the parish. In these and another public school about 330 children are educated, and about 900 are taught in 19 private schools; there are also four Sunday schools. In the vicinity of Carricklake are the ruins of a church; and near Churchhill are the remains of Castle Tully, the inhabitants of which were slaughtered in the war of 1641. Several Danish raths or forts exist here, some of which are very perfect. There is a sulphureous spring at Braad, and a chalybeate spring at Rosslemonough.

IRVINESTOWN, or LOWTHERSTOWN, a market and post-town, in that part of the parish of DERRYVULLEN which is in the barony of LURG, county of FERMANAGH, and province of ULSTER, 7¾ miles (N. W.) from Enniskillen, and 88¼ (S. W.) from Dublin, on the road from Enniskillen to Kesh; containing 1047 inhabitants. It consists of one street of 217 houses, and contains the parish church, a handsome modern building with a spire, erected in 1831, at an expense of £2300 of which £1385 was granted as a loan by the late Board of First Fruits. There are also two Methodist meeting houses, a school on Erasmus Smith's foundation, and a dispensary. It is a constabulary police station, and petty sessions are held on alternate Wednesdays. The market is on Wednesday, and fairs are held on the 8th of each month and on the 12th of April

KESH, a village and post-town, in the parish of MAGHERACULMONEY barony of LURG, county of FERMANAGH, and province of ULSTER, 12 miles (N. by W.) from Enniskillen, and 93 miles (N. W.by N.) from Dublin, on the road from Enniskillen to Donegal; containing 28 houses and 139 inhabitants. It is a constabulary police station, and has fairs on Jan. 28th, March 28th, June 1st, July 28th, Sept. 28th, and Nov. 21st.

KILLESHER, a parish, in the barony of GLENAWLEY, county of FERMANAGH, and province of ULSTER; containing, with the post-town of Florence-Court, 5114 inhabitants. According to the Ordnance survey it comprises, with certain islands in Lower Lough McNean, 24,936¼ statute acres, of which 24½ are in the river Erne and small loughs, and 642½ are in Lower Lough McNean: there is a considerable quantity of bog and mountain land. Fairs are held at Whitehill on May 13th, July 13th, Sept. 11th, and Nov. 11th. Florence Court, the beautiful mansion of the Earl of Enniskillen, stands in a large and finely planted demesne. The living is a rectory and vicarage, in the diocese of Kilmore, and in the patronage of the Bishop: the tithes amount to £200. The church is a small building, and was repaired in 1819, by aid of a loan of £600 from the late Board of First Fruits. There is no glebe-house: the glebe comprises 1300 acres. The R. C. parish is co-extensive with that of the Established Church, and has a chapel at Whitehill, and one at Crossroads: there are also two places of worship for Wesleyan Methodists. About 460 children are educated in six public schools, to two of which the Earl of Enniskillen subscribes, and about 100 in two private schools; there are also five Sunday schools. Here are some mineral springs and remarkable caves, also the ruins of the old church.

KINAWLEY, a parish, partly in the barony of TULLAGHAGH, county of CAVAN, partly in that of GLENAWLEY, but chiefly in that of KNOCKNINNY, county of FERMANAGH, and province of ULSTER, 6 miles (N. W.) from Ballyconnell, on the road to Enniskillen; containing, with the post-town of Swanlinbar, which is separately described, 16,077 inhabitants. According to the Ordnance survey it comprises 51,004 statute acres, of which 15,346½ are in the county of Cavan; and, including islands, 35,657½ are in the county of Fermanagh; of the latter number, 2895 acres are in Upper Lough Erne, and 645¼ in small loughs. Agriculture is in a good state; there is a considerable quantity of bog, and limestone and freestone are abundant. Cuilcagh mountain, which, according to the Ordnance survey, is 2188 feet high, is in the Cavan part of the parish. The river Shannon rises at the base of this mountain from a deep circular gulph, 20 feet in diameter, and there is another deep gulph about three-quarters of a mile from this, in which the flowing of water may be heard. The elevation of the source of the Shannon above Lough Allen is 115 feet, and above the sea 275 feet. Petty sessions are held every fortnight at Derrilin, where fairs are held on May 27th and Oct. 27th. The principal seats are Mount Prospect, the residence of Blaney Winslow, Esq.; Dresternan, of D. T.

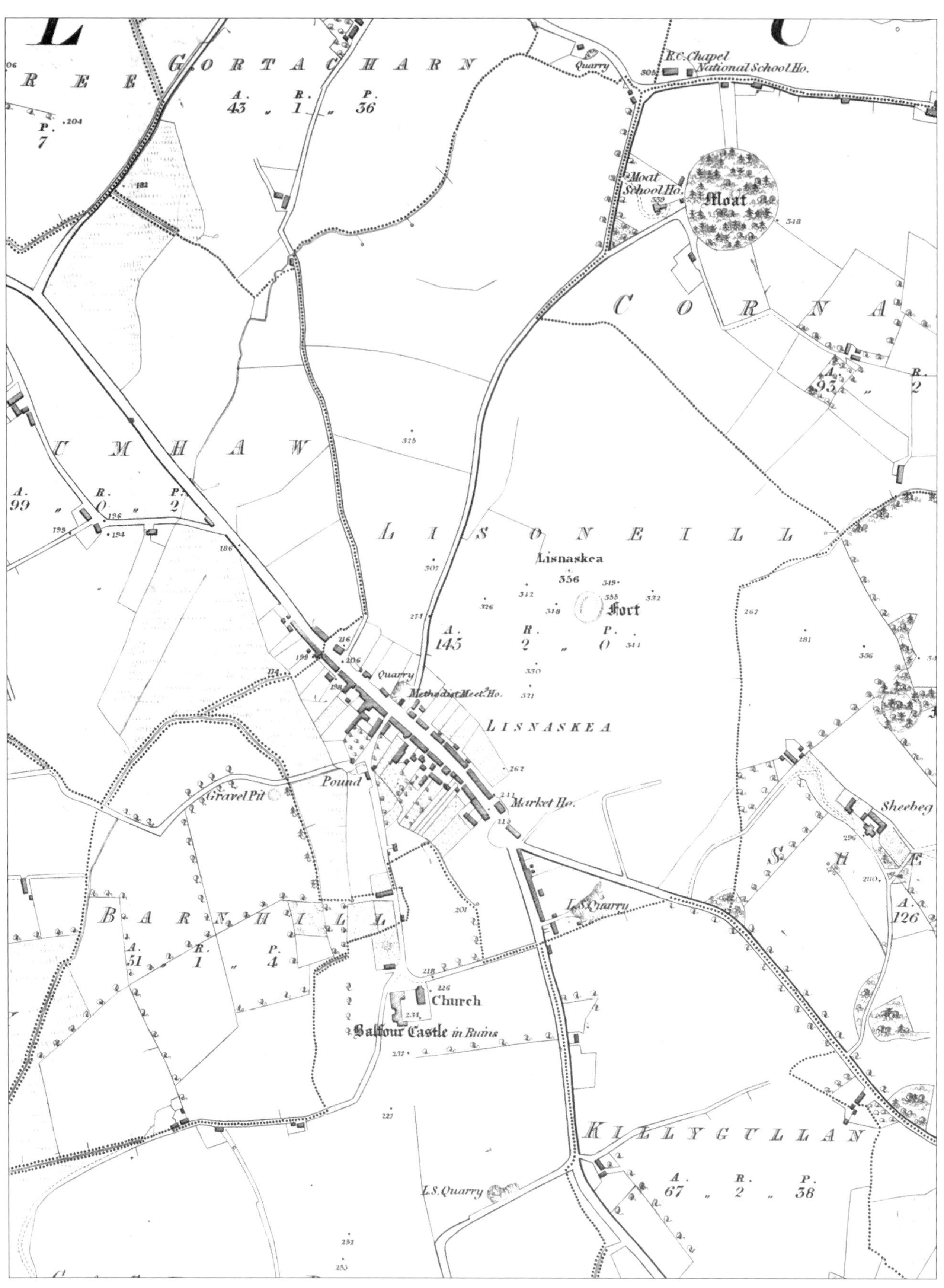

Lisnaskea. Part of O.S. map of Co. Fermanagh, sheet 34, published 1835 (reproduced at 140%).

Winslow, Esq.; Prospect Hill, of A. Maguire, Esq.; and Cloghan, of D. Winslow, Esq. The living is a rectory and vicarage, in the diocese of Kilmore, and in the patronage of the Bishop; the tithes amount to £369.4.7$^1/_2$. The glebe-house was erected in 1822, by aid of a loan of £787 from the late Board of First Fruits. There is a church at Derrilin, and one at Swanlinbar, which is in a ruinous state. In the R. C. divisions the parish forms two unions or districts, called Kinawley, in which are chapels at Kinawley and Swanlinbar; and Knockaninny, in which are chapels at Knockaninny, Glassmullen, and Drumderrig. There are eight public schools, in which about 850 children are educated, and 13 private schools, in which are about 570, also seven Sunday schools.

LISBELLAW, a village, in a detached portion of the parish of CLEENISH, barony of TYRKENNEDY, county of FERMANAGH, and province of ULSTER, 3$^1/_2$ miles (E. S. E,) from Enniskillen, on the road to Clogher; containing 45 houses and 242 inhabitants. Tradition states that on a hill above the village a battle was fought between some of the troops of King William and James II, when the latter were defeated. The Lisbellaw estate was the property of the late Earl of Rosse, on whose demise the title became extinct, and the property passed to the Rev. Grey Porter, the present proprietor. The village is picturesquely situated amidst conical-shaped hills, in a highly cultivated district, and in the vicinity of Lough Erne: it has a penny post to Enniskillen. The inhabitants are chiefly employed in weaving linen and making mats from bulrushes; and there are corn-mills with drying-kilns attached. Fairs are held on May 11th, June 20th, July 20th, Aug. 18th, Oct. 12th, Nov. 11th, and Dec. 23rd, chiefly for cattle and pigs: those in May and November are much frequented for hiring servants. Petty sessions are held on alternate Saturdays; and a baronial court was formerly held, but has been discontinued: here is a station of the constabulary police. The church, or chapel of ease to the parochial church of Cleenish, is a neat edifice, built in 1764 by Lord Rosse, who was interred in a vault beneath. The R. C. chapel is a large plain building, attached to the district of Enniskillen. Here are also a meeting-house for Presbyterians of the Seceding Synod (of the second class), built on a site given by the late Sir R. Hardinge; and a small meeting-house for Methodists. A school, formerly in connection with the Kildare-place Society, but now supported by the parents of the children, is held in a commodious house, which also contains apartments for the master. In the vicinity of the village are several ancient raths or forts; and on a finely wooded island in Lough Erne, connected by a causeway with the mainland, is Bellisle, the ruined seat of the late Earl of Rosse.

LISNARRICK, a village, in the parish of DERRYVULLEN, barony of LURG, county of FERMANAGH, and province of ULSTER, 3$^1/_2$ miles (S.) from Kesh, on the road to Enniskillen; containing 171 inhabitants. It consists of three rows of irregularly built houses, disposed in a triangular form; and has fairs on Jan. 12th, on the 22nd of Jan., Feb., and March, April 5th, May 9th and 23rd, 22nd of June and July, and Oct. 15th, for general farming stock.

LISNASKEA, or LISNESKEA, a market and post-town, in the parish of AGHALURCHER, barony of MAGHERA-STEPHANA, county of FERMANAGH, and province of ULSTER, 9 miles (S. E.) from Enniskillen, and 71 (N. E.) from Dublin, on the road to Enniskillen; containing 89 houses and 430 inhabitants. It consists chiefly of comfortable houses and shops, and contains a handsome market-house, corn and butter stores, a savings bank, and a large hotel. From its proximity to Lough Erne, which reaches to Lake Head, within a quarter of a mile of the town, great facility is afforded for the conveyance of corn, butter, linen, and yarn, of which considerable quantities are supplied from the thickly inhabited islands on the lake, and sold in this market: it is stated that a short canal could be constructed at a moderate expense that would enable boats to come up to the town. The market is on Saturday, and fairs are held on the Monday before Easter, April 13th, Monday after Ascension, June 1st, and Oct. 10th, for general farming stock. The church, or chapel of ease to Aghalurcher, was rebuilt in 1814, at an expense of £369 British, defrayed by the parishioners; and in 1829 the late Board of First Fruits gave £450, and lent £50 for the erection of a glebe-house in the vicinity. The curate, who is appointed by the rector of Aghalurcher, has a stipend of £73.16.8, exclusively of the marriage fees, and the glebe-house, which is valued at £20 per annum. The R. C. chapel, called the Monte Chapel, stands on a hill near the town: it was built in 1814, at an expense of about £700: attached is a national school. In the town is a meeting-house for Primitive Methodists; also a school endowed by Major Leslie, with three acres of land and £14 per annum, an infants' school, and a dispensary. In the vicinity are Green Hill, the residence of Major Irvine; Snow Hill, of J. D. Johnstone, Esq.; Fairview, of Alex. Robinson, Esq.; The Hill, of the Rev. M. Herbert; and the ruins of Castle-Balfour. – See AGHALURCHER.

MAGHERACROSS, a parish, partly in the barony of OMAGH, county of TYRONE, and partly in the barony of LURG, but chiefly in that of TYRKENNEDY, county of FERMANAGH, and province of ULSTER, 5$^1/_2$ miles (N. by E.) from Enniskillen, on the road to Omagh; containing 5313 inhabitants. It comprises, according to the Ordnance survey, 10,452$^1/_4$ statute acres, of which 343$^3/_4$ are in the barony of Omagh, 170$^1/_4$ in Lurg, 71 water, and 7505 are applotted under the tithe act, and valued at £6015.2.9 per annum. About 50 acres are woodland, 1500 waste and bog, and the remainder good arable and pasture land; the soil is fertile, the system of agriculture improved, and there is a good supply of peat for fuel. The principal seats are Jamestown, the residence of G. Lendrum, Esq.; Crocknacrieve, of H. M. Richardson, Esq.; and Barn, of the Rev. J. Irwin. A large fair, chiefly for horses, is held on Feb. 12th at Ballinamallard. The living is a rectory and vicarage, in the diocese of

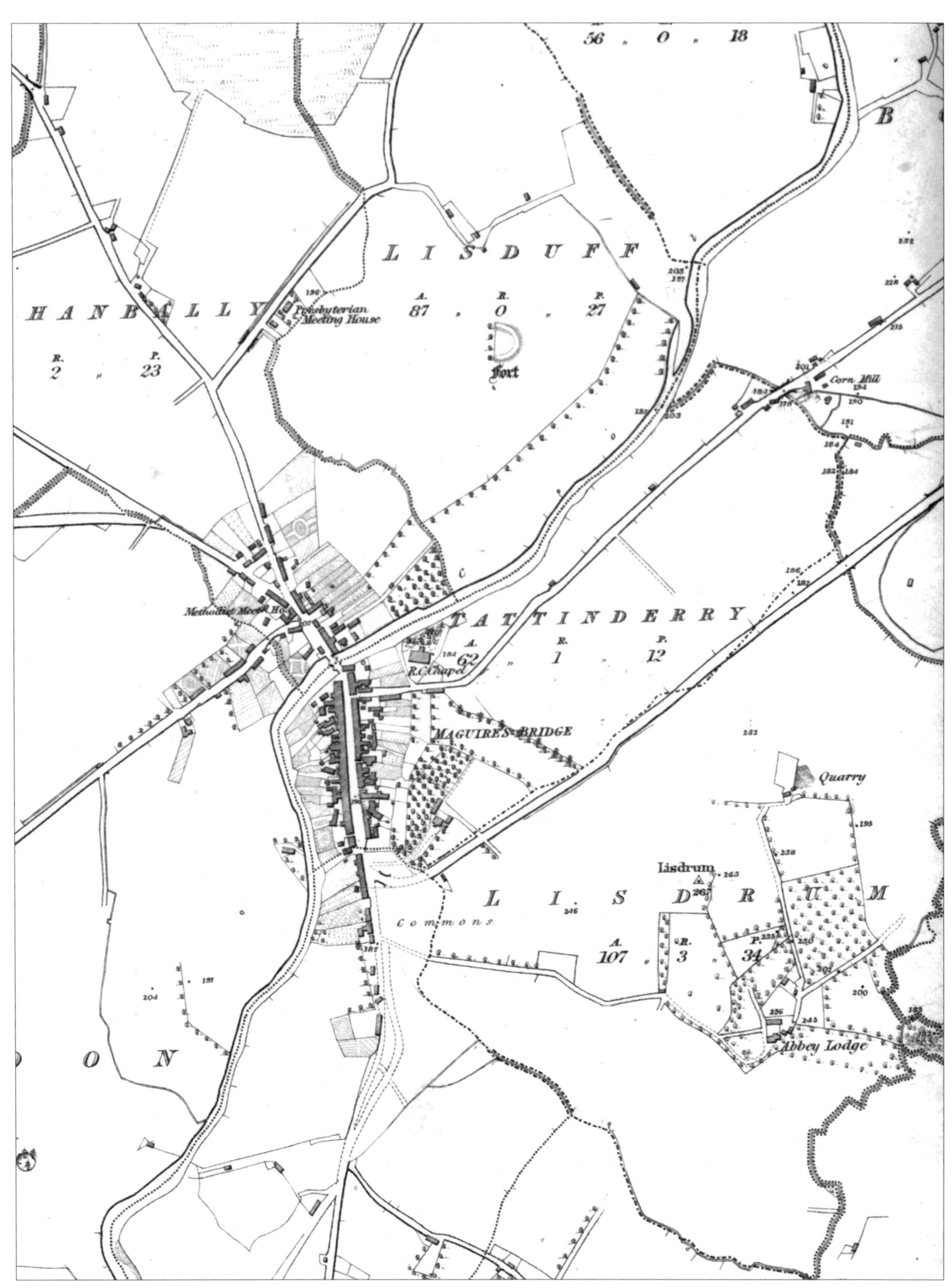

Maguiresbridge. Part of O.S. map of Co. Fermanagh, sheet 28, published 1835 (reproduced at 140%).

Clogher, and in the patronage of the Bishop: the tithes amount to £328.4.2. There is no glebe-house; the glebe comprises 300 acres, valued at £176 per annum. The church is a plain neat edifice in good repair, and was erected about 50 years since. In the R. C. divisions the parish forms part of the union or district of Whitehall, or Derryvullen; the chapel is a small thatched building. There are places of worship for Wesleyan and Primitive Wesleyan Methodists in connection with the Established Church. About 400 children are taught in the parochial and six other public schools, of which a female school is supported by G. Lendrum, Esq.; and there are five private schools, in which are about 200 children; two Sunday schools, and a dispensary.

MAGHERACULMONY, a parish, in the barony of LURG, county of FERMANAGH, and province of ULSTER, on the road from Ballyshannon to Omagh; containing, with the post-town of Kesh, 6451 inhabitants. This parish is situated on Lough Erne, and, according to the Ordnance survey, comprises, including islands, 18,577 statute acres, of which 3843$^3/_4$ are in Lower Lough Erne, and 9973 are applotted under the tithe act. With the exception of about 1500 acres of mountain or turbary, the land is of good quality and chiefly in pasture; that portion of it which is under tillage produces good crops, and the system of agriculture is improving. There are some quarries of excellent limestone, which are worked for agricultural purposes, and also of freestone of good quality, which is raised for building; and coal is found in the parish, but not worked. Fairs are held at Ederney and Kesh, which see; and petty sessions are also held at the latter place on alternate Mondays. The living is a rectory and vicarage, in the diocese of Clogher, and in the patronage of the Bishop; the tithes amount to £255. The glebe-house was built in 1780, at an expense of £808.4, the glebe comprises 374 acres, valued at £326, and 46 acres in the possession of the incumbent, valued at £69, per annum. The church, a plain neat building, was repaired and enlarged by the addition of a gallery, in 1825, at an expense of £276.18.5$^1/_2$, for which a loan was granted from the Consolidated Fund. In the R. C. divisions the parish, with the exception of three townlands, forms part of the union or district of Drumkeeman. About 450 children are taught in the parochial and four other public schools; and there are three private schools, in which are about 150 children. In the deer-park of Gen. Archdall are the ruins of some monastic buildings; there are also some remains of Crevenish Castle, near which is a strongly impregnated sulphuric spring, the water of which is similar to that of Harrogate.

MAGUIRE'S-BRIDGE, a market-town, in the parish of AGHALURCHER, barony of MAGHERASTEPHENA, county of FERMANAGH, and province of ULSTER, 2$^1/_2$ miles (N. W.) from Lisnaskea, on the road to Fintona; containing 854 inhabitants. It is situated on Maguire's river, here crossed by a bridge which gives name to the town, and consists of one street comprising about 200 houses, and containing a R. C. chapel, meeting-houses for Presbyterians and Methodists, and a dispensary. It has a penny post to Lisnaskea. The market is on Wednesday; and fairs are held on the first Wednesday in each month, and on Jan. 17th, the third Wednesday in May, July 5th, and Oct. 2nd. It is a station of the constabulary police. The R. C. chapel is a large building, erected in 1822 at an expense of £800; it is lighted with pointed windows, and the altar is embellished with a painting. Attached to the chapel is a school. The seats in the vicinity are Drumgoon, the residence of R. Graham, Esq.; Green Hill, of Major Irvine; Abbey Lodge, of J. Macartney, Esq.; and Aghavea, of the Rev. T. Birney.

NEWTOWN-BUTLER, a town, in the parish of GALLOON, barony of COOLE, county of FERMANAGH, and province of ULSTER, 4$^1/_2$ miles (W. by S.) from Clones, on the road to Enniskillen; containing 412 inhabitants. In 1641, the Enniskilleners defeated the army commanded by Mac Carthy-more, about one mile north of the town, in retreating through which the latter set fire to the church and burned it to the ground, together with several inhabitants who had sought refuge there; they were afterwards totally defeated at Kilgarret Hill, half a mile to the south, and their leader made prisoner. The village consists of two streets, and in 1831 contained 76 houses: it has a penny post to Clones and Lisnaskea. There is a market on Friday; fairs for yarn and butter are held on the second Friday in each month, and on May 12th is a large fair for cattle. General sessions are held four times in the year, and petty sessions on alternate Wednesdays, in the court-house, to which a bridewell is attached. A constabulary police force is stationed in the town. Here are the parochial church, and a large R. C. chapel; a handsome meeting-house was recently erected for the Primitive Wesleyan Methodists, one-half the expense of which was defrayed by J. Butler Danvers, Esq. The old meeting-house has been converted into a school for gratuitous daily instruction, and is also used as a Sunday school; a national school is held in the chapel; and there is also a parochial school. This place gives the inferior title of baron to the family of Butler, Earls of Lanesborough, and it was once the seat of that family, of whose mansion no vestige can now be traced.

ROSSLEA, or ROYSLEA, a village, in that part of the parish of CLONES which is in the barony of CLONKELLY, county of FERMANAGH, and province of ULSTER, 4 miles (N. N. E.) from Clones, on the road from Lisnasken to Monaghan; containing 355 inhabitants. The place is romantically situated near the celebrated mountain of Carnmore, in a fine meadow district, several townlands of which are rich pastureland, especially those of Lisnabrack and Salloo, where vast numbers of oxen are annually fed for the English market. The village consists of one irregularly built street, containing 71 houses, and is connected with the new line of road on the mountain from Enniskillen to Belfast by a bridge over the river Fin. In the vicinity is Lake View, the residence of the Rev. T. Bogue, P. P., a beautiful

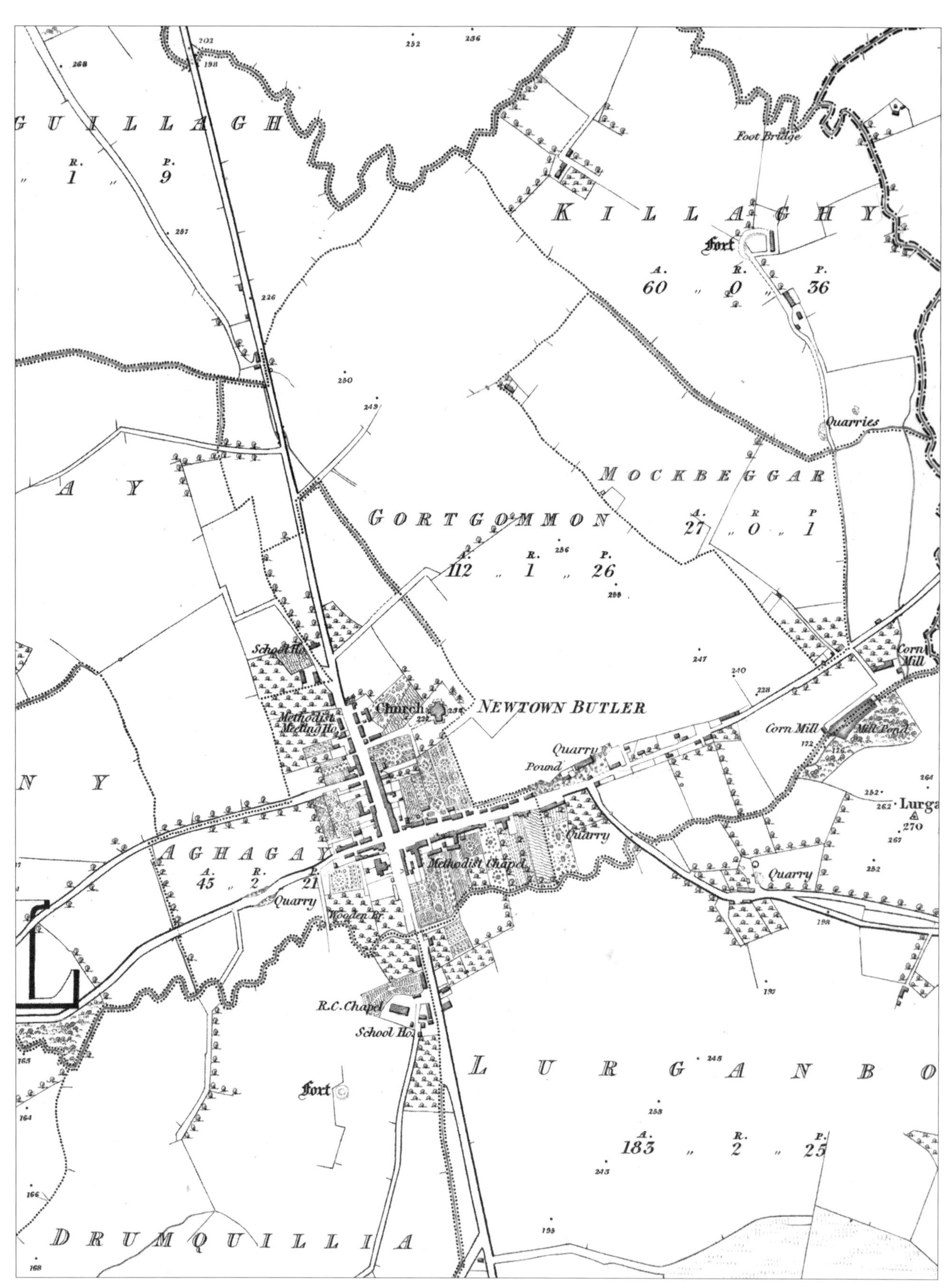

Newtownbutler. Part of O.S. map of Co. Fermanagh, sheet 40, published 1835 (reproduced at 140%).

villa, overlooking the lake of Island Hill and commanding a fine view of several other small lakes in the neighbourhood; it is surrounded with grounds tastefully laid out and richly embellished. Here is a flax-mill belonging to Mr. Lynch. Fairs are held on the 8th of every month; a constabulary police force is stationed here, and petty sessions and manorial courts are held in the court-house, a neat building in the centre of the village. The R. C. chapel is a very handsome edifice of stone, with a tower and campanile turret: the interior is highly embellished; the windows are enriched with stained glass, and over the altar-piece is a fine painting. Carnmore mountain is of lofty elevation, and abounds with wild and romantic scenery; from its summit are seen 32 lakes, including Lough Erne; and its deep glens are inhabited by a numerous class of peasantry of singular habits and of great originality of character.

ROSSORY, a parish, partly in the barony of GLENAWLEY, but chiefly in that of MAGHERABOY, county of FERMANAGH, and province of ULSTER; containing, with part of the suburbs of Enniskillen, 4338 inhabitants. This parish, which is situated on the shores of Lough Erne, and on the roads leading respectively from Enniskillen to Sligo and Ballyshannon, comprises, according to the Ordnance survey, 7654 statute acres, of which $2302^1/_4$ are in the barony of Glenawley, and in Magheraboy: of these, about 494 acres are water, and by far the greater portion of the remainder is meadow and pasture. The land is of good quality, and that portion of it which is under tillage is in a state of profitable cultivation: there is a moderate proportion of bog, and limestone is quarried for agricultural purposes and also for repairing the roads; the system of agriculture is much improved, and there is no waste land. The principal seats are Lisgoole Abbey, the residence of M. Jones, Esq.; and Gortudrate, of A. Crawford, Esq. The living is a rectory and vicarage, in the diocese of Clogher, and in the patronage of the Bishop: the tithes amount to £240. The glebe-house, a handsome residence, was erected at an expense of £1107, for which purpose the late Board of First Fruits granted a gift of £323 and a loan of £461; the glebe comprises 78 acres, valued at £136.10 per annum. The church is an ancient edifice. In the R. C. divisions the parish forms part of the union or district of Enniskillen. At Portora, within the limits of the parish, is the Royal endowed school of Enniskillen, a handsome building, erected at an expense of £4000. About 120 children are taught in three public schools; and there are three private schools, in which are about 220 children, and a Sunday school. The interest of a bequest of £50 by Mrs. Noble is annually divided among twelve aged women. A very ancient religious foundation appears to have subsisted here, upon the site of which Lisgoole abbey was afterwards founded for Canons Regular by Mac Noellus Mackenleff, King of Ulster, about the year 1106. This establishment was destroyed by fire in 1360, and in the reign of Hen. VIII, having fallen into ruin, it was surrendered by the last abbot to Maguire, tanist of Fermanagh, by whom it was assigned to the Franciscans, and the abbey rebuilt as a place of sepulture for the principal families of that country; at the dissolution it was granted to Sir John Davies. Here is a sulphureous spring in great repute.

TEMPO, a post-town, in that part of the parish of ENNISKILLEN which is in the barony of TYRKENNEDY, county of FERMANAGH, and province of ULSTER, 6 miles (E. N. E.) from Enniskillen, on the road to Five-mile-town, and $86^1/_2$ miles (E. N. E.) from Dublin; containing 335 inhabitants. It is a station of the constabulary police, has a market on Wednesday for butter, and a fair on the 28th of each month. Here is a chapel of ease to the parochial church at Enniskillen; also the R. C. chapel giving name to the district, which comprises the greater part of the parish of Enniskillen, and three townlands of Aughavea; it is a neat structure, erected in 1826. A meeting-house for Wesleyan Methodists has been recently completed; and a dispensary is about to be established.

TOMREGAN, a parish, partly in the barony of KNOCKNINNY, county of FERMANAGH, and partly in that of LOWER LOUGHTEE, but chiefly in the barony of TULLAGHAGH, county of CAVAN, and province of ULSTER, on the road from Belturbet to Swanlinbar; containing, with the post-town of Ballyconnell (which is separately described), 4118 inhabitants. This parish, which is situated on the river Woodford, comprises, according to the Ordnance survey, 10,678 statute acres, of which $3200^3/_4$ are in the county of Fermanagh, and of the remainder $2256^1/_4$ are in Lower Loughtee, and 5221 in Tullaghagh, county of Cavan; 6644 statute acres are applotted under the tithe act, and 275 are under water. The river Woodford has its source in the county of Leitrim, and after reaching Woodford, formerly the residence of the Gore family, and from which it takes its name, passes through two lakes, and becoming deep and broad might at a very trifling expense be made navigable to Lough Erne, a distance of nearly nine miles. The lands are in a very indifferent state of cultivation; a large portion that might be rendered profitable is allowed to remain waste: there is abundance of bog, affording a good supply of fuel. The mountainous parts abound with iron ore and coal, which might be easily raised, but no regular works have been established, though some of the coal has been sent to Ballyhays, Cavan, and to the great iron-works at Arigna. Slieve Russell, which borders on Fermanagh, and is the highest land in this county, is partly within the parish; it is chiefly waste and barren, the surface being in some parts very rocky, and in others a mere swamp. Lead and silverore have been brought down the stream which flows from the mountain of Ortnacullagh, in the vicinity of the parish. There are some quarries of excellent limestone and granite, and marble is also found in some of the townlands; the materials for Cavan court-house, Clancorris castle, and the episcopal palace of Kilmore, were supplied from these quarries. Ballyconnell House, the residence of John Enery, Esq., beautifully situated in a fine demesne on the

Woodford river, is within the parish. There are a small bleaching-mill and flour-mill.

The living is a rectory and vicarage, in the diocese of Kilmore, and in the patronage of the Bishop: the tithes amount to £129.13.4. The glebe-house was built in 1812, at an expense of £1385 British, of which £969 was a loan and £92 a gift from the late Board of First Fruits: the glebe comprises 380 acres, valued at £381.13.3, of which 50 acres are bog, and the remainder arable and pasture land. The church was built about 80 years since at the expense of the late Col. Montgomery, and was enlarged in 1820 at an expense of £923 British, of which half was a gift and half a loan from the same Board; it has recently been further improved at an expense of £70, of which £60 was contributed by the Rev. Mr. Carson, and the remainder by the Rev. J. Storey, the incumbent; it occupies a picturesque situation on the road to Ballinamore, and with the adjacent school-house forms a pleasing object as seen from the mountains. In the R. C. divisions the parish is partly in the union or district of Knockninny, and partly in that of Drumlaine, but chiefly in that of Kildallon; the chapel, at Ballyconnell, is a plain building roofed with thatch. There is a place of worship for Wesleyan Methodists. The school-house at Ballyconnell was built at an expense of £227, of which part was defrayed by the incumbent, part by Government, and part from the Ballyconnell estate; it contains school-rooms for boys and girls, and residences for the master and mistress, and is open to the children of all the poor. There are also schools at Cranaghan, Corramore, Mulnagorman, Gorteree, Gortenedden, and Killiwilly, aided by private subscriptions: about 600 children are educated in these schools, and about 70 in two private schools. In the mountains are some curious caves.

TROREY, or ST. MICHAEL'S, TRORY, a parish, partly in the barony of LURG, but chiefly in that of MAGHERABOY, county of FERMANAGH, and province of ULSTER, 4 miles (N.) from Enniskillen, on Lough Erne; containing 2012 inhabitants. It comprises, according to the Ordnance survey, 6068$^{3}/_{4}$ statute acres, of which 1564$^{1}/_{2}$ are in Lurg and the remainder in Magheraboy; 1832 acres are in Lower Lough Erne, 135$^{3}/_{4}$ in the river Erne and small loughs, upwards of 100 are woodland, and 100 bog; the remainder is arable, and one-third of it was abbey land and is tithe-free. A bridge with an arch of 30 feet span crosses the river here; it was erected in 1817, at an expense of £1100. Adjoining it, on the river Ballycassidy, and on the banks of the lough, are the extensive flour-mills of John Halliday, Esq., employing 25 persons, and worked by water equal to a 35-horse power: small boats, of about 10 tons burden each, ply up the lake to these mills. The parish was constituted, in 1778, by disuniting some townlands from the parish of Devenish: the living is a perpetual cure, in the diocese of Clogher, and in the patronage of the Prebendary of Devenish. The tithes amount to £116.10.3$^{1}/_{2}$, payable to the perpetual curate. The glebe comprises 60 acres, valued at £90 per ann.: the glebe-house was built in 1820, at an expense of £461, being a gift of £415 and a loan of £46 from the late Board of First Fruits. The church is a plain building, erected in 1778, at the cost of £300, defrayed by assessment on the parish. There is a place of worship for Wesleyan Methodists; also five schools, in which about 240 children are taught; and a Sunday school.

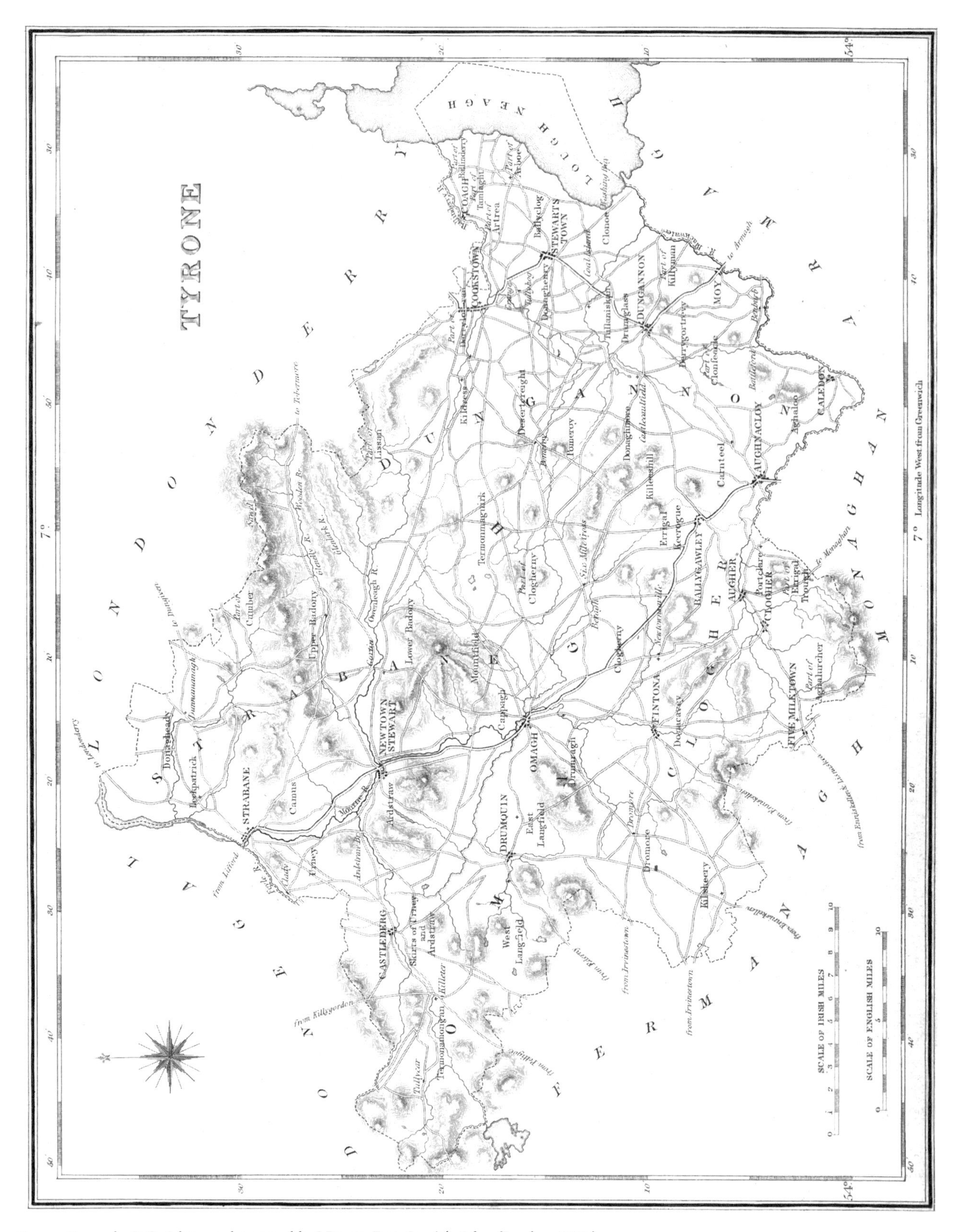

Tyrone. Drawn by R.Creighton and engraved by I.Dower. From Lewis's Atlas *(London, 1837).*

COUNTY TYRONE

A

TOPOGRAPHICAL DICTIONARY

TYR

TYRONE (County of), an inland county of the province of ULSTER, bounded on the east by the county of Armagh and Lough Neagh, on the north by the county of Londonderry, on the west by the counties of Donegal and Fermanagh, and on the south by those of Fermanagh and Monaghan. It extends from 53° 59′ to 54° 37′ (N. Lat.), and from 6° 28′ to 7° 50′ (W. Lon.); comprising an area, according to the Ordnance survey, of 754,395 statute acres, of which 555,820 are cultivated land, 171,314 are unimproved mountain and bog, and 27,261 are covered with water. The population, in 1821, amounted to 261,865; and in 1831, to 302,943.

In the time of Ptolemy it was inhabited by the Scoti, which tribe extended itself over most of the inland regions; though some writers place the Erdini here, as well as in the neighbouring maritime county of Donegal. It was afterwards known as the district or kingdom of Cineal Eoghain, frequently called Tyr-Oen, whence its present name of Tyrone is derived: a portion of its southern border embraces the northern parts of the ancient district of Orgial or Uriel. According to Camden it was divided into Upper and Lower, or North and South Tyrone by the Slieve Gallion mountain; but as this range is now wholly included within Londonderry, it is probable that the name of Tyrone was then extended to the greater part of that county also. This district was from the earliest period of the Irish annals the chief seat of the power of the O'Nials, the princes or kings of the country, who traced their origin from Nial of the nine hostages, and several of whom obtained the sovereignty over the whole island. In the tenth century, Hugh O'Nial, lord or chief of Tyr-Oen, was solicited by Malachy, King of Ireland, to assist him against Brian Boroimhe, then claiming the rank of King of Ireland, and was offered a large portion of Meath as the reward of his acquiescence. O'Nial of Tyrone was one of the chiefs in Roderic O'Conor's army in his unsuccessful attempt to drive the English out of Dublin. In 1177, his death is recorded under the title of King of Tyrone. On the second arrival of King John in Ireland, O'Nial, who had been a formidable opponent to De Courcy during his invasion of Ulster, was prevailed on to give his personal attendance on the king, but not until two hostages had been sent for the security of his person. Hen. III., in a letter to the Irish subordinate princes who had done homage to the English sovereign, styles him O'Ne'l regi de Kinelum sive Tir-Oen. The O'Nial family was also one of the five Irish septs which were specially entitled to the enjoyment of English rights and privileges. On the first arrival of Rich. II. in Ireland, O'Nial met him in Drogheda, being the first of four native princes who waited on that king.

During this period and for many years after, this territory, of which Tyrone was the principal part and the usual seat of the ruling prince's residence, was untouched by the English; while, on the contrary, their borders were exposed to his predatory incursions. O'Nial was one of the adherents of Edward Bruce in his attempt to conquer Ireland. In 1333, on the death of the Earl of Ulster, who was assassinated at Carrickfergus by his own servants, O'Nial crossed the Bann and seized part of the counties of Down and Antrim, which he parcelled out into the districts of the Upper and Lower Claneboy, and these continued subject to the family till the reign of Jas. I. In the reign of Hen. VIII., Hugh Baccagh, or the Lame, invaded Meath, but was afterwards induced to submit to that monarch, by whom he was honoured with a collar of gold; and though he had supported the Kildare family during its rebellion, he was not only pardoned but had the title of Earl of Tyrone conferred on him, with remainder to his illegitimate son Matthew. On his death, however, his legitimate son John, better known by the name of Shane O'Nial, assumed the family title and seized on the inheritance, claiming the sovereignty of the province, and arrogating the supremacy over all the subordinate clans; after maintaining a desultory warfare against the English government, he was assassinated by Alexander Oge McConnell, or McDonnell, the leader of the Scots in Ulster, to whom he had recourse for protection when unable to give effectual resistance to the English. The title was claimed after his death by Tirlogh Leinagh O'Nial, a nephew of the first Earl of Tyrone, but being advanced in years and of a peaceable disposition, he suffered it to be wrested from him by Hugh, the son of Matthew O'Nial, who, after performing some services to the English in the war against Desmond, was admitted to the title and rank of Earl of Tyrone and to the estate of his ancestors, in virtue of the grant made to his grandfather; a fort on the Blackwater being the only place excepted from his jurisdiction.

He afterwards became one of the bitterest and most formidable enemies of the English. In consequence of alleged grievances, he raised forces and suddenly seized on the above-named fort, which was the key of his territory on that side; but being hard pressed by Sir John Norris, he evacuated that position, burnt the town of Dungannon, and the neighbouring villages, together with the greater part of his own fortress there, and endeavoured to preserve his life by concealment. Afterwards, being buoyed up with promises of succours from Spain, he joined a league of all the northern chieftains against the English. In 1597, the whole of Ulster, except the castles along the coast, was in the possession of O'Nial or his adherents; and in an attempt made to relieve the fort of the Blackwater, then hard pressed by his army, Sir Henry Bagnall, Marshal of the English, his inveterate enemy, was utterly routed and slain. After having baffled the celebrated and unfortunate Earl of Essex by a succession of affected submissions and unexpected hostilities, and joined in the expedition to Munster to aid the Spaniards at Kinsale, he was invaded in turn by the royal forces under Lord Mountjoy, who, by seizing on the passes and erecting forts at Charlemont, Mountjoy, and other important positions, reduced him to such extremities that he surrendered at Mellifont, and attended Mountjoy to Dublin, who proposed to send him thence to the Queen. Her death changed his destination for that time; but in the beginning of the ensuing reign, being suspected of an attempt to excite a new insurrection in Ulster, he fled to Spain; and his princely property being consequently confiscated, was parcelled out into six counties, which were modelled, divided, and planted with English settlers under special instructions from the king.

According to the rules of this settlement, the whole county, which was estimated to contain 1571 balliboes, or 98,187 acres, being at the rate of 1000 acres to 16 balliboes, was divided into 78 portions, which, after deducting a portion for the church and some lands for Trinity College, Dublin, were granted to English and Irish undertakers, that is, settlers, who engaged to build, fortify, and stock the lands with British tenantry. Five borough towns, Dungannon, Clogher, Omagh, Strabane, and Mountjoy were allowed a certain portion of the surrounding grounds; and another portion was assigned to some of the members of the O'Nial family. The Irish were distributed as tenants among the undertakers, the swordsmen excepted, who were to be removed to the waste parts of Connaught or Munster, where they were to be dispersed and not suffered to settle together in one place. On an inspection of the progress of the plantation, made by Captain Pynnar under the king's direction in 1618, it appeared that the county was divided into the five precincts of Strabane, Omy, Clogher, Mountjoy, and Dungannon: the first of these, Strabane, was allotted to Scotch undertakers, of whom those then in possession of the lands granted to the original patentees were the Earl of Abercorn, Sir Geo. Hamilton, Sir William Stewart, Sir Robert Newcomen, and Sir John Drummond; Omy, allotted to English undertakers, was in the possession of the Earl of Castlehaven and Sir John Davies; Clogher, also allotted to English undertakers, was held by Lord Ridgwaie, George Ridgwaie, Sir Gerard Lowther, Lord Burleigh, John Leigh, Sir William Stewart, Sir William Cope, and William Parsons; Mountjoy, allotted to Scotch undertakers, was held by Sir Robert Heyburne, Lord Vehiltree, Captain Sanderson, Mrs. Lindsey, Alex Richardson, Andrew Stewart (son to Lord Vehiltree), and David Kenedaie; Dungannon, allotted to servitors and natives, was held by Lord Chichester, Lord Ridgwaie, Sir Toby Caulfield, William Parsons, Sir Francis Ansley, Lord Wingfield, and Tirlagh ONial. The only towns in the erection of which any progress had been made were those of Strabane and Augher. The county continued to improve during the reign of Jas. I. and in the commencement of that of Chas. I., but it suffered greatly during the war of 1641, at the termination of which, much of the lands fell into the hands of new proprietors; and in the subsequent war of 1688 it was the scene of many military events connected with the siege of Londonderry.

The county is partly in the diocese of Clogher, partly in that of Armagh, but chiefly in that of Derry. For purposes of civil jurisdiction it is divided into the baronies of Clogher, Dungannon, Strabane, and Omagh. It contains the borough and market-town of Dungannon, the assize and market-town of Omagh, the disfranchised boroughs and market and post-towns of Strabane and Clogher; the disfranchised borough and market-town of Augher; the market and post-towns of Cookstown, Stewartstown, Newtown-Stewart, Aughnacloy, Caledon, Ballygawley, Castlederg, and Moy; the market-towns of Drumquin, Beregh, and Trillick; and the post-towns of Fintona, Five-mile-town, Dunamanagh, and Coal-Island. The principal villages are Claudy, Coagh, Dromore, Gartin, Pomeroy, Six-mile-cross (each of which has a penny post), Killeter, Newmills, Termonmaguirk, and Tullyhoge. It sent ten members to the Irish parliament, two for the county, and two each for the boroughs of Dungannon, Strabane, Augher, and Clogher. Since the Union its representatives in the Imperial parliament have been two for the county, and one for the borough of Dungannon: the election for the county is held at Omagh. The county constituency, as registered to the commencement of the year 1837, was, 322 freeholders of £50, 346 of £20, and 1805 of £10; 1 rent-charger of £50, and

30 of £20; 50 leaseholders of £20, and 46 of £10; making a total of 2600 electors. Tyrone is included in the north-west circuit: the assizes are held at Omagh, where the county gaol and court-house are situated: general sessions of the peace are held alternately at Omagh and Strabane, for the Omagh district, which comprises the baronies of the same name: those for the district of Dungannon, which comprises the baronies of Dungannon and Clogher, are held at Dungannon and Clogher alternately. The local government is vested in a lieutenant, 13 deputy-lieutenants, and 106 other magistrates, together with the usual county officers, includinig two coroners. There are 29 constabulary police stations, having in the whole a force of an inspector, a paymaster, 2 stipendiary magistrates, 5 officers, 32 constables, 189 men, and 5 horses. The district lunatic asylum is in the city of Londonderry, the county infirmary at Omagh, the fever hospital at Strabane; and there are dispensaries at Termonmaguirk, Stewartstown, Augher, Clogher, Castlederg, Caledon, Dungannon, Newtown-Stewart, Strabane, Dunamanagh, Drumquin, Fintona, Coagh, Dromore, Trillick, Omagh, Gortin, Ballygawley, and Cookstown, supported by equal Grand Jury presentments and private subscription. The Grand Jury presentments for 1836 amounted to £35,331.13.2, of which £4031.11.10 was for roads, bridges, &c., being the county charge; £18,952.1.2$^1/_2$ for the same, being the baronial charge; £5450.17.8 for public buildings, charities, officers' salaries, and incidents; £2574.6.2$^1/_2$ for the police; and £4322.16.3 for the repayment of advances made by Government. In the military arrangements the county is in the northern district, and contains one barrack for infantry at Omagh.

The surface is greatly diversified by a continued variety of hill and dale, rising into elevated mountain tracts in the north and west, which are known by the general name of the Munterlowny mountains: the most elevated is Sawell, part of which is in the county of Londonderry, 2235 feet high; the next is Mullaghearn, 1778 feet. Bessy Bell and Mary Grey are the fanciful names of two mountains detached from this range and standing prominently remarkable on each side of the river Mourne: the former is said to derive its name from Baal or Bel, whose religious rites called Baase were performed on its summit; hence the expression Baase Bell, which by a natural corruption has been moulded into its present popular appellation: the origin of the name of the other has not been ascertained. To the west of the barony of Dungannon are the mountains of Ballygawley, and still further south-west are those of Morley or Murley, both so high as to preclude the possibility of cultivation, though not so lofty as the northern range. The less elevated districts present many views of rich tranquil scenery. The mountainous parts, particularly near the courses of the numerous rivers and streams, abound with picturesque and romantic prospects: the central part of the county from Omagh to Ballygawley is mostly a dreary expanse of bog and heath. The lakes are few and small; in the demesne of Baronscourt are three, in one of which is an artificial islet, clothed with timber, called McHugh's island, from a chieftain of that name who constructed it and erected a fortress on it. Not far from Baronscourt is Lough Creevy; Lough Frae or Fry is in Lissan parish: there are others, small but interesting for their scenery, near Pomeroy, Donoughmore, Fairlough, and Dunamanagh; the border of one in the demesne of Pomeroy presents an exact miniature resemblance of the outline of Ireland.

The climate is very variable: the prevalence of western winds occasions a constant humidity of the atmosphere, which is a frequent cause of rheumatism and paralysis; but the county is improving greatly in this respect; disease is much more uncommon than it was formerly, and those who are well fed and clothed are as free from sickness here as the similar class in any other part of the country. In the mountain districts to the north, the soil is cold and shallow, seldom exceeding six inches in depth: in some parts the subsoil is a tenacious clay, rendering the surface wet and spongy; in others it is a compact bog, equally tenacious of moisture, and therefore equally injurious by retaining the surface water; yet even amidst these elevated cold and moory districts in the north and west, some spots of excellent land appear, well cultivated and highly productive. At Strabane the lands are of a dry and fertile description, and also in a high state of cultivation; near Urney are some meadow lands of the richest quality. The eastern parts are a deep alluvial soil based upon limestone, adequate also to produce excellent crops. The vale of the Blackwater is exceedingly picturesque and also of the greatest fertility.

Agriculture has made rapid advances of late years, particularly in the eastern districts, where crops of every kind are raised of the best quality. The culture of wheat is universal, except in the mountainous parts: the farmers are peculiarly skilful in the management of flax and potatoes. The lands in the more fertile districts are much subdivided, the general size of farms varying from 5 to 50 acres: the fields are judiciously laid out; the fences generally of white thorn, except in the hilly country, where they are mostly of dry stone, sometimes 8 feet broad at the bottom, very carelessly built and much neglected: where stones are scarce, walls built of sods, and often topped with furze, are used. Draining and irrigation form part of the general system in many parts, but the water is not good for irrigation. The improvements in the agricultural implements and carriages have kept pace with those in tillage. Spade cultivation is not so prevalent here as in the hilly districts of other counties. An implement called a "skroghoge," for cutting scraws or sods, is peculiar to this part of the country: it is in the form of a large spade, with a blade of ten inches both in length and breadth, and a handle about four feet and a half long. The sods used in the covering of houses, to lay between the wattles and the thatch, are cut with it about two feet broad and from an inch to two inches thick; the length is determined by that of the slope of the roof: when cut, they are rolled upon a stick like a roll of parchment, and thus carried to the place on which they are to be laid. The mode formerly general here of allowing land to rest for a few years, to recover itself naturally, without the assistance of clover or hayseeds, prevented the pastures from being of a rich quality, but it is no longer practised except by the poorest class of farmers. A pernicious custom exists in many parts of turning the cattle into the potato grounds before the stalks are withered, thus checking the growth of the bulb and injuring the land. Red and white clover are the most common kind of artificial grasses.

The native cattle are mostly reared on the mountains; they are of various colours and shapes, but generally small, as heavy stock could not subsist on the scanty vegetation produced there, being principally heath and a coarse kind of sedge grass which springs up immediately after burning the heath, a common practice in many parts. In no other county in Ireland has there been a greater improvement in the breed of cattle than in the low country of Tyrone. Some of the best description in England and Scotland have been brought over. The numerous crosses thus produced have occasioned a great variety of stock, which, however, appears necessary to suit the various soils. In the valley of the Blackwater and some other similar districts, the Durham breed thrives remarkably well, and in many parts a judicious cross with the Kerry cow has been introduced to great advantage. Though there are few extensive dairy farms, butter is made in large quantities, and some cheese: the butter is usually salted and made up in firkins for the Scotch market. The native horse, though ill-shaped, is hardy and well suited to agricultural purposes: a superior description, for the road or field sports, is brought in from other counties: the great mart for the purchase of good horses is the fair of Moy; yet some very fine horses are now reared in the county from British sires. The native sheep are small and ill-shaped, and very inferior both as to fleece and carcass: these are confined to the mountainous districts; in the fertile parts the breed is good; but, strictly speaking, Tyrone is not a sheep-feeding county. The vicinity of Strabane is the only part in which pigs are kept in great numbers; and little improvement has taken place in this kind of stock.

The county exhibits some very striking geological features. The red sandstone formation embraces a con siderable portion of its southern and eastern parts, while the greatest part of the north and west belongs to the clay-slate formation. In both districts there are considerable exceptions. The clay-slate is intersected by a vein of micaceous limestone, which first appears in the bed of the river Poe; thence passing near Newtown-Stewart and crossing the Munterlowney mountains, it terminates near the village of Dunamanagh, in the northern extremity of the county. Detached portions of limestone, similar to that of the great central field of Ireland, are to be met with in many parts: white limestone, containing numerous nodules of flint, similar to that of Antrim, is found near Coagh. Near Cookstown is a species dissimilar to all the others, and containing a great variety of organic remains: the vein extends southwards to Stewartstown and is disposed in strata varying from five inches to four feet in thickness. But the most remarkable geological feature of the county is its coal formation, in which, though the field is of small extent as compared with those in the south and west, it surpasses them in the thickness of the seams and quality of the mineral. The district around this coal field contains rocks of every class, from the more ancient of the primary to the latest of the secondary or alluvial formations. In the Coal Island works the coal rests on fire-clay, in Drumglass on soft porous sandstone, and in Annahoe on blue clunch; but as the country in which the collieries are situated is covered with alluvial soil to the depth of from 20 to 30 feet, it is often difficult to trace the various beds. In its external aspect it is in general similar to that composed of sandstone; the surface exhibiting an assemblage of low hills with steep acclivities and flattened summits, rarely exceeding 100 feet in height: when higher, their upper part is generally composed either of new red sandstone or of trap. The Coal Island district is 8 miles long by an average breadth of $2^1/_2$ miles, and therefore comprehends an area of about 1140 acres; the Annahoe district is little more than a mile long by half a mile in breadth, and may therefore contain about 500 acres. Both districts contain sandstone, sandstone slate, shale, argillaceous iron-stone, and fire-clay. The composition and external character both of the coal and of its accompanying strata are nearly similar in the two divisions: it burns rapidly, giving out a bright blaze and intense heat, like that of Ayrshire. The shale, called by the miners metal, varies in colour from light blueish white to black, is extremely soft, and decomposes rapidly on exposure to the atmosphere: it sometimes contains impressions of ferns, myrtle, and gigantic reeds. An uncommon species of clay-stone, extrennely compact and difficult to break, occurs interstratified with the shale. Argillaceous iron-stone is not abundant; when found, impressions of a large species of fern are frequently detected in the interior. The fire-clay, which lies immediately beneath the bed of coal, is so soft as to form a pulpy mass on the admixture of the slightest moisture, and by allowing the pillars of coal which support the roof to sink into it, immediately swells and would close the workings were not great precautions adopted. This clay makes fire-bricks equal to those of Stourbridge.

Great irregularity prevails in the direction and inclination of the coal strata: the main dip in the southern extremity is north-east; in the northern, south-west; but it is frequently altered by wavings or undulations, which are generally north and south. Besides these undulations, which throw the strata into confusion, the continuity of the beds is often broken by slips or faults. The average angle of the strata with the horizon is about 11° 30′, or one foot of fall for five of length, but in many places it increases to 50°: the

Killymoon Castle. Engraved by Branston. From The Irish Penny Journal, *vol. 1, 1841.*

difficulty of clearing off the water is much increased by this increase of angle. The quantity of coal capable of being produced from the Coal Island district may be estimated from the fact that, in the immediate vicinity of the village, there are seven workable beds of coal, amounting, in the aggregate, to 34 feet of coal in a depth of 244 yards: no instance occurs in the great mining districts of England of an equal number of beds so near each other. From the sulphureous and ferruginous appearance of the water in many places, it is evident that large quantities of iron ore are deposited here. Clay, of various colours, for making bricks, may be procured in all parts of the county. Good flooring and ridge tiles, garden pots, and coarse earthenware are made in the neighbourhood of Moy and Killyman. Excellent pottery is manufactured near Coal Island: the clay, which is of a muddy white before it is baked, is made up into small oblong wedges of about a pound each, and sold as a substitute for fullers' earth, for which purpose it is sent to all parts and brings back a profitable return. A line of escars proceeds from Killyman, by Dungannon, Ballygawley, and Clogher, to Five-mile-town, where it enters the county of Fermanagh. Those in this county are formed of nodules of basalt, greenstone, porphyry, limestone, chalcedony, jasper, and agate: a branch of them near Fintona is almost exclusively formed of chalcedony, jasper, agates, and quartz. At Killeshill and Newtown-Saville the formation of the escars is as regular as if they had been artificially arranged. In the sandstone formation in Killyman, fossil fishes of several species are found, among which the trout and pike can be distinctly recognised: on raising the stone from the quarry, the fish is found imbedded in it, one side of it being raised in high relief, and the concave impress of it in the lower stone exhibits the marks of the gills, eyes, and scales with the utmost accuracy.

The linen manufacture has long been the staple of the county, and though it has declined considerably, large quantities are annually manufactured and bleached, principally for the English market. Bleach-greens were numerous in every part, but nearly two-thirds of them are unemployed or converted to other purposes. The linens are all carried in a brown state to the towns of Omagh, Dungannon, Cookstown, Ballygawley, Fintona, and Strabane, and sold in the markets there. The wool of the county, and all that is brought into it, is made up into cloth, blankets, and druggets. The farmers, who are in general linen-weavers, consume the greater part of the cloth and blankets; the druggets are worn by the poorer class of women; the cloth is generally yard wide, and of very good quality. The people are all expert at dyeing for their domestic purposes; they dye various colours, but blue is the favourite. Excellent druggets of two parts wool and one linen are much esteemed. An economical practice of the wool-spinners is worthy of notice: the root of the common fern is replete during summer with an oily glutinous substance, an excellent substitute for oil or butter; and as wool cannot be manufactured without the aid of some substance of this nature, a pound of wool requiring a quarter of a pound of butter, the common people supply the want of it by cutting the fern root into small pieces, bruising it in a mortar, and pressing out the juice through a cloth. Spades, shovels, and other farming implements, crucibles and other chymical vessels, and fire-bricks, are manufactured very extensively at Coal Island. Tanning is carried on in several places, as is also the manufacture of tobacco, soap, and candles. There is a good ale brewery at Donoughmore; distilleries are worked in various parts. There are large flour-mills at Caledon and Coal Island, plating-mills at Leckpatrick, Fintona and New-mills, and scutch-mills in most parts.

The county is copiously watered by the numerous branches of the Foyle, which, under the names of the Munterlony, the Poe, the Mourne, the Carnown, the Owenkellow, and the Owenreagh, rise in the mountainous central districts: the Derg joins the Mourne from a lough of its own name; the Dennet empties itself into the Foyle near the northern boundary of the county. The Foyle, which forms part of the western boundary, is navigable to St. Johnstown, and thence by an artificial navigation between three and four miles farther up to Strabane. The Ballinderry river forms part of the north-eastern boundary. The Blackwater, which forms part of the southern boundary, and discharges itself into Lough Neagh, is navigable to Moy and Blackwatertown: near the mouth of this river a canal proceeds from the lake to Coal Island, and more than half a century since was partially opened above New Mills, but this latter part of the undertaking was abandoned before the canal was completed. The beauty of the scenery in several parts is much enhanced by woods and plantations. Large tracts of land near Baron's Court, and Rash or Mountjoy forest, have been planted since 1795. Near Augher and Favour Royal there are considerable natural woods, and throughout the greater part of the county the soil appears disposed to throw up a spontaneous growth of timber, but in too many instances the young trees are neglected and the cattle suffered to browse upon them. Near Strabane are many large and well-stocked orchards. The roads are numerous, and in general judiciously laid out and kept in good repair. A new line is now in progress of formation from Omagh by Mountfield, Kildress, and Cookstown to Belfast. The roads are all made and repaired by county presentments.

The remains of antiquity are neither numerous nor peculiarly interesting. Raths are scattered over almost every part: near the western border of the mountain named Mary Gray, more than twelve of them may be seen within the compass of a mile: they are generally in pairs; many are now scarcely discernible, in consequence of the farmers having drawn off the mould for manure. The most perfect has a parapet six feet high, with stepping-stones projecting from the inner sides in an oblique direction to the top, like the winding of a staircase: its diameter is 33 yards. A very remarkable Druidical monument, called Clogh-togle, or the "lifted stone," stands on a hill a mile north of Newtown-Stewart: it consists of three large stones set upright in a triangular position, about 7 feet high each, and covered with a broad horizontal flag, 11 feet long, 7' broad, and 15 inches thick. On an opposite hill, at the distance of about 100 yards, was a similar relic of larger dimensions, now lying on the ground. There is a large and very beautiful one, also called Clogh-togle, at Tamlaght near Coagh; it consists of six upright stones standing about 5 feet above the ground, on which is a large slab whose greatest diameter is 10 feet, its circumference 28, and its greatest thickness 7 feet; and there is another, but less perfect, in the demesne of Loughry, and a very noble one, 12 feet high, a quarter of a mile above Castle Derg. At Kilmeillie, near Dungannon, are two circles of stones, each about 20 yards in diameter, in the form of the figure 8. On the same hill was found a kind of altar of dry stones, with the charcoal and bones fresh among the stones, which retained the marks of fire.

An urn was found in a little sandy hill near Cookstown, covered with a large lime-stone slab, and surrounded by six others. Near Omagh, three small chests containing as many urns were found in 1712, under two heaps of stones. In the parish of Errigal-Keroge is a fiat stone set upright, about three feet broad and of the same height above ground, having one side covered with carvings of a regular design, consisting of waving and circular lines: it had been the cover of a vault formed of flags set edgeways: in the vault were found two earthen vessels containing ashes. Near Dungannon were found several brazen trumpets of an uncommon construction, with a hole in the side, and the smaller end stopped, supposed to have been Danish. The monastic institutions, of which traces yet remain, are those of Ardboe, Ardstraw, Cluin-Dhubhain, Garvaghkerin, Puble, Grange, and Donoughmore. Those of Clogher, Airecal-Dachioroc or Errigal-Keroge, Corock, Ballinasagart, Dungannon, Omagh, Maghclair, Strabane, and Trillick exist only in the records of history. The remains of ancient castles are numerous, but few of them are of much importance. Benburb is the largest: near it are the ruins of one of the residences of Shane O'Nial; those of Newtown-Stewart, Dungannon, Strabane, and Ballygawley are, together with the modern mansions of the nobility and gentry throughout the county, noticed under their respective parishes.

The peasantry are very industrious. The houses of the farmers are built in some parts of stone, in others of clay;

slating is becoming more prevalent than thatch for roofing. The want of native timber has also been much felt in the construction of the houses of the small farmers and cottiers. The cabins are generally built at the joint cost of landlord and tenant, in which case the latter has an abatement of rent: when the whole is executed at the tenant's cost, a year's rent is usually allowed him. The use of turf for fuel is universal, except in the immediate neighbourhood of the collieries. The food consists of potatoes and oatmeal, and in seasons of scarcity, barley-meal; milk is used in summer and autumn; in winter, herrings. Sometimes a pig is killed at Christmas, or several labourers join in the purchase of a cow. The Donagh, which is kept at Brookborough, near Five-mile-town, is a box or casket about the size of a thick quarto volume, containing a representation of Christ and the Apostles in high relief on brass coated with silver, under which are some relics; it is used as a test of veracity in taking evidence among the people. A belief in fairies, called here the Wee People, is universal among the poorer peasantry; as is the custom of driving their cattle round fires lighted on Midsummer eve. A kind of hurling, here called "common," is a favourite amusement of the young men: formerly they devoted eleven days at Christmas to this exercise, now they give only one; a proof of the increase of habits of industry. There are chalybeate springs at Dunbonrover, in Badony parish; at the foot of Douglas mountain; besides several of less note among the Munterlowny mountains. At Aghaloo is a sulphureous water stronger than that at Swanlinbar; and a very valuable mineral water at Scarvey, two miles from Aughnacloy. Tyrone gives the inferior titles of Earl and Viscount to the Marquess of Waterford, the head of the Beresford family.

AGHALURCHER – see entry in Co. Fermanagh section.

ARBOE, or ARDBOE, a parish, partly in the barony of LOUGHINSHOLIN, county of LONDONDERRY, but chiefly in the barony of DUNGANNON, county of TYRONE, and province of ULSTER, 5 miles (E. N. E.) from Stewartstown; containing 8148 inhabitants. A monastery was founded here by St. Colman, son of Aidhe, and surnamed Mucaidhe, whose reliques were long preserved in it: it was destroyed in 1166, by Rory Makang Makillmory Omorna, but there are still some remains. The parish is situated on the shore of Lough Neagh, by which it is bounded on the east, and comprises, according to the Ordnance survey, 33,504 statute acres, of which 21,000 form part of Lough Neagh, and 56 are in small islands. The greater portion is under tillage, and there are some tracts of good meadow, about 50 acres of woodland, and 1000 acres of bog. The system of agriculture is improved; the soil is fertile, and the lands generally in a high state of cultivation. There are several large and handsome houses, the principal of which is Elogh, the residence of Mrs. Mackay. The living is a rectory, in the diocese of Armagh, and in the patronage of the Provost and Fellows of Trinity College Dublin: the tithes amount to £507.13.10$^1/_2$. The church, a neat small edifice, was erected in the reign of William and Mary, on a site two miles westward from the ruins of the ancient abbey. The glebe-house is a handsome building; and the glebe comprises 212 acres. The R. C. parish is co-extensive with that of the Established Church; the chapel, a spacious and handsome edifice, is situated at New Arboe; and there are two altars in the open air, where divine service is performed alternately once every Sunday. There is a place of worship for Presbyterians in connection with the Seceding synod. There are four public schools, in which about 320 boys and 240 girls are taught; and there are also five private schools, in which are about 140 boys and 50 girls, and five Sunday schools. On the western shore of Lough Neagh are the ruins of the ancient abbey; which form an interesting and picturesque feature; and the remains of an old church, of which the walls are standing. Near them is an ancient ornamented stone cross in good preservation.

ARDSTRAW, or ARDSRATH, a parish, partly in the barony of OMAGH, but chiefly in that of STRABANE, county of TYRONE, and province of ULSTER; containing, with the post-town of Newtown-Stewart, 21,212 inhabitants. This place was distinguished, under the name of Ardsrath, as the seat of an ancient bishoprick, over which St. Eugene, or Oen, presided about the year 540. At a very early period a small stone church or chapel existed here; and the names are recorded of several bishops who presided over the see, which, in 597, was removed to Maghera, and finally to Derry, in 1158. This place suffered repeatedly by fire, and appears to have been destroyed about the close of the twelfth century. The parish, which is situated on the road from Dublin to Londonderry, comprises, according to the Ordnance survey, 44,974 1/4 statute acres, of which 5374 are covered with water. The surface is pleasingly diversified with hill and dale, and enlivened by the rivers Struell, Glenelly, and Derg, which, after flowing through the parish, unite in forming the river Morne, which abounds with trout and salmon; and also with several large and beautiful lakes, of which three are within the demesne of Baron's Court. The land is chiefly arable, with pasture intermixed; and the soil in the valleys is fertile; but there are considerable tracts of mountain and several extensive bogs. Limestone is found in several places at the base of the mountain called Bessy Bell, the whole of the upper portion of which is clay-slate; on the summit of another mountain, called Mary Gray, it is found with clay-slate at the base; and round the southern base of the former are detached blocks of freestone scattered in every direction. There are also some quarries of limestone at Cavandaragh; the stone is raised in blocks, or lamina, from a quarter of an inch to three feet in thickness. The mountains within and forming a portion of the boundary of the parish are Bessy Bell, Douglas, and Mary Gray, which present beautiful and romantic scenery, particularly in the neighbourhood of Newtown-Stewart; and the view from the high grounds, including the lakes and rivers by which the parish is diversified, is truly picturesque. There are five bridges; one at Moyle, of three elliptic arches; a very ancient bridge at Newtown-Stewart, of six arches; another of six arches at Ardstraw, and a modern bridge of three arches on the Derry road. The principal seats are Baron's Court, the residence of the Marquess of Abercorn; Castlemoyle, of the Rev. R. H. Nash, D. D.; Woodbrook, of R. M. Tagert, Esq.; Newtown-Stewart Castle, of Major Crawford; Coosh, of A. Colhoun, Esq.; and Spa Mount, of E. Sproule, Esq. There were formerly several bleach-greens in the parish, but at present there is only one in operation, which is at Spa Mount, on the river Derg, and in which about 16,000 pieces are annually bleached and finished, principally for the London market.

The living is a rectory, in the diocese of Derry, and in the patronage of the Provost and Fellows of Trinity College, Dublin: the tithes amount to £1094. The church is a large and beautiful edifice with a handsome spire, and is situated in the town of Newtown-Stewart; a grant of £478 for its repair has been lately made by the Ecclesiastical Commissioners. A new church, or chapel of ease, is about to be built at Baron's Court, or Magheracreegan, for which the late Board of First Fruits granted £600, now in the hands of the Ecclesiastical Commissioners. The glebe-house has a glebe of 681 acres attached to it, of which $461\frac{3}{4}$ are in a state of cultivation. The R. C. parish is co-extensive with that of the Established Church, but is divided into East and West Ardstraw; there are chapels at Newtown-Stewart, Dragish, and Cairncorn. There are five places of worship for Presbyterians in connection with the Synod of Ulster, at Ardstraw, Newtown-Stewart, Douglas Bridge, Clady, and Garvetagh; that of Ardstraw is aided by a second class grant, and those of Newtown-Stewart, Douglas-Bridge, and Clady have each a third class grant. There are also two places of worship for Presbyterians of the Seceding Synod, one at Drumligagh of the first class, and the other at Newtown-Stewart of the second class; and there are a meeting-house for Primitive and two for Wesleyan Methodists. The parochial school at Newtown-Stewart is aided by an annual donation from the rector; and there are fifteen other public schools in different parts of the parish, and seventeen private schools; in the former are 1600, and in the latter about 780, children: and thirty-five Sunday schools. The poor are supported by voluntary contributions, aided by the interest of £100 in the $3\frac{1}{2}$ per cents, being a sum due to the parish, which was recovered about twenty years since by process of law, and by act of vestry added to the poor fund.

There are numerous interesting remains of antiquity in the parish, the most ancient of which are those of the monastery and cathedral of Ardsrath, near the village, consisting chiefly of the foundations of that part of the building which was formerly used as the parish church, the remains of some very beautiful crosses of elaborate workmanship, and several upright stones and columns richly fluted; but the churchyard, which was very extensive, has been contracted by the passing of the public road, in the formation of which many remains of antiquity were destroyed. Nearly adjoining is a ruin which tradition points out as the bishop's palace, and which was occupied as an inn when the Dublin road passed this way. About three miles above Ardstraw Bridge, and situated on a gentle eminence, are the picturesque ruins of Scarvaherin abbey, founded by Turloch Mac Dolagh, in 1456, for Franciscan friars of the third order, and on its dissolution granted by Queen Elizabeth to Sir Henry Piers; and near Newtown-Stewart is the site of the friary of Pubble, which appears to have been an appendage to Scarvaherin, and was granted at the same time to Sir Henry Piers; of the latter, nothing but the cemetery remains.

In Newtown-Stewart are the extensive and beautiful remains of the castle built by Sir Robert Newcomen, in 1619; it is in the Elizabethan style, with gables and clustered chimneys. Jas. II. lodged in this castle, on his return from Lifford in 1589, and by his orders it was dismantled on the day following; with the exception of the roof, it is nearly perfect. At the foot of the mountain called Bessy Bell are the ruins of an ancient building called Harry Ouree's Castle, concerning which some remarkable legends are preserved by the country people; they consist of two circular towers, with a gateway between them, and some side walls, which overhang their base more than 8 feet. Near the end of the bridge at Newtown-Stewart is a large mound of earth, evidently thrown up to protect the ford, which in early times must have been of importance as the only pass through the vast range of the Munterlony mountains. There was a similar fort on the ford of Glenelly, near Moyle Castle, and another at the old ford at the village of Ardstraw. On the summit of Bessy Bell, or Boase-Baal, on which in pagan times sacrifice is supposed to have been offered to Baal or Bel, is a large and curious cairn; there are also cairns on the summit of Mary Gray, and more than thirty forts in the parish, nearly in a line from east to west, which were designed to guard the passes on the rivers of Glenelly and Derg. About a mile below Newtown-Stewart, in the bed of the river, is a single upright stone, called the "Giant's Finger," and lately "Flinn's rock," respecting which many strange traditions are preserved in the neighbourhood. – See NEWTOWN-STEWART.

ARDSTRAW-BRIDGE, a village, in the parish of ARDSTRAW, barony of STRABANE, county of TYRONE, and province of ULSTER, 3 miles (W. N. W.) from Newtown-Stewart: the population is returned with the parish. This place, formerly Ardsrath, is of high antiquity, and was distinguished for its ancient and greatly celebrated abbey, noticed in the preceding description of the parish of Ardstraw. The village is situated on the river Derg, which is here wide and rapid, and is crossed by an ancient stone bridge of six arches, over which the old road from Londonderry to Dublin formerly passed: it contains 32 houses, some of which are well built, but several of them are old and in a neglected state. There were formerly six fairs held in the village, which were large and well attended, but they have been discontinued for some time. There is a place of worship for Presbyterians in connection with the Synod of Ulster, and a public school.

ARDTREA, or ARTREA, a parish, partly in the barony of DUNGANNON, county of TYRONE, and partly in the barony of LOUGHINSHOLIN, county of LONDONDERRY, and province of ULSTER; containing, with the district or perpetual curacy of Woods-chapel, and the greater part of the market and post-town of Moneymore, 12,390 inhabitants, of which number, 7471 are in the district of Woods-chapel. During the rebellion of the Earl of Tyrone, in the reign of Elizabeth, this place was the scene of numerous conflicts; and in the parliamentary war, in 1641, it was involved in many of the military transactions of that period. In 1688–9, a sanguinary battle took place here between the adherents of Jas. II., who were in possession of the forts of Charlemont and Mountjoy, and the forces of Wm. III., commanded by Lord Blayney, who, having possession of Armagh, was desirous of assisting the garrisons of Inniskillen and Derry, and for this purpose determined to force a passage to Coleraine, which he accomplished, after defeating a detachment of the enemy's forces at the bridge of Ardtrea. The parish, which is also called Ardtragh, is situated partly on Lough Beg, but chiefly on Lough Neagh, and is intersected by the Ballinderry river and by numerous roads, of which the principal are those leading respectively from Armagh to Coleraine, from Omagh to Belfast, and from Stewarts-town to Moneymore. It contains, according to the Ordnance survey, 20,962$^3/_4$ statute acres, of which 18,679$^1/_4$ are in the county of Londonderry, including 2181$^1/_2$ in Lough Neagh, 317$^1/_2$ in Lough Beg, and 26$^1/_2$ in the river Bann. The soil is very various; the land is chiefly arable, and is fertile and well cultivated, especially around Moneymore, on the estate belonging to the Drapers' Company, and on that belonging to the Salters' Company round Ballyronan.

There are several extensive tracts of bog in various parts, amounting in the whole to nearly 3000 acres, and affording an ample supply of fuel. Freestone of every variety, colour and quality, is found here in abundance; and there is plenty of limestone. At a short distance from the church, on the road to Cookstown, is an extraordinary whin-dyke, which rises near Ballycastle in the county of Antrim, passes under Lough Neagh, and on emerging thence near Stewart Hall, passes through this parish and into the mountain of Slievegallion, near Moneymore. Spring Hill, the pleasant seat of W. Lenox Conyngham, Esq., is an elegant and antique mansion, situated in a rich and highly improved demesne, embellished with some of the finest timber in the country. The other principal seats are Lakeview, the residence of D. Gaussen, Esq.; Warwick Lodge, of W. Bell, Esq.; and Ardtrea house, of the Rev. J. Kennedy Bailie, D.D. The farm-houses are generally large and well built; and most of the farmers, in addition to their agricultural pursuits, carry on the weaving of linen cloth for the adjoining markets. There is an extensive bleach-green, which, after having been discontinued for some years, has been repaired and is now in operation. The primate's court for the manor of Ardtrea is held at Cookstown monthly, for the recovery of debts under £5; and its jurisdiction extends over such lands in the parishes of Lissan, Derryloran, Kildress, Arboe, Desertcreight, Ardtrea, Clonoe, Tamlaght, Ballinderry, and Donaghendrie, as are held under the see.

The living is a rectory, in the diocese of Armagh, and in the patronage of the Provost and Fellows of Trinity College, Dublin: the tithes amount to £738.9.3$^3/_4$. The church, an elegant edifice in the later English style, was erected in 1830, near the site of the ancient church; the principal entrance is a composition of very elegant design, and, from its elevated site, the church forms a very pleasing object in the landscape. The glebe-house is a large and handsome residence, built of hewn freestone by the late Dr. Elrington, then rector of the parish and subsequently Bishop of Ferns, aided by a gift of £100, and a loan of £1030, from the late Board of First Fruits: the glebe comprises 115$^1/_4$ acres. The district church, called Woods-chapel, is situated at a distance of 10 miles from the mother church: the living is a perpetual curacy, in the patronage of the Rector. In the R. C. divisions the parish is the head of a union or district, called Moneymore, which comprises this parish and part of that of Desertlyn, and contains three chapels, one at Moneymore, one at Ballynenagh, and a third at Derrygaroe. There are two places of worship for Presbyterians at Moneymore, one for those in connection with the Synod of Ulster, of the first class, built by the Drapers' Company at an expense of £4000; and one for those in connection with the Seceding Synod, of the second class, built by subscription on a site given by the Drapers' Company, who also contributed £250 towards its erection. There are three schools aided by the Drapers' Company, and one at Ballymulderg, the whole affording instruction to about 170 boys and 170 girls; and there are also two pay schools. An ancient urn very elaborately ornamented was found in a kistvaen, on opening a tumulus in the townland of Knockarron, in 1800, and is now in the possession of John Lindesay, Esq.. of Loughry. – See MONEYMORE, and WOODS-CHAPEL.

AUGHALOO, or AUGHLOE, a parish, in the barony of DUNGANNON, county of TYRONE, and province of ULSTER; containing, with the post-town of Caledon, 10,140 inhabitants. This parish, which is the most easterly in the county, is bounded on the east by the river Blackwater, and is situated on the mail coach road from Armagh to Aughnacloy; it contains, according to the Ordnance survey, 19,583$^3/_4$ statute acres, of which 140 are under water. The surface is pleasingly undulated and well planted and watered; the lands are in a high state of cultivation, the system of agriculture is greatly improved, and' there is little waste land and only a small portion of bog. There are several gentlemen's seats, of which the principal are Caledon Hill,

Augher Castle. Drawn by Francis Grose. From Francis Grose, Antiquities of Ireland *(London, 1791).*

the seat of the Earl of Caledon; Crilly, of R. Pettigrew, Esq; Rahaghy, of N. Mayne, Esq.; and Drummond, or Cottage Hill, of H. Moore, Esq. It is in the diocese of Armagh, and is a rectory and vicarage, forming part of the corps of the archdeaconry of Armagh and the union of Carrenteel; the tithes amount to £609.4.7. The church is situated in the town of Caledon. A perpetual curacy was founded here in 1807, by the archdeacon, who endowed it with £50 per annum and $26^1/_2$ acres of glebe; it has also an augmentation from Primate Boulter's fund, and is in the gift of the Archdeacon. In the R. C. divisions this parish is the head of a union or district, comprising the parishes of Aughaloo and Carrenteel; the chapel is at Caledon. There are three places of worship for Presbyterians, at Minterburn, Crillig, and Caledon, the last in connection with the Seceding Synod and of the second class: there is also an Independent meeting-house, but no regular service is performed in it. The parochial school is at Caledon; there are male and female schools at Ramakit, Curlough, Minterburn, and Dyan, built and chiefly supported by the Earl of Caledon; a school near the demesne was built and is supported by the Countess of Caledon, in which 40 girls are clothed and educated; and a school at Rahaghy is under the National Board. These schools afford instruction to about 580 boys and 370 girls; and there are also five private schools, in which are about 100 boys and 150 girls, and 14Sunday schools. Close to a stream that separates the union of Carrenteel from the parish of Errigal-Kerogue is a sulphuric spring, resembling in its properties the Harrogate waters, but wanting their purgative quality: it has been enclosed in a small house erected over it by an individual who had received benefit from the use of the water. At Glenarb are the remains of a monastery with a burial-ground, and numerous stone crosses have been discovered. – See CALEDON

AUGHER, a market-town (formerly a parliamentary borough), in the parish and barony of CLOGHER, county of TYRONE, and province of ULSTER, 2 miles (N. E. by E.) from Clogher, and $75^1/_4$ (N. N. W.) from Dublin; containing 726 inhabitants. Of the origin and early history of this place but very little is known. In the reign of Elizabeth, Lord-Deputy Mountjoy placed in it a powerful garrison to defend the pass through the valley in which it is situated, that retained possession for some time, constantly harassing the army of the Earl of Tyrone till his final surrender at Mellifont. From this place the queen's army marched when it crossed the mountains to give battle to the earl at

Magheralowney, where that chieftain's principal magazine was taken, in June 1602. At the time of the English settlement of Ulster, by virtue of a decree by James I. in 1611, Sir Thomas Ridgway, Knt., Treasurer at War for Ireland, received, in 1613, a grant of 315 acres of land in the barony of Clogher, under an agreement that he should, within four years, settle on a parcel of land called Agher twenty Englishmen or Scots, chiefly artificers and tradesmen, to be incorporated as burgesses and made a body politic within the said four years; and should set apart convenient places for the site of the town, churchyard, market-place, and public school; he was likewise to assign to the burgesses houses and lands and 30 acres of commons. Sir Thomas received also, in 1611, the grant of a market and two fairs to be held here; and in 1613, the town and precincts, with the exception of a fort and bawn called Spur Royal castle, which had been erected, were created a borough. Besides the 315 acres of land on which he was to found the borough, Sir Thomas received a grant of 2000 acres called Portclare; and according to Pynnar's report in 1619, it appears that, besides the fort and bawn, he had built 16 houses of stone in the town, which were inhabited by English artificers who were burgesses, and had each two acres of land, and commons for their cattle. In 1630, Sir James Erskine, Knt., then proprietor of the manor, received a grant of two additional fairs. On the breaking out of the war in 1641, a garrison was stationed here by Col. Chichester and Sir Arthur Tyringham, and the castle was gallantly defended against the insurgent forces, who, in an attempt to take it by storm, were repulsed. This defeat so exasperated their leader, Sir Phelim O'Nial, that in revenge he ordered his agent, Mac Donnel, to massacre all the English Protestants in three adjacent parishes. Sir James Erskine dying without male issue, the extensive manor of Portclare, which in 1665 was confirmed in the family by Chas. II., under its present name of Favour Royal, was divided between his two daughters, who married into the families of Richardson and Moutray, and the respective portions are still in the possession of their descendants, of whom the present proprietor of Augher castle has assumed the additional surname and arms of Bunbury. The castle was finally dismantled by order of parliament, and continued in a state of dilapidation and neglect till 1832, when it was restored and a large and handsome mansion built adjoining it by Sir J. M. Richardson Bunbury, Bart. The ancient building consisted of a pentagonal tower surrounded by a wall 12 feet high and flanked by four circular towers: the wall has been removed, but one of the round towers has been restored; and the entrance gateway has also been removed and rebuilt on an elevated situation commanding some fine views, in which the remains of the old castle form an interesting object: the mansion is situated in a well-wooded demesne of 220 acres, and upon the margin of a beautiful lake.

The town is situated on the river Blackwater, over which is a bridge adjoining it, and in a fertile valley between two ridges of lofty mountains clothed with verdure to the summit, of which the highest, Knockmany, is covered on its south side with thriving plantations. It consists of one principal street, from which another branches at right angles on the south leading to Clogher; and has a penny post to Aughnacloy. Several new roads have been lately formed; and not far distant is an excellent bog. The lands in the neighbourhood are well cultivated. Besides Augher Castle, there are several gentlemen's seats near the town, described in the article on the parish of Clogher, which see. The market is on Monday, and has lately become a good market for oats; and fairs for the sale of cattle, sheep, pigs, and other commodities, are held on the last Monday in every month, in the market-place set apart under the original grant at the bottom of Clogher-street; the market-house is the only public building in the town. The collection of tolls and customs has been discontinued by the proprietors of the manor. Here is a chief station of the constabulary police.

The charter granted in 1613 incorporated the inhabitants under the style of "The Burgomaster, Free Burgesses, and Commonalty of the Borough of Agher," with the privilege of holding a civil court of record with jurisdiction to the extent of five marks, and of returning two members to the Irish parliament, which they continued to exercise till the Union, when the £15,000 compensation money for the abolition of its franchise was awarded to James, Marquess of Abercorn. Since that period no corporate officers have been appointed, and the town is now entirely within the jurisdiction of the county magistrates, who hold petty sessions irregularly. The seneschal of the manor holds a court here every third Monday, for the recovery of debts to the amount of 408, the jurisdiction of which extends into the parishes of Errigal-Kerogue, Errigal-Trough, Ballygawley, and Clogher; and a manorial court leet is held once in the year. Divine service is performed in the market-house every Sunday by the officiating clergyman of Clogher. A school for boys was built on part of the Commons Hill, or Fair Green, granted by the proprietors of the manor to the deans of Clogher, in trust for a school-house, and with funds provided from the Lord-Lieutenant's School Fund it is supported by private subscriptions and by a weekly payment of ld. from each pupil; and a school for girls is supported in a similar manner.

AUGHNACLOY, a market and post-town, in the parish of CARRENTEEL, barony of DUNGANNON, county of TYRONE, and province of ULSTER, 16 miles (S. E.) from Omagh, and $75^1/_2$ (N. N. W.) from Dublin; containing 1742 inhabitants. This place, which is on the confines of the county of Monaghan, is situated on the river Blackwater, and on the mail coach road from Dublin to Londonderry. The town was built by Acheson Moore, Esq., who also erected the parish church, and it is now the property of R. Montgomery Moore, Esq., his descendant: it consists of one principal street of considerable length, from which three smaller streets branch off, and contains 363 houses, of

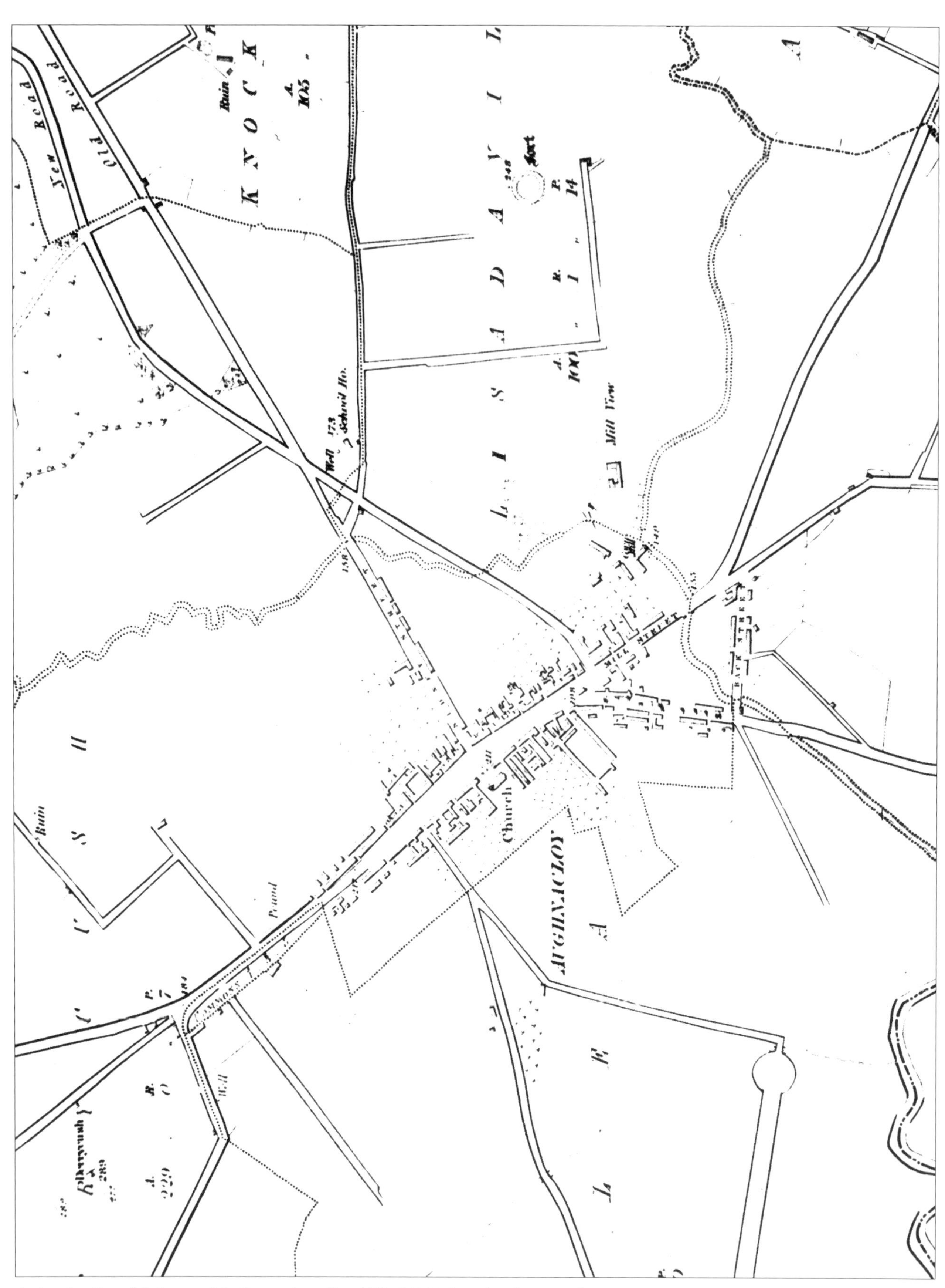

Aughnacloy. Part of O.S. map of Co.Tyrone, sheet 60, published 1834 (reproduced at 140%).

which the greater number are thatched buildings, although there are several good houses of brick roofed with slate, and in the immediate neighbourhood are several gentlemen's seats, which are described in the articles on their respective parishes. The market is on Wednesday, and is very well attended; and fairs for live stock are held on the first Wednesday in every month. There is a convenient market-house. A constabulary police station has been established here; and petty sessions are held every alternate Monday. The church, a spacious and handsome edifice, was erected in 1736. There are a R. C. chapel, and places of worship for Presbyterians in connection with the Synod of Ulster, and for Primitive and Wesleyan Methodists. The parochial school is supported by the archdeacon, and there are three other schools. At Garvey, one mile distant, is a very valuable mineral spring, which has been found efficacious in dyspeptic and cutaneous diseases; it is enclosed within a large building, and near it is a house affording excellent accommodation to those who frequent it for the benefit of their health. Dr. Thomas Campbell, author of *Strictures on the History of Ireland*, was a native of this place.

BADONY (LOWER), a parish, in the barony of STRABANE, county of TYRONE, and province of ULSTER, 8 miles (N. N. E.) from Armagh; containing 7024 inhabitants. This place is situated on the Munterlowney Water, and is bounded on the north by the Spereen mountains, which are the highest in the county, and among which the mountain of Mullaghcairn rises to a very considerable height above the rest; its summit, according to the Ordnance survey, being 1778 feet above the level of the sea. The base of this mountain is a vast accumulation of sand and water-worn stones, rising to an elevation of 900 feet, and in it is an extraordinary fissure called Gortin Gap, through which the road from Omagh leads to the village of Gortin. The parish, according to the same survey, comprises 47,921¾ statute acres (including 178½ under water), of which the greater portion is mountain and bog, but the former affords good pasturage and the latter an abundance of fuel: the vale of Gortin is fertile and well cultivated. Through the range of mountains opposite to Mullaghcairn is a pass called Barnes Gap, in which various indications of copper ore have been discovered. In these mountains is Beltrim, the handsome residence of A. W. C. Hamilton, Esq., proprietor of the principal part of the parish; and in a large bog is the ancient fortress of Loughnacranagh, where the Earl of Tyrone sheltered himself from the British troops under Lord-Deputy Mountjoy, who despatched Sir Henry Dockwra from Omagh, in June 1602, to give battle to the Irish prince, whom he defeated. The inhabitants are principally employed in agriculture and in the breeding of cattle; and the weaving of linen cloth is carried on in several of the farm-houses. The living is a rectory, in the diocese of Derry, separated from Upper Badony by order of council in 1706, arid in the patronage of the Bishop: the tithes amount to £750. The church, situated in the village of Gortin, is a small neat edifice with a campanile turret at the west end. There is neither glebe nor glebe-house at present, but a house is about to be built on a glebe of 30 acres of land granted for that purpose by Mr. Hamilton. The R. C. parish is co-extensive with that of the Established Church, and contains two chapels, one at Ruskey, the other at Greencastle. There is a place of worship for Presbyterians in connection with the Synod of Ulster. The parochial school is supported by the rector and Mr. Hamilton; and there is a school at Ruskey under the trustees of Erasmus Smith's charity, arid others at Liscable Winneyduff, Caronhustion, and Broughderg. These schools afford instruction to about 180 boys and 120 girls: there are also eleven private schools, in which are about 450 children; and eight Sunday schools.

BADONY (UPPER), a parish, in the barony of STRABANE, county of TYRONE, and province of ULSTER, 4 miles (N. N. E.) from Newtownstewart; containing 5715 inhabitants. A monastery for Franciscans of the third order was founded at Corrick about the year 1465; it continued to flourish till the dissolution, and in the reign of Jas. I. was given, with all its possessions, to Sir Henry Piers, who soon after sold it to Sir Arthur Chichester; it was subsequently granted to the Hamilton family, whose descendant is the present proprietor. There are some highly picturesque remains of this abbey, affording an idea of the original extent and elegance of the buildings. Here was also a strong castle or fortress, of which there are some remains. The district appears to have been distinguished at an early period as the scene of various important battles, and in the fastnesses of its mountains the lawless and daring found a secure asylum. In the reign of Elizabeth, O'Nial was defeated here with the loss of all his baggage, plate, and treasures, and compelled to make his escape across the river Bann to his castle of Roe. The parish comprises, according to the Ordnance survey, 38,208¼ statute acres, including 150½ under water: nearly three-fourths are mountain and bog, and the remainder, with the exception of a small portion of woodland, is arable. The state of agriculture is progressively improving; extensive tracts of mountain have been recently enclosed and brought into cultivation, and great portions of bog and mountain may still be reclaimed. Part of the Sawel mountain is within its limits, and, according to the Ordnance survey, rises to an elevation of 2235 feet above the level of the sea. Most of the farmers and cottagers unite with agricultural pursuits the weaving of linen; and great numbers of cattle and horses are bred and pastured in the extensive mountain tracts. Fairs are held on the 16th of every month for the sale of cattle, horses, and pigs, and are in general numerously attended. A constabulary police force has been stationed here. A manorial court is held monthly, at which debts under £2 are recoverable; and a court of petty sessions is held every alternate week at Gortin.

This parish was formerly much more extensive than it is at present; an act of council was obtained, by which it was divided into the parishes of Upper and Lower Badony, and a church was soon afterwards built for the latter at Gortin. The living is a rectory, in the diocese of Derry, and in the patronage of the Bishop: the tithes amount to £396.18.6. The church is an ancient structure, in the early English style: for the repair of which a grant of £108 has been lately made by the Ecclesiastical Commissioners. The glebe-house, a handsome residence, was built in 1821, by aid of a loan of £225 from the late Board of First Fruits; the glebe comprises 195 acres, of which 86 are mountain. The R. C. parish is co-extensive with that of the Established Church; there are two chapels, of which one, near the foot of the mountain, is a spacious building. There are places of worship for Presbyterians of the Synod of Ulster and of the Seceding Synod; the minister of the former officiates also in the adjoining parish of Lower Badony. The parochial male and female school is aided by a small annual payment bequeathed by the late C. Hamilton, Esq., but is chiefly supported by the rector. There are two schools situated respectively at Castledamp and Clogherney; a school at Corrick, supported by - Gardiner, Esq.; a male and female school at Glenroan, built and supported by Major Humphreys; and a school at Plumb Bridge, supported by subscription: there are also four pay schools, and two Sunday schools.

BALLINDERRY, or BALLYDERRY, a parish, partly in the barony of DUNGANNON, county of TYRONE, but chiefly in the barony of LOUGHINSHOLIN, county of LONDONDERRY, and province of ULSTER, 7 miles (S. E. by E.) from Moneymore; containing 3163 inhabitants. This parish is situated on the Ballinderry river, which here separates the above-named baronies and counties, and falls into the north-western portion of Lough Neagh. It comprises, according to the Ordnance survey, 8177 statute acres, of which $2268\frac{1}{2}$ are in the county of Tyrone, and $5908\frac{1}{2}$ are in Londonderry; 2978 acres form a portion of Lough Neagh. The greater part belongs to the Salters' Company, of London; part belongs to the see of Derry; and some of the lands are held under Cromwellian debentures, and are the only lands in the county of Londonderry, west of the river Bann, that are held by that tenure. A castle was built by the Salters' Company at Salterstown, in 1615, soon after they had obtained the grant of those lands from Jas. I.; and in the insurrection of 1641 it was surprised by Sir Phelim O'Nial, who put all the inmates to death, with the exception of the keeper, who, with his wife and family, effected their escape to Carrickfergus, where, taking refuge in the church, they were finally starved to death. It continued for some time in the possession of the insurgents, who, being ultimately driven from their post, destroyed it, together with the church adjoining. Nearly the whole of the land is arable and under an excellent system of cultivation; a valuable tract of bog produces excellent fuel, and there is no wasteland. There are several large and well-built houses in the parish; but the only seat is Ballyronan, that of J. Gaussen, Esq. The inhabitants combine with agricultural pursuits the weaving of linen and cotton cloth; and at Ballyronan an extensive distillery has been lately established by Messrs. Gaussen, situated on the shore of Lough Neagh, close to the little port of Ballyronan. The living is a rectory, in the diocese of Armagh, and in the patronage of the Lord-Primate: the tithes amount to £192.6.2. The church, a large edifice in the later English style of architecture, was erected in 1707. The glebe-house, nearly adjoining, was built at an expense of £980, of which £100 was a gift from the late Board of First Fruits, in 1795: the glebe comprises 413 acres of well-cultivated arable land. The R. C. parish is co-extensive with that of the Established Church; there is a chapel at Ballylifford, and at Derryaghrin is an altar in the open air. Near the church is a place of worship for Wesleyan Methodists. The parochial school, in which are about 40 boys and 20 girls, is aided by a donation of £10 per annum from the rector; and there are three Sunday schools, one of which is held in the R. C. chapel, and three daily pay schools, in which are about 80 children. The ruins of the castle at Salterstown, situated on the margin of the lake, present a picturesque and interesting appearance, but are fast mouldering away. Adjoining the bridge over the river are the remains of an ancient iron forge, erected by the Salters' Company in 1626, but which soon after fell into disuse. At Salterstown, near the site of the old church and close to the shore of Lough Neagh, is a chalybeate spring, which has been found efficacious in cutaneous disorders, and was formerly much resorted to; but having become mixed with other water, its efficacy is greatly diminished. At Ballyronan is a large ancient fortress in good preservation.

BALLYCLOG, or BALLYNECLOG, a parish, in the barony of DUNGANNON, county of TYRONE, and province of ULSTER, 2 miles (N.) from Stewarts-town, on the road to Moneymore; containing 2786 inhabitants. This place formed part of the lands granted by Jas. I. to Sir Andrew Stewart, and with the exception of the lands belonging to the primate, which are in the manor of Cookstown, is wholly included within the manor of Stewarts-town. The parish is situated on Lough Neagh, and comprises, according to the Ordnance survey, $7796\frac{3}{4}$ statute acres, of which $3092\frac{1}{4}$ are in the lough. The lands are chiefly under tillage; there are about 15 acres of woodland and 20 of bog; the system of agriculture is in a highly improved state, and there is not a single acre of waste land in the parish. Coal, limestone, freestone, basalt, and quartz prevail; and many rare plants grow here, which are not found in any other part of the country. Among the gentlemen's seats the principal are Steuart Hall, the residence of the Earl of Castlesteuart; Belmont, of A. T. Bell, Esq. and Drumkirn, of E. H. Caulfield, Esq. The lands of Belmont are an original freehold held by the Bells and Darraghs for more than three hundred years by allodial tenure, being the only lands in the country held by that title. The living is a rectory, in the diocese of Armagh, and in the patronage of the Lord-Primate; the tithes amount to £184.12.$3\frac{3}{4}$. The church is a small plain ancient structure with a tower and spire; and in the churchyard are the family vaults of the Steuarts of Steuart Hall, and the Bells of Belmont, to whom some handsome monuments of freestone have been erected. The glebe-house was built by aid of a gift of £100 from the late Board of First Fruits, in 1792: the glebe comprises 97 acres, of which 7 are exhausted bog and altogether unprofitable. In the R. C. divisions this parish forms part of the union or district of Stewart's-town: the chapel is situated at the northern extremity of the parish. The Presbyterians have a place of worship at Brae. There is a school under the Trustees of Erasmus Smith's Charity; also three schools, situated respectively at Upper Back, Eirey, and Ochill, aided by annual donations from the Countess of Castlesteuart; and a school at Drumkirn supported by Mrs. Caulfield. These schools afford instruction to about 230 boys and 200 girls; and there is also a private school of about 30 children at Drumbanaway. A considerable rivulet in this townland disappears beneath a hill and appears again on the shore of Lough Neagh, at a distance of three miles; and in the townland of Brae is a spring of excellent water issuing from between the basalt, freestone, and limestone strata, producing 290 gallons per minute, and ebbing and flowing at the new moon.

BALLYGAWLEY, a market and post-town, and a parish, partly in the barony of CLOGHER, and partly in that of DUNGANNON, county of TYRONE, and province of ULSTER, 13 miles (S. E.) from Omagh. and 74 miles (N. W. by N.) from Dublin; containing 4428 inhabitants, of which number, 972 are in the town. The lands and manor of Moyenner and Balegalle were granted by Jas. I. to Capt. William Turvin, but he neglecting to comply with the conditions of the grant, they were afterwards granted, in 1614, to Sir Gerard Lowther, who erected on the bank of a small river a very extensive castle, which he enclosed within a bawn of stone and lime and made a place of great strength. This castle was destroyed, in 1642, by the insurgents under Sir Phelim O'Nial: the walls and two towers of the bawn, with part of the castle walls, are still remaining and a modern house has been recently erected on the site. The town is situated on the mail coach road from Dublin to Londonderry, and consists of three streets and a market-place; it contains about 250 houses, some of which are large and well built, and is the property of Sir Hugh Stewart, Bart., whose handsome mansion, Ballygawley House, is about two miles distant from the town. Innismagh, the seat of Col. Verner; Anahoe, of H. Crossle, Esq.; and Martray, of Mervyn Stewart, Esq., are within the parish. A small manufacture of gloves is carried on in the town, which, from the goodness of the materials and the neatness of the workmanship, are in general demand. There is an extensive brewery, that has acquired celebrity for the quality of its ale, and a large distillery of malt whiskey has been established. The market is on Friday; it is amply supplied with provisions of all kinds, and every alternate week a large quantity of linen cloth is exposed for sale. Fairs are held on the second Friday in every month, principally for the sale of cattle, sheep, and pigs. A constabulary police force has been stationed here; petty sessions are held once a fortnight; and as the head of the manor of Moyenner or Ballygawley, manorial courts are held in the town for the recovery of debts not exceeding 40s. This district was constituted a parish in 1830, by an order of council under the provisions of an act of the 7th and 8th of Geo. IV., when eighteen townlands were separated from the parish of Errigal-Kerogue, in the barony of Clogher, and twelve from that of Carrenteel, in the barony of Dungannon, and formed into the parish of Ballygawley. These townlands are situated near the mountains and contain some good land, particularly on the north-east, where the soil is good and well cultivated. The living is a perpetual curacy, in the diocese of Armagh, and in the alternate patronage of the Rectors of Errigal-Kerogue and Carrenteel. The curate's income is £70 per annum, contributed in moieties by the rector of Errigal-Kerogue and the archdeacon of Armagh, as incumbent of Carrenteel. The church is a small but handsome edifice, in the later English style, erected at an expense of £1000, of which sum, £900 was a gift from the late Board of First Fruits. There is a place of worship in the town for Presbyterians in connection with the Synod of Ulster, of the third class; also a Baptist meeting-house in the parish. A boys' school is supported by Sir Hugh Stewart, and there is a school at Knockany, together affording instruction to about 130 boys and 130 girls; there is also a private school at Lisgonnell of about 70 boys and 30 girls.

BENBURB, or BINBURB, a small village, in the parish of CLONFEACLE, barony of DUNGANNON, county of TYRONE, and province of ULSTER, $5^3/_4$ miles (N. N. W.) from Armagh: the population is returned with the parish. The first notice of this place under its present name occurs during the rebellion of the Earl of Tyrone, when the Lord-Deputy Boroughs crossed the river Blackwater at Bean-Bhorb, at the head of the English forces, in June 1597; and being seized with a sickness of which he died a few days after at Newry, was succeeded in the command of the army by the Earl of Kildare, between whom and the Earl of Tyrone a severe engagement took place, in which the English were defeated, the Earl of Kildare mortally wounded, and his two foster brothers slain; many of the English were killed in battle, and numbers perished in the river. Sir Henry Bagnall, with 4500 foot and 400 horse, marched against the Earl of Tyrone's army, with which he had a severe conflict; many of the English cavalry were dreadfully mangled by falling into pits dug by the enemy and covered with branches of trees; but after surmounting these and other obstacles, Bagnall made a vigorous attack upon the right wing of the Irish army commanded by the earl himself, and on the left under O'Donnell of Tyrconnell; a dreadful carnage ensued, the two armies being wholly engaged; but just when victory seemed to incline towards the English forces, Bagnall was shot by a

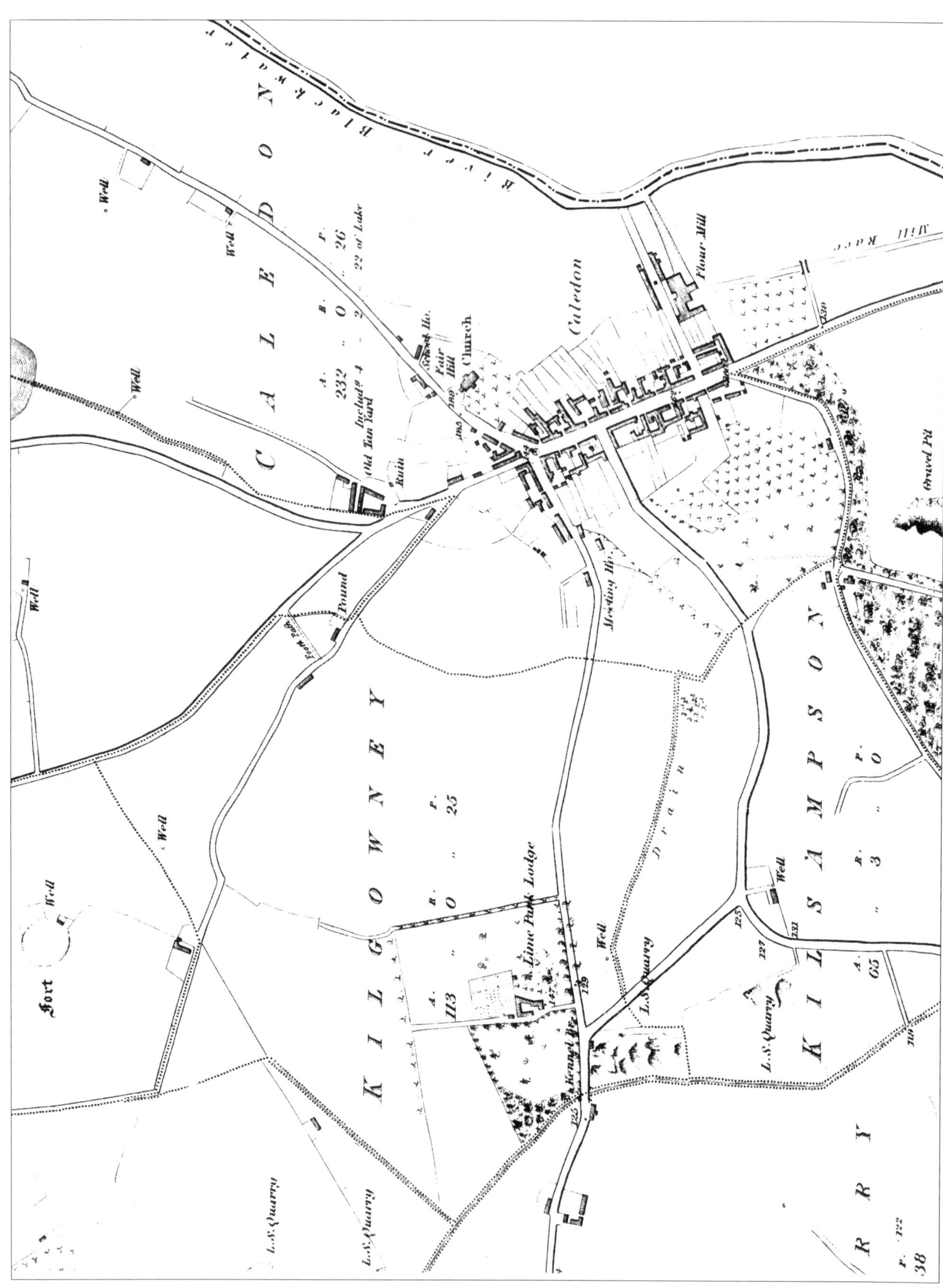

Caledon. Part of the O.S. map of Co. Tyrone, sheet 67, published 1834 (reproduced at 140%).

musket ball in the forehead and fell dead on the field. The English, thrown into confusion by the loss of their leader, were defeated, and in their retreat to Armagh, many were trodden down by the Irish cavalry. This triumph of Tyrone was but of short duration; the Lord-Deputy Mountjoy defeated him in several battles, and had driven him back to the camp at Bean-Bhorb, where, on the 15th of July, 1601, a battle was fought, in which Tyrone was totally defeated and his army compelled to retreat in confusion to his chief fortress at Dungannon.

On the plantation of Ulster, Sir Robert Wingfield received from James I. a grant of 1000 acres of land at Benburb, by a deed dated Dec. 3rd, in the 8th year of that monarch's reign; and previously to the year 1619 he had erected a castle on these lands, built the present church, and founded the village, which at that time contained 20 houses. This new establishment continued to flourish till the breaking out of the war in 1641, when the castle was surprised by order of Sir Phelim O'Nial, on the night of the 22nd of October, and the whole of the inmates put to death. On the 5th of June, 1646, this place became the scene of a battle between Sir Phelim O'Nial and Gen. Monroe; the former, with a large body of men, took up a position between two hills, with a wood in his rear and the river Blackwater, at that time difficult to pass, on his right. Monroe, with 6000 foot and 800 horse, marched from Armagh and approached by the opposite bank of the river, where, finding a ford, now called Battleford Bridge, he crossed and advanced to meet O'Nial. Both armies were drawn up in order of battle, but instead of coming to a general engagement, the day was spent in skirmishing, till the sun, which had been favourable to the British, was declining, when, just as Monroe was beginning to retreat, he was attacked by the Irish, who made a furious onset. An English regiment commanded by Lord Blayney fought with undaunted resolution till they were cut to pieces and their leader slain; the Scottish horse next gave way, and the infantry being thrown into disorder, a general rout ensued. More than 3000 of the British forces were slain and their artillery and stores taken, while, on the part of O'Nial, not more than 70 were killed. The castle was soon after dismantled, and has ever since remained in ruins; it was the largest in the county, and, though weakly built, occupies a remarkably strong position on the summit of a limestone rock rising perpendicularly from the river Blackwater to the height of 120 feet. In the village is a small ancient out-post strongly built and probably forming an entrance to the castle, which on every other side was defended by natural barriers. Near the village are Tullydoey, the seat of J. Eyre Jackson, Esq., where also is the residence of T. Eyre, Esq.; and Castle Cottage, of Capt. Cranfleld. There were formerly very extensive bleach-greens near the village, and the mills and engines are still remaining; but the principal part of the business is carried on at Tullydoey, where large quantities of linen are finished for the English markets; the weaving of linen is also carried on to some extent. The Ulster canal, now in progress, passes on the eastern side of the river and village, and is here carried through a hill of limestone, which has been excavated to the depth of 80 feet, and is conducted longitudinally over the mill-race by an aqueduct of considerable length. A court is held on the first Friday in every month for the manor of Benburb, which extends over 47 townlands and comprises 9210 acres, for the recovery of debts not exceeding £2. The parish church is situated close to the village, in which is also a place of worship for Presbyterians in connection with the Synod of Ulster. The ruins of the castle are extensive and highly picturesque; and near the walls was found a signet ring hearing the arms and initials of Turlogh O'Nial, which is now in the possession of Mr. Bell, of Dungannon. The O'Nials had a strong hold here of greater antiquity than the castle erected by Sir R. Wingfield. See CLONFEACLE.

BEREGH, or LOWRYSTOWN, a market-town, in the parish of CLOGHERNEY, barony of OMAGH, county of TYRONE, and province of ULSTER, 7 miles (S. E.) from Omagh: the population is returned with the parish. It is situated on the road from Omagh to Dungannon, and consists of one long wide street containing about 70 houses, most of which are well built, though rapidly falling into decay. The former residence of the Belmore family, proprietors of the town, an elegant and spacious mansion, is now in ruins; and the town exhibits every appearance of neglect. The inhabitants are principally employed in agriculture, with which they combine the weaving of linen cloth. The patent for the market and fairs was granted under the name of Lowrystown; the market is on Wednesday, and fairs are held regularly on the first Monday in every month for cattle, sheep, and pigs. A constabulary police force is stationed here; and petty sessions are held every alternate week. One of the chapels for the R. C. parish of Clogherney is situated in the town. – See CLOGHERNEY.

CALEDON, a market and post-town, in the parish of AUGHALOO, barony of DUNGANNON, county of TYRONE, and province of ULSTER, 7 miles (W.) from Armagh, and 70 miles (N. N. W.) from Dublin; containing 1079 inhabitants. This town, which was formerly named Kennard, as it is still frequently called by old people, although its manor, markets, and fairs, are all known by the modern name of Caledon, appears to have been more anciently called Aghaloo, it being the head of the parish of that name, and the site of its venerable church, which was destroyed in the insurrection of 1641. It appears to have been an important military post from a very early period, having been the property and principal residence of one of the princely sept of O'Nial. The first direct mention of it is in 1498, when the Lord-Deputy Kildare marched against Mac Art O'Nial, and having defeated and driven him from his strong hold in Kennard, presented the fortress and territory to the British ally, Tirlagh O'Nial, whose descendants seem never to have been found in arms against

England, until Sir Phelim O'Nial headed the insurgents in 1641; for, in the settlement under Jas. I., Tirlagh O'Nial had a grant of Kennard, with 4000 acres. Tirlagh built here a bawn of lime and stone, some time prior to 1619, near which he erected a castle. This was afterwards the residence of Sir Phelim, from which he sallied on the evening of the 22nd of October, 1641, having invited himself to supper with Lord Caulfield, at Charlemont. While at the supper table he made Lord Caulfield a prisoner, and having separated his lordship's family and the garrison, carried than prisoners to Kennard, in the castle of which he put his lordship to death. Sir Phelim, who had been educated as a Protestant in England, soon found himself at the head of 30,000 men, and waged a sanguinary warfare against the English. The whole of the county of Tyrone remained in the possession of the insurgents till 1646, when Gen. Monroe, at the head of 6000 foot and 800 horse, marched against the Irish under Owen Roe O'Nial. Having passed through Armagh, Munroe, on the 6th of June, crossed the Blackwater at the ford near Kennard, and fought the battle of Benburb, or, as it is here called, Batterford Bridge, in which he was defeated and many British officers and men were slain.

This town, which is situated on the river Blackwater, and on the road from Armagh to Omagh, was, before 1816, a mean village, but is now, through the exertions of the Earl of Caledon, one of the best built towns in the North of Ireland: it contains 226 houses, nearly all of which are built of stone. The neighbourhood presents gentle swells and fertile vales, producing abundant crops. Close to the town are extensive flour-mills, erected by Lord Caledon in 1823, where above 9000 tons of wheat are ground annually, all of which is grown in the vicinity, where scarcely an acre of wheat was sown at the beginning of the century. The Ulster canal, now in the course of formation, passes through the Earl of Caledon's demesne, a little to the westward of the town. The market is on Saturday, and is well attended; and a fair is held on the second Saturday in every month. A constabulary police force has been stationed here and there are barracks for the militia. A court for the recovery of debts under 40s. is held in the market-house, on the first Monday in each month, for the manor of Caledon, which extends into the parishes of Aughaloo and Clonfeacle, in the county of Tyrone, and of Tynan, in that of Armagh; and petty sessions are held in the town once a fortnight. There are several large and elegant houses in the neighbourhood, the principal of which is Caledon Hill, the seat of the Earl of Caledon, which stands in a richly ornamented demesne of 650 Irish acres, extending beyond the Blackwater into the county of Armagh. Not, far distant are Tynan Abbey, the residence of Sir James Stronge, Hart.; Glasslough, of Mrs. Wynne Leslie; Crilley, of R. Pettigrew, Esq. Rahaghy, of N. Mayne, Esq. Annagh, of C. Richardson, Esq.; Drummond, of H. Moore, Esq.; and the glebe-house, of the Rev. E. A. Stopford; besides several large and good houses in the town.

The living was made a perpetual curacy in 1807, and 20 acres were then added to the old glebe, which consisted only of $6^1/_2$ acres. It is in the diocese of Armagh, and patronage of the Archdeacon. The income is £100 per annum, arising from a salary of £50 paid by the archdeacon; £15, the estimated value of $26^1/_2$ acres of glebe land; and £35.2, paid by the trustees of Primate Boulter's augmentation fund. The present church occupies the site of the ancient building, and is the parish church of Aughaloo: it was erected by Primate Robinson, in 1767, during the incumbency of the Rev. C. W. Congreave; the spire was built by the present Lord Caledon, by means of a bequest by his late father; and the church was enlarged and otherwise improved by his lordship. It is a large and handsome edifice, in the later English style of architecture, comprising a nave, chancel, and south transept, and for repairing it the Ecclesiastical Commissioners recently granted £175.8.11. There are a R. C. chapel and a place of worship for Wesleyan Methodists. The parochial school is situated near the church: it was built in 1776 by Mr. Congreave, and is endowed with 3 acres of land and 3 tenements given by Primate Robinson, and also with £8 per annum by Lord Caledon. Schools at Ramakit, Curlough, Dyan, and Minterburn, are principally supported by Lord Caledon; there are national schools at Rahaghy and Mullinahorn; and near the demesne is a female school built and supported by the Countess of Caledon, in which 40 girls are clothed and educated.

Here is a dispensary; and a mendicity association was established in 1829, to which Lord Caledon subscribes £100 per annum. Among the charitable bequests is £100 left by Alex. Pringle, Esq., and vested in the funds, in the name of Lord Caledon; the interest, with that of several smaller sums, is applied to the relief of the poor. Two extensive lakes existed here formerly, one on the north and the other on the south side of the town, with an island in the centre of each; that on the south has been drained and brought into cultivation; the north lake remains, and the island in it, which borders on the glebe is beautifully planted. Almost the last vestiges of the ancient castle of the O'Nials were removed a few years since, and a clump of trees planted to mark the entrance into the courtyard some of the flooring of the castle was subsequently discovered, about four feet beneath the surface of the ground, in forming the new road to Aughnacloy. Some old swords and other military instruments have been found in the neighbourhood, and are preserved at Caledon Hill. Caledon gives the titles of Baron, Viscount, and Earl to the family of Alexander, in which the proprietorship of the town is vested. – See AUGHALOO.

CAMUS-juxta-MORNE, a parish, in the barony of STRABANE, county of TYRONE, and province of ULSTER; containing, with part of the town of Strabane, 6570 inhabitants. This parish, which is situated on the old road from Dublin to Londonderry, and on the river Morne, comprises, according to the Ordnance survey (including $20^3/_4$ acres in Lyons island), $7505^3/_4$ statute acres, of which

103 are water, about 4540 are arable and pasture land, and the remainder mountain and bog; 6743 acres are applotted under the tithe act, and valued at £3078 per annum. The land, although in some places rocky, is generally very fertile, producing abundant crops, particularly in the vale of Morne. The inhabitants combine the weaving of linen with their agricultural pursuits. The principal houses are Milltown Lodge, the residence of Major Humphries, and the glebe-house, of the Rev. J. Smith. The living is a rectory, in the diocese of Derry, and in the patronage of the Bishop: the tithes amount to £468. The church is in the town of Strabane, and is a large and handsome edifice, for the repairs of which the Ecclesiastical Commissioners have recently granted £184.4.2: it was originally built as a chapel for the new town of Strabane, by the Earl of Abercorn in 1619, and has been used as the parish church since the destruction of the mother church, about the middle of the 17th century. The glebe-house was built by aid of a gift of £100 and a loan of £800 from the late Board of First Fruits, in 1832, upon the townland of Bierney, which constitutes the glebe, comprising 300 acres, and is more than three miles from the church. In the R. C. divisions the parish is the head of a union or district called Clonleigh and Camus, and comprising both those parishes: there are two chapels in the union, of which that of Camus, in the town of Strabane, is a large plain edifice. There is a large meeting-house for Presbyterians in connection with the Synod of Ulster, of the first class; and there are places of worship for Wesleyan and Primitive Methodists. The parochial school, on the glebe of Bierney, is supported by the trustees of Erasmus Smith's charity, and the master has a rent-free residence and two acres of land. At Milltown is a school for boys and girls, erected by the Marquess of Abercorn, a large and handsome building, with a separate residence for the master and mistress, each of whom receives £20 a year from the Marquess, who also aids a school established at Edymon; and there is a national school at Strabane. About 160 boys and 100 girls are educated in these schools. Prior to 1829 a blue-coat school existed here, with an income of £30 per annum, which sum is now applied to clothing 12 boys. Near Milltown school are the dispensary and fever hospital belonging to Strabane; they are large and well ventilated buildings, admirably arranged for their purposes. The ruins of the old parish church are situated on the banks of the Mourne: it was founded by St. Colgan in 586, and destroyed during the insurrection of 1641. – See STRABANE.

CAPPAGH, a parish, partly in the barony of OMAGH, but chiefly in that of STRABANE, county of TYRONE, and province of ULSTER, 2 miles (N.) from Omagh; containing, with the district parish of Mountfield, 13,589 inhabitants. This parish, according to the Ordnance survey, comprises 37,670½ statute acres, of which 34,626¾ are in Strabane, and 3043¾ in Omagh; the applotment under the tithe act embraces 16,097 acres, and 266¾ are water. The greater part of the laud is reclaimed bog or mountain, and about 1500 acres are woodland: in some places the land is remarkably good, particularly in the eastern part of the parish, but not more than one-fourth is cultivated. Part of the mountains of Bessy Bell, Mary Gray, and Mullaghcairn are in this parish, and afford good pasturage for cattle to their very summits. The inhabitants combine with agricultural pursuits the spinning of flax and weaving of linen. There is abundance of freestone, with limestone of inferior quality, and several indications of coal are met with. Gortin gap, through which a road runs from Omagh to Gortin, is a deep ravine stretching in a northern and southern direction through Mullaghcairn or Cairntogher, which is the highest mountain in the county. There are several handsome houses in the parish, the principal of which are Mountjoy Cottage, the residence of C. J. Gardiner, Esq.; Mount Pleasant, of the Rev. C. Cregan; Facary Lodge, of Sir W. McMahon, Bart.; Mountfield Lodge, of the Rev. Mr. Stack; Lislimanahan, of Capt. Hill; Lisanally, of G. Norris, Esq.; Millbank, of H. Peebles, Esq.; Mullaghmore, of R. Burges, Esq; and Ergennagh glebe-house, of the Rev. H. H. Harte. The improvements made during the last 50 years are very extensive; the late Lord Mountjoy commenced planting the demesne of Rash, now called Mountjoy Forest, in 1780, and much of the timber is large and very promising. The late Sir W. McMahon built a very handsome house, surrounded by extensive plantations, at Facary, and also laid out a town at Mountfield, where markets and fairs will be held. A new road has been opened through the parish, direct from Omagh to Belfast.

The living is a rectory, in the diocese of Derry, and in the patronage of the Provost and Fellows of Trinity College, Dublin: the tithes amount to £1000. The church is a large and handsome edifice, in the Grecian style, with a lofty and beautiful octagonal spire: it was erected in Mountjoy Forest in 1768, at the sole expense of Dr. Gibson, then rector. The glebe-house is being rebuilt upon an enlarged scale: the glebe consists of 573 acres, about half a mile from the church, and of two other portions containing 999 acres, making a total of 1572 acres, only 410 of which are under cultivation. There is a chapel of ease at Mountfield, four miles from the church; it is a small but very beautiful edifice, with a lofty spire, standing on the south side of a high mountain, and was built at an expense of £1000 by the late Board of First Fruits, in 1828: the living is a perpetual curacy, endowed with £25 per ann. from Primate Boulter's fund, and in the gift of the Rector. Divine service is also performed, every second Sunday, in the school-houses of Calkill, Carrigan, Castletown, Taercur, and Mayne. The R. C. parish is co-extensive with that of the Established Church, and has two chapels, one at Knockmoyle, the other at Killyclogher. There are places of worship for Baptists and Presbyterians of the Synod of Ulster, the latter of the third class. The male and female parochial schools are situated on the glebe, and are supported by the rector, who has given the master a house and three acres of land. Mountfield male and female schools were supported by the late Sir W. McMahon;a school at Knockmoyle was founded under the will of John McEvoy, who endowed it with £16 per annum, for the gratuitous education of the poor children in Mountjoy Forest, and vested its management in the Rector for ever. There are also schools at Carrigan, Taercur, Killynure, Common, Crevenagh, and Lislap; six under the National Board, at Castlerody, Killyclogher, Carrigan, Tetraconaght, Beltony, and Rathcarsan; and other schools at Edenderry, Calkill, and Drummullard. In these schools are about 770 boys and 450 girls; and there are also four private schools, containing about 90 boys and 40 girls, and six Sunday schools. The ruins of the old church are scarcely discernible, but the cemetery is much used. There are several forts on Mary Gray mountain, close to each other.

CARRENTEEL, a parish, in the barony of DUNGANNON, county of TYRONE, and province of ULSTER; containing, with the post-town of Aughnacloy, 7459 inhabitants. This place formed part of the manor of Portclare, a very extensive district granted to Sir Thomas Ridgeway, in 1611, by Jas. I., by whose order a fortress called Lismore Bawn was erected here in 1619, of which there are extensive ruins. During the war in 1641, this parish was visited by the contending parties and the church was destroyed; some vestiges of it may still be traced in the ancient cemetery adjoining the village. The parish is situated on the river Blackwater, and on the mail coach road from Dublin to Londonderry including twelve townlands forming part of the district parish of Ballygawley, it comprises, according to the Ordnance survey, 13,431¾ statute acres, of which 13,080 acres are applotted under the tithe act, and 61 are water; the land is chiefly under an excellent system of cultivation, and produces good crops. The northern side of the parish is mountainous, and contains a tract of bog; and there are extensive quarries of limestone and freestone of very good quality. The seats are Storm Hill, that of K. Montgomery Moore, Esq.; the Bawn, of B. Moore, Esq.; Millview, of S. Simpson, Esq.; and the glebe-house, the residence of the Rev. Archdeacon Stopford. The inhabitants, in addition to their agricultural pursuits, employ themselves at home in weaving linen and cotton. Fairs are held in the village on the first Wednesday in every month, chiefly for cattle and horses. By order of council under the provisions of an act of the 7th and 8th of Geo. IV., twelve townlands were separated from this parish, in 1830,to form part of the district parish of Ballygawley.

The living is a rectory and vicarage, in the diocese of Armagh, united by charter in 1637 to the rectory and vicarage of Aghaloo, together constituting the union of Carrenteel and corps of the archdeaconry of Armagh, in the patronage of the Lord-Primate. The tithes amount to £406.3.1, and of the union to £1015.7.8. It is recommended by the Ecclesiastical Commissioners to dissolve this union on the next avoidance, and to make each parish a separate benefice. After the destruction of the church of Carrenteel, in 1641, a church was erected at Aghaloo, but it was taken down after the erection of the present church at Aughnacloy, which was built in 1736, at the sole expense of the late Acheson Moore, Esq., to which, in 1796, his daughter and heiress, Mrs. Malone, added a tower surmounted by a lofty octagonal spire; and to the repairs of which the Ecclesiastical Commissioners have recently granted 190.18. The glebe-house, about half a mile from the church, was erected in 1790, and £2000 has been expended on its repair and improvement; the glebe comprises 1046 statute acres, valued at £969 per annum. The R. C. parish is coextensive with that of the Established Church, and is called Aughby; there are chapels at Aughnacloy, Caledon, and Killin. There are two meeting-houses for Presbyterians, one in connection with the Synod of Ulster, of the second class, and the other with the Seceding Synod; and places of worship for Wesleyan and Primitive Methodists. The parochial male and female school is wholly supported by Archdeacon Stopford, and there are four other schools; in these about 240 boys and 150 girls are instructed, and there are also a private school of 60 boys and 20 girls, and five Sunday schools. At Garvey are the ruins of an extensive and elegant castle, erected by the late Col. Moore, which, very soon after its completion, was suffered to fall into decay; they are situated near those of Lismore Bawn. In this townland, which is about a mile from Aughnacloy, is a very valuable mineral spring; the water contains sulphur, nitre, magnesia, and steel held in solution with carbonic acid; it has been found efficacious in cutaneous diseases and in dyspeptic complaints; a large room has been erected over the spring, and the water issues from a fountain of marble in the centre. Near it is a good house for the accommodation of personsfrequenting the spa. – See AUGNACLOY.

CASTLE-CAULFIELD, a village, in the parish of DONAGHMORE, barony of DUNGANNON, county of TYRONE, and province of ULSTER, 3 miles (W.) from Dungannon; containing 212 inhabitants. This town was founded by Sir Toby Caulfield, afterwards Lord Charlemont, to whom Jas. I. granted the lands called Ballydonnell, or the town of O'Donnell, in 1610. Sir Toby, in 1614, began building a mansion-house in the Elizabethan style, which afterwards acquired the name of Castle-Caulfield, and around which he located 41 British families, and mustered 30 men at arms. The second Lord Charlemont added a large gatehouse with towers, and a keep or donjon. In Pynnar's Survey it is described as the fairest house in all these parts; it is now a stately ruin, the gables and clustered chimneys producing a fine effect. The village is situated in a fertile valley, on the road from Dungannon to Omagh, and consists of one small street containing about 50 houses; the inhabitants are generally engaged in agriculture and the weaving of linen; a daily penny post to Dungannon has been established. Limestone and coal are found in the neighbourhood; and fairs, held on the second Monday in every month, for the sale of live stock, are numerously

Castlecaulfield. From The Irish Penny Journal, *vol. 1, 1841.*

attended. A court for the manor of Castle-Caulfield is held by the seneschal; and petty sessions are held every alternate Saturday. Besides Castle-Caulfield, the seat of the Earl of Charlemont, here are several elegant houses, enumerated in the article on Donaghmore, which see.

The parish church is in this village, and was built in 1685 it is a large and handsome edifice, in the Grecian style of architecture, except the south windows, which are in the later English style, and were brought from the old church of Donaghmore, which was destroyed in the war of 1641.A neat mural monument, in memory of the Rev. G. Walker, was erected on the south side of the altar, by his widow, in 1703. This distinguished man, while residing here in 1688, raised a regiment of infantry at his own expense, to act against the adherents of Jas. II., and proceeded to Londonderry, in the defence of which he had the principal share, and subsequently, on the death of Major Baker, became sole governor of the city. After the siege was raised, he resigned the command of the garrison, came to England, where he was most graciously received by their Majesties, and in Nov., 1689, received the thanks of the House of Commons, having just before published an account of the siege. A letter, written by Archbishop Tillotson, is extant, in which he says, "the king, besides his first bounty to Mr. Walker, hath made him bishop of Londonderry, that so he may receive the reward of that great service in the place where he did it." He returned to Ireland with King William, and having resolved to serve a campaign before he took possession of his bishoprick, was killed at the head of his regiment at the battle of the Boyne, on the 1st of July, 1690. In the village is a chapel belonging to the Seceding Synod, of the first class. Near the church is the male and female parochial school, capable of accommodating 300 children; it is endowed with two acres of land and £5 per annum from the rector, and was built in 1823 at an expense of £253, with apartments for the master and mistress. The ruins of the castle, and a very large and perfect fort near Parkanour, are the only vestiges of antiquity; but tradition points out the site of a friary, near the latter, although no remains are visible.

CASTLEDERG, or DERG-BRIDGE, a market and post-town, in the parish of SKIRTS, barony of OMAGH, county of

TYRONE, and province of ULSTER, 8 miles (S.) from Strabane, and $107^1/_4$ (N.) from Dublin; containing 575 inhabitants. The town is indebted for its origin to Sir John Davis, attorney-general for Ireland to Jas. I., to whom a grant of 2000 acres of land, then called Garertagh, was made in 1609, on which Sir John, prior to 1619, built a castle and established 16 British families; he also erected a stone bridge over the river Derg, adjoining the castle, which, being the first built over that river, gave the town the name of Derg-Bridge, by which it is still frequently called. Sir John had another grant of land at Claraghmore, upon which he built a castle, called Kerlis, and constructed a causeway, seven miles long and eight feet wide, in a straight line over mountains and through bogs, from one castle to the other. Several parts of this road are still traceable, but others have been broken up to make the road from this town to Drumquin. In the war of 1641, Sir Phelim O'Nial besieged the castle of Derg; and although he was driven away with disgrace and considerable loss of men, horses, and ammunition, yet he so greatly injured it that it was never afterwards repaired, and remains a noble pile of ruins on the northern bank of the river. The bridge erected by Sir John Davis remained till 1835, when it was taken down, and a handsome bridge of hewn stone, of four arches, has been erected.

The town, which is also called Castle-Derrick and Churchtown, is situated on the road from Newtown-Stewart to Pettigo, and on the new line of road from Londonderry to Enniskillen, between which places two coaches running daily pass through it. It consists of one principal and two smaller streets, containing 105 houses, many of which are large and well built, and has much improved under the patronage of Sir R. A. Ferguson, Bart., its proprietor, who has lately built a very handsome inn. The market is on Friday, and is large and well attended; a fair is held on the first Friday in every month. A constabulary police force has been stationed here; petty sessions are held on alternate Saturdays; a court for the manor of Hastings every third Saturday, in which debts under 40s. are recoverable; and a monthly court for the manor of Ardstraw, for debts to a similar amount. There was anciently a church in the town, which was in ruins in 1619, when it was rebuilt by Sir John Davis; but being destroyed by Sir Phelim O'Nial in 1641, there was no church till 1731, when the present neat edifice was built by Hugh Edwards, Esq., of Castle-Gore, and was much improved in 1828. There is a national school for boys and girls, and a dispensary. Hugh Edwards, Esq., in 1735, bequeathed an acre of land on which to build a schoolhouse, and £24 annually for the support of a master, to teach eight poor boys, but the school was not built; it is now, however, about to be erected and endowed. Not far from the town are the ruins of Castle-Gore, formerly the residence of the proprietors of the Manor-Hastings estate.- See SKIRTS.

CLAUDY, a village, in the parish of URNEY, barony of STRABANE, county of TYRONE, and province of ULSTER, 3 miles (S. S. w.) from Strabane; containing 176 inhabitants. It is situated on the road from Londonderry to Sligo, and on the river Finn, comprising one irregularly built street containing 44 houses, most of which are old. Fairs for the sale of cattle, sheep, and pigs, are held on Aug. 1st and Nov. 16th. Close to the village is a handsome bridge of seven arches over the Finn, connecting Claudy with the county of Donegal. Prior to the erection of this bridge, there was an important ford here, which was contested with great slaughter by the partisans of William and James, in 1688; and at the time of the siege of Londonderry it was a strong post under Col. Skeffington, who was driven from it by the Duke of Berwick, a short time before Jas. II. crossed the Finn at this place. - See URNEY.

CLOGHER, an incorporated market and post-town, a parish, and the head of a diocese (formerly a parliamentary borough), in the barony of CLOGHER, county of TYRONE, and province of ULSTER, 7 miles (W.) from Aughnacloy, and $82^1/_2$ (N. W. by N.) from Dublin; containing, with the towns of Augher and Five-mile-town, and the village of Newtown-Saville (all separately described) 17,996 inhabitants, of which number, 523 are in the town. This place is said to have derived its name from a stone covered with gold, which in pagan times is reported to have made oracular responses. The Clogh-or, or "golden stone," was preserved long after the abolition of paganism; for McGuire, canon of Armagh, who wrote a commentary on the registry of Clogher, in 1490, says "that this sacred stone is preserved at Clogher, on the right of the entrance into the church, and that traces of the gold with which it had been formerly covered by the worshippers of the idol called Cermaed Celsetacht are still visible." There is still a very ancient stone lying on the south side of the cathedral tower, which many believe to be the real Clogh-or. It appears to have some very ancient characters engraved on it, but is evidently nothing more than the shaft of an antique cross of rude workmanship, of which there are several in the ancient cemetery. Clogher is called by Ptolemy Rhigia or Regia; and according to some authors, St. Patrick founded and presided over a monastery here, which he resigned to St. Kertenn when he went to Armagh, to establish his famous abbey there; but according to others, it was built at the command of St. Patrick in the street before the royal palace of Ergal, by St. Macartin, who died in 506, and from its vicinity to this palace both the abbey and the town appear anciently to have been called Uriel or Ergal. In 841, the abbot Moran Mac Inrachty was slain by the Danes.

In 1041 the church was rebuilt and dedicated to St. Macartin. In 1126 the Archdeacon Muireadhach O'Cuillen was killed by the people of Fermanagh. Moelisa O'Carrol, Bishop of Clogher, in 1183, on his translation of the archbishoprick of Armagh, presented to this abbey a priest's vestments and a mitre, and promised a pastoral staff; he also consecrated the abbey church. Bishop Michael Mac Antsair, in 1279, exchanged with the abbot the episcopal residence that had been built near the abbey by Bishop Donat O'Fidabra, between 1218 and 1227, for a piece of land outside the town, called Disert-na-cusiac, on which he erected another episcopal palace. His immediate successor, Matthew Mac Catasaid, erected a chapel over the sepulchre of St. Macartin. In 1361 the plague miserably afflicted Ireland, particularly the city of Clogher, and caused the death of the bishop. In April 1395, while Bishop Arthur Mac Camaeil was employed in rebuilding the chapel of St. Macartin, the abbey, the cathedral, two chapels, the episcopal residence, and 32 other houses, were destroyed by fire; but the bishop applied himself with unwearied diligence to the rebuilding of his cathedral and palace. In 1504, another plague ravaged Clogher and caused the death of the bishop. Jas. I., in 1610, annexed the abbey and its revenues to the see of Clogher, by which it was made one of the richest in the kingdom. Between 1690 and 1697, Bishop Tennison repaired and beautified the episcopal palace; and his successor, Bishop St. George Ash, expended £900 in repairing and improving the palace and lands, two-thirds of which was repaid by his successor. Bishop Sterne, in 1720, laid out £3000 in building and other improvements of the episcopal residence, £2000 of which was charged on the revenues of the see.

The town is situated on the river Blackwater, the source of which is in the parish, and consists of one row of 90 houses, the northern side only being built upon. Some of the houses are large, handsome, and well built with hewn stone, and slated. The episcopal palace is a large and handsome edifice close to the cathedral, on the south side of the town, and consists of a centre with two wings: the entrance is in the north front by an enclosed portico, supported by lofty fluted columns. It is built throughout of hewn freestone, and standing on elevated ground commands extensive views over a richly planted undulating country. Its erection was commenced by Lord John George Beresford, Primate of Armagh, while Bishop of Clogher, and completed by Lord Robert Tottenham, the present bishop, in 1823. Attached to the palace is a large and well-planted demesne of 566 acres, encircled by a stone wall; and within it are the remains of the royal dwelling-place of the princes of Ergallia, a lofty earthwork or fortress, protected on the west and south by a deep fosse; beyond this, to the south, is a camp surrounded by a single fosse, and still further southward is a tumulus or cairn, encircled by a raised earthwork. The market is on Saturday; the market-house was built by Bishop Garnett. Fairs for live stock are held on the third Saturday in every month. The market was granted to the bishop by letters patent dated April 20th, 1629: he was also authorised to appoint two fairs and receive the profits of the market and fairs. The old fairs, which are supposed to have been granted by the charter, are held on May 6th and July 26th.

At the solicitation of Bishop Spottiswood, Chas. I., in 1629, directed that, "for the better civilizing and strengthening of these remote parts with English and British tenants, and for the better propagation of the true religion, the lord-lieutenant should by letters patent make the town of Clogher a corporation." This was to consist of a portreeve and 12 burgesses, to be at first nominated by the bishop; the portreeve was afterwards to be elected on Michaelmas-day, by and from among the burgesses. No freemen were created, and the bishops appear to have connected a burgess-ship with each of the stalls in the cathedral. Prior to March 29th, 1800, the bishops had nominated the members of parliament for the borough without opposition, and the senesehal of their manor had been the returning officer; but at that time the Irish House of Commons resolved that the limits of the borough were coextensive with the manor, and as the freeholders of the manor had tendered their votes in favour of two candidates, they were declared by the Irish parliament to be duly elected, and the bishop's nominees were unseated. At the Union, the £15,000 granted as compensation for abolishing the elective franchise was claimed by the bishop, the dean and chapter, and prebendaries of the cathedral, and the Rev. Hugh Nevan, senesehal of the manor; but their claim was disallowed and the money paid to the Board of First Fruits. By the charter a grant was to be made to the corporation by the bishop of 700 Irish acres near the town, for which a rent of 8d. per acre was to be paid. Out of the profits of 200 acres of this land the corporation was, within two years, to erect a school-house and maintain a schoolmaster, with a servant, for a grammar school. English was to be taught by the master, who was always to be appointed by the bishop. The portreeve was to have 200 acres of the grant assigned for his support while holding the office, and for the payment ofa steward and serjeant or bailiff; and the profits of the remaining 300 acres were to be divided among the burgesses. This grant appears not to have been made. The charter granted a civil court of record to the corporation, with a jurisdiction extending to a circle of three miles in every direction round the cathedral, and to the amount of £5 English, with a prison for debtors. Since the death of the last senesehal, about 1823, this court has not been held. Quarter sessions are held here twice a year in the sessions house, alternately with Dungannon, for the baronies of Dungannon and Clogher; and there is a bridewell.

The SEE of CLOGHER is one of the most ancient in Ireland, and had its origin in the religious foundation instituted by St. Patrick, or his friend St. Macartin, a descendant of Fiachus Araidh, King of Ulster, who was succeeded in the mingled abbacy and prelacy by St. Tigernach, St. Laserian, St. Aidan (who converted the Northumbrians to Christianity, and was the first bishop of

Lindisfarne), and other celebrated ecelesiastics of the early ages. So late as the 12th century, Edan O'Killedy, bishop of this see, subscribed his name as Bishop of Uriel to the great charter of Newry. The equally ancient see of Clones was at a remote period annexed to it, as also were those of Ardsrath and Louth. About 1240, Hen. III. sent a mandatory letter to Maurice Fitzgerald, Lord-Justice of Ireland, commanding him to unite the bishoprick of Clogher to the archiepiscopal see of Arinagh, on account of the poverty of both. This union was not then effected, but under the Church Temporalities act it will take place on the death of the present bishop. About 1266, the bishoprick of Ardsrath was taken possession of by the Bishop of Derry, and Louth by the Archbishop of Armagh; and on the death of Bishop Arthur Mac Camaeil, the archbishop claimed his best horse, ring, and cup as an heriot. Clogher, being situated in a part of the island to which the English arms or laws had scarcely ever extended, had not a bishop of English extraction before the time of Edmund Courcey, who was consecrated in 1485. The last bishop who held the see and its temporalities from the court of Rome was Hugh or Odo O'Cervallan, promoted by Paul III., amid confirmed by Hen. VIII., in 1542. The first Protestant bishop was Miler Magragh, who had been a Franciscan friar and was made Bishop of Down by Pope Pius V., but afterwards becoming a Protestant, was placed in this see by Queen Elizabeth in 1570, and soon afterwards was made Archbishop of Cashel. From the time of his translation, owing to the disturbances in this part of the country, there was no bishop till 1605, when George Montgomery, a native of Scotland, was made bishop by Jas. I., and held the see with those of Derry and Raphoc, and afterwards with that of Meath. On the death of Bishop Boyle, in 1687, the episcopal revenues were paid into the exchequer, and the see continued vacant about three years, when King William translated Dr. Tennison to it.

This diocese is one of the ten which constitute the ecclesiastical province of' Armagh: it comprises a small portion of the county of Louth and parts of the counties of Donegal and Tyrone, the greater part of Fermanagh, and the whole of Monaghan; and is 76 British miles long and 25 broad, comprehending a superficies of about 528,700 plantation acres, of which 1850 are in Louth, 25,000 in Donegal, 68,100 in Tyrone, 254,150 in Fermanagh, and 179,600 in Monaghan. The chapter consists of a dean, archdeacon, precentor, chancellor, and the five prebendaries of Kilskerry, Findonagh, Tullycorbet, Tyhallon, and Devenish. According to the registry, the ancient chapter consisted of twelve canons, of which the dean and archdeacon were two: this was altered by Bishop Montgomery, and the offices of precentor amid chancellor were added; and hence it is that the archdeacon of this diocese, as the more ancient officer, ranks next the dean. The lands belonging to the see amount to 22,591 statute acres, of which 18,851 are profitable land; and the gross average annual income, as returned by the Commissioners of Ecclesiastical Inquiry, is £10,371, and the net revenue £8686.11.6. There is no economy fund connected with the cathedral; it was for many years kept in repair out of a fund bequeathed for charitable purposes by Bishop Sterne, but the trustees have lately withdrawn the grant.

The consistorial court of the diocese is held at Monaghan: its officers are a vicar-general, a surrogate, two registrars and a deputy, and two proctors; the registrars are keepers of the records, which consist of copies of wills from 1659 to the present time, (locuments relating to inductions to benefices, &c. The diocesan school is at. Monaghan, and is described in the article on that place; and there are free schools connected with the diocese at Carrickmacross and Enniskillen. The total number of parishes in the diocese is 45, which are either rectories and vicarages, or vicarages, the rectorial tithes of which are partly appropriate to the see, and partly impropriate in lay persons. The benefices are also 45, of which, one is in the gift of the Crown, 37 in that of the Bishop, four in that of Trinity College, Dublin, one in that of the Marquess of Ely, and one in that of Sir Thomas B. Lennard, Bart.; the remaining one is a perpetual curacy, in the gift of the prebendary of Devenish. The only union is that of Currin and Drumkrin, which will be dissolved on the next avoidance. The number of churches is 61, and of glebe-houses, 38. In the R. C. divisions this diocese, as originally constituted, forms a distinct bishoprick, and is one of the eight suffragan to Armagh: it comprises 37 parochial unions or districts, containing 81 chapels served by 37 parish priests and 51 coadjutors or curates. The bishop's parish is Carrickmacross, where he resides; and the dean's, Monaghan.

The parish is of great extent, and comprehends the manors of Augher, in which is the town of that name; Clogher (granted by Chas. I. to the bishop), in which is the town of Clogher; Blessingburne, in which is the town of Five-mile-Town; Mount-Stewart; and part of the manor of Killyfaddy, granted to Sir Wm. Cope, and the rest of which is in the adjoining parish of Donagheavy: there are eight townlands of the manor of Clogher, called abbey lands, which are tithe-free. It contains 49,761 statute acres, according to the Ordnance survey, of which 30,000 are good arable and pasture land, 2131/4 are water, and 19,761 are waste heath and bog, the greater part of which is, however, highly improvable; of its entire surface, 43,754 acres are applotted under the tithe act. The land in the vicinity of the town is remarkably fertile and well cultivated; freestone and limestone are abundant, and, there are indications of coal and lead ore. Clogher is situated on a lofty eminence, in the midst of a rich and diversified country encircled by mountains, which on the south approach within one mile, and on the north within two miles of the town, and the highest of which is Knockmany. Slieve Beagh, on the southern border of tire parish, rises to an elevation of 1254 feet above the level of the sea. Besides the episcopal palace, the parish contains several fine residences. The deanery or glebe-house, which is about a quarter of a mile west of the cathedral, is a handsome house in a fertile and well-planted glebe. Not far distant from it is Augher Castle, the splendid residence of Sir J. M. Richardson Bunbury, Bart.; Cecil, the seat of the Rev. Francis Gervais; Corick, of the Rev. Dr. Story; Killyfaddy, of R. W. Maxwell, Esq.; Blessingburne Cottage, of Col. Montgomery; Daisy-hill, of A. Millar, Esq.; Fardross, the ancient seat of A. Upton Gledstanes, Esq.; Ballimagowan, of A. Newton, Esq.; Waring Bank, of J. McLannahan, Esq.; and Corcreevy House, of Lieut.Col. Dickson.

The living is a rectory and vicarage, in the diocese of Clogher, constituting the corps of the deanery of Clogher, in the patronage of the Crown: the tithes amount to £850, and the income of the dean, including tithes and glebe, is £1374.17.3. The cathedral, which is dedicated to St. Macartin, and from time immemorial has been used as the parish church, was built in the ancient style of English architecture by Bishop Sterne, in 1744, at his own expense, but was remodelled in the Grecian style by Dean Bagwell, in 1818, who erected stalls for the dignitaries and a gallery for the organist and choir, also galleries in the two transepts; and about the same time the whole was newly roofed and ceiled. The Ecclesiastical Commissioners have recently made a grant of £197 for repairs. It is a large and handsome cruciform structure, with a lofty square tower rising from the west front, in which is the principal entrance: the throne, which is very beautiful, occupies the western angle of the south transept, and the whole of the interior is handsomely fitted up. There are several elegant monuments, among which are Bishop Garnett's, who died in the year 1783, and Bishop Porter's, who died in 1819. The chapter-house is near the entrance, on the right.

There are two chapels of ease in the parish, one at Five-mile-Town, or Blessingburne, and one at Newtown-Saville; and divine service is regularly performed every Sunday in the market-house at Augher, in several of the school-houses in distant parts of the parish, and also at Lislie during the summer. The glebe-house, or deanery, is about a quarter of a mile from the cathedral. The glebe comprises 556a. 1r. 24p. statute measure, of which l00a. ir. 28p. are annexed to the deanery, and 455a. 3r. 36p. are leased, at a rent of £337.15.6$^1/_2$ and renewal fines amounting to £20.7 per annum. The R. C. parish is co-extensive with that of the Established Church, and there are chapels at Aghadrummond, Escragh, and Aghentine; there are also places of wor ship for Presbyterians at Longridge amid Aghentine. The free school in the town is under the patronage of the Bishop: the master's salary is derived from the proceeds of a bequest of £420 by Bishop Garnett, which the existing bishop augments to £40 per annum. The schoolhouse was built in 1780, by Bishop Garnett, at an expense of £300. At Beltany there is a male and female school, on Erasmus Smith's foundation, endowed with two acres of land by the Rev. F. Gervais, who, in conjunction with the trustees of that charity, built the school-house, at an expense of £658.19.6. There are a female school at Cecil, built and supported by Mrs. Gervais; and schools for both sexes at Escragh, supported by Cal)t. Maxwell at Five-mile-Town, supported by Col. Montgomery, and at Bailyscally, supported by J. Trimble, Esq., all under the National Board; there are also four other schools. In these schools are about 490 boys and 330 girls; and there are seventeen private schools, in which are about 540 boys and 350 girls, and thirteen Sunday schools. A dispensary is maintained in the customary manner. At Lumford Glen is a deep ravine, in which a small stream of water flows through a cleft in the rock and forms a beautiful cascade. A carriage drive, edged with fine plantations, has been made to this waterfall.

CLOGHERNY, or CLOUGHENRY, a parish, in the barony of OMAGH, county of TYRONE, and province of ULSTER, 6 miles (S. E.) from Omagh; containing 6785 inhabitants. This parish, anciently Donaghaneigh, is situated on the road from Dungannon to Omagh, and contains, according to the Ordnance survey, 17,791$^1/_2$ statute acres (including a detached portion of 2368$^1/_2$ acres), about 8000 of which are arable, mostly under a good system of cultivation. There is a market at Beregh on Wednesday, and a fair on the first Monday in every month; and fairs are also held at Seskinore, on the second Monday in every month, for hive stock. The principal seats are Gortmore, the residence of J. Galbraith, Esq.; Mullaghmore, of R. Burges, Esq.; Seskinore, of Mrs. Perry; and Somerset, of the Rev. J. Lowry. The living is a rectory, in the diocese of Armagh, and in the patronage of the Provost and Fellows of Trinity College, Dublin, who purchased the advowson in 1830: the tithes amount to £692. The church is a large and handsome edifice, built about 1746, and enlarged arid much improved in 1773. The glebe-house was built in 1774, about which time the parish was disunited from Termon: it is large and handsome, and is on a glebe of 154 acres; there is also a glebe at Upper Clogherny, comprising 429 acres, and another called Mullaghollin, in the parish of Termon, comprising 508 acres, making a total of 1084 acres of arable land, besides about 850 acres of mountain and bog. The R. C. parish is co-extensive with that of the Established Church, and is called Beregh; there are chapels at Beregh, Liskmore, and Brackey. At Dervethroy is a meeting-house for Presbyterians in connection with the Synod of Ulster, of the third class; and at Seskinore is one in connection with the Associate Synod. The parochial school, situated near the church, is a large and handsome edifice, built by the inhabitants, at a cost of £800, and is supported by the rector; and there are 11 other schools in the parish, also four Sunday schools. About a mile from the church are the ruins of the old church of Donaghaneigh, in a large townland, which is extra-parochial, and belongs to the Bishop of Clogher.

CLONFEACLE, a parish, partly in the barony of ARMAGH, and partly in that of O'NEILLAND WEST, county of ARMAGH, but chiefly in the barony of DUNGANNON,

Benburb Castle. From The Dublin Penny Journal, *vol. 1, 1834.*

county of TYRONE, and province of ULSTER, 5½ miles (N. N. W.) from Armagh; containing, with the districts of Derrygortrevy, Moy, and Blackwatertown, (each of which is separately described) 19,547 inhabitants. This place was distinguished at a very remote period as the seat of a religious establishment of great reputation, of which St. Lugud, or Lugaid, was abbot about the year 580. It was soon after vested in the Culdean monks, whose chief establishment in Ireland was at Armagh, and with it this house became united about the middle of the 10th century. The Culdees kept possession of the Church, and several large tracts of land in the parish, till the Reformation, when the whole became forfeited to the Crown, and were granted by Jas. I., on the 13th of May, 1614, to Primate Hampton, and his successors for ever, under the denomination of the "Termon, or Erenach lands of Clonfeicle," together with the church and rectory, which latter has since passed from the Primate, and is now vested in the Provost and Fellows of Trinity College, Dublin. During the Irish wars, and more especially in the rebellion of the Earl of Tyrone, this district was the scene of numerous sanguinary battles, the details of which are given in the article on Benburb.

The parish is intersected by the river Blackwater, over which are several large and handsome stone bridges; and comprises, according to the Ordnance Survey, 26,218 statute acres, of which 21,582 are in Tyrone, and 4636 in Armagh. The surface is diversified by several small and beautiful lakes, the principal of which is Lough Curran, on an artificial island in which have been discovered the remains of buildings and warlike and domestic implements; and near it is the old camp of the O'Nials, now Fort Magarrett. The land is chiefly arable: the soil is light but generally fertile, producing excellent crops; the system of agriculture is improved, and there is no wasteland, except a tract of bog or marsh, about 400 acres in extent. Limestone and freestone abound in the parish: there are extensive and valuable limestone quarries at Benburb. The Ulster canal passes for three miles through the parish, on the Armagh or eastern side of the Blackwater. At Benburb a rock has been excavated to the depth of 86 feet, and the Canal carried longitudinally over a mill-race for a very considerable distance, by a handsome aqueduct. The scenery is pleasingly diversified and beautifully picturesque; the glen through which the Blackwater flows is highly romantic, and the canal, when completed will add to the interest of the landscape. The principal seats are Dartrey Lodge, the residence of W. Olpherts, Esq.; the Argory, of W. McGeough Bond, Esq.; and Tullydoey, of J. Eyre Jackson, Esq., at which place is also the residence of T. Eyre, Esq. The weaving of linen is carried on extensively by the farmers and cottiers at their own dwellings; and at Tullydoey is an extensive bleach-green.

The living is a rectory and vicarage, in the diocese of Armagh, and in the patronage of the Provost and Fellows of Trinity College, Dublin: the tithes amount to £1030. The glebe-house is a good building; the glebe comprises 532a. 3r.17p. of good arable land. The church was destroyed during the rebellion of Tyrone, since which tmne the village of Clonfeacle has been neglected and now forms part of Blackwatertown; and, in the same rebellion, the church of Eglish was destroyed, and that parish has ever since been included in the parish of Clonfeacle. The present parish church is situated close to the village of Benburb, on the confines of the counties of Armagh and Tyrone; it was built by Sir R, Wingfield, in 1619, and repaired and enlarged in 1815, by a gift of £800 from the late Board of First Fruits; the Ecclesiastical Commissioners have recently granted £526.11 towards its further repair. There are also a church at Moy and one at Derrygortrevy; the latter stands near the site of the old church of Eglish. In the R. C. divisions the parish is called Upper and Lower Clonfeacle, and includes the whole parish of Eglish; there are chapels at Eglish, Moy, and Blackwatertown. There is a place of worship at Benburb for Presbyterians in connection with the Synod of Ulster of the second class; and one at Crew in connection with the Associate Synod: and at Blackwatertown is a place of worship for Wesleyan Methodists. The parochial school, near the church at Benburb, was built in 1832, by the Rev. Henry Griffin, the present rector, by whom it is principally supported; there are also schools at Blackwatertown and Derrycrevy, and near the old churchyard at Clonfeacle is a national school. At Benburb, Gorestown, Drummond, Mullycarnan, and Carrowcolman, schools were built and are supported by funds arising from a bequest, by Lord Powerseourt, of £2000 for charitable uses, and are conducted under the moral agency system. The sum of £4 per annum is paid to the poor of this parish from Drelincourt's charity, and two children are eligible to the Drelincourt school at Armagh. A bequest of £100 was made to the poor by a person whose name is now unknown. The ruins of Benburb castle, situated on the summit of a limestone rock overhanging the river, have a very picturesque appearance; and near them was found a silver signet ring, bearing the arms and initials of Turlogh O'Nial, which is now in the possession of Mr. Bell, of Dungannon. Several interesting relics of antiquity have been found in various parts; a large well-formed canoe was found in the bed of the river at Bhackwater-town, in 1826, and is now in the garden of C. Magee, Esq.; it is scooped out of an oak tree, and is in good preservation. The same gentleman has also some very perfect querns, an altar of rude construction, several stone hatchets, and the horns of an elk, which were found a few years since at Drumlee. At Tullydoey are some inconsiderable vestiges of an ancient fort.

CLONOE, a parish, in the barony of DUNGANNON, county of TYRONE, and province of ULSTER, 2 miles (S. by E.) from Stewartstown, on the road to Lurgan; containing 5555 inhabitants, and comprising, according to the Ordnance survey, 12,070$^{3}/_{4}$ statute acres, of which 29$^{1}/_{2}$ are part of the Blackwater, and 2940$^{3}/_{4}$ are part of Lough Neagh (called Washing bay), by which the parish is bounded on the east. A large tract of marshy ground and bog extends from the shore of the lough to the Blackwater, and the remainder is good arable and pasture land. Near the north-western extremity of the parish are the extensive ruins of Mountjoy castle, built by the Earl of Mountjoy, when lord-deputy of Ireland, in 1601, to check the Earl of Tyrone. This castle, which was built of brick made on the spot, is situated on a gentle eminence close to the shore of the lake, and was thought of so much importance, on the plantation of Ulster, that Jas. I. made this place a corporate borough, and granted 300 acres of land for its support, and 300 acres more to maintain a garrison. In the war of 1641 it was taken by Turlogh O'Nial, who kept possession of it till his total defeat by Gen. Monroe, in 1643; it was dismantled by order of parliament in 1648, since which time it has been in ruins. The Earl of Tyrone built a strong castle on the shore of Lough Neagh, towards the close of the 16th century, and called it Fuith-na-gael, of the "Abomination of the Stranger;" but it was soon after taken by the English, and no traces of it remain.

The living is a rectory, in the diocese of Armagh, and in the patronage of the Provost and Fellows of Trinity College, Dublin: the tithes amount to £461.10.9$^{1}/_{4}$. The glebe-house was built by aid of a gift of £200 and a loan of £550 from the late Board of First Fruits: the glebe comprises 78 acres. The church is a small ancient edifice; it was repaired in 1699, and the Ecclesiastical Commissioners have recently granted £197.6 for its further repair. The R. C. parish is co-extensive with that of the Established Church; there are two chapels, one at Clonoe and one at Mountjoy; the latter was built in 1835. The parochial school is aided by the rector; a manor school is supported by A. Annesley, Esq., lord of the manor, at whose expense a large and handsome school-house was erected; there is also a school at Aughamullan. In these schools are about 170 children; and there is a pay school, in which are about 70 children. The late Dr. E. Sill bequeathed his estate, called Barn Hill, at Stewartstown, together with all his real and personal property, to build and support an hospital in this parish, at Washing bay, near the influx of a stream called the "Holy River" into Lough Neagh; the funded property exceeded £3000, and the lands produce more than £100 per annum, but no hospital has yet been built.

COAGH, a village, in that part of the parish of TAMLAGHT which is in the barony of DUNGANNON. county of TYRONE, and province of ULSTER, 3 miles (S. by E.) from Moneymore; containing 393 inhabitants. This place formed part of the estate granted to the Hon. Andrew

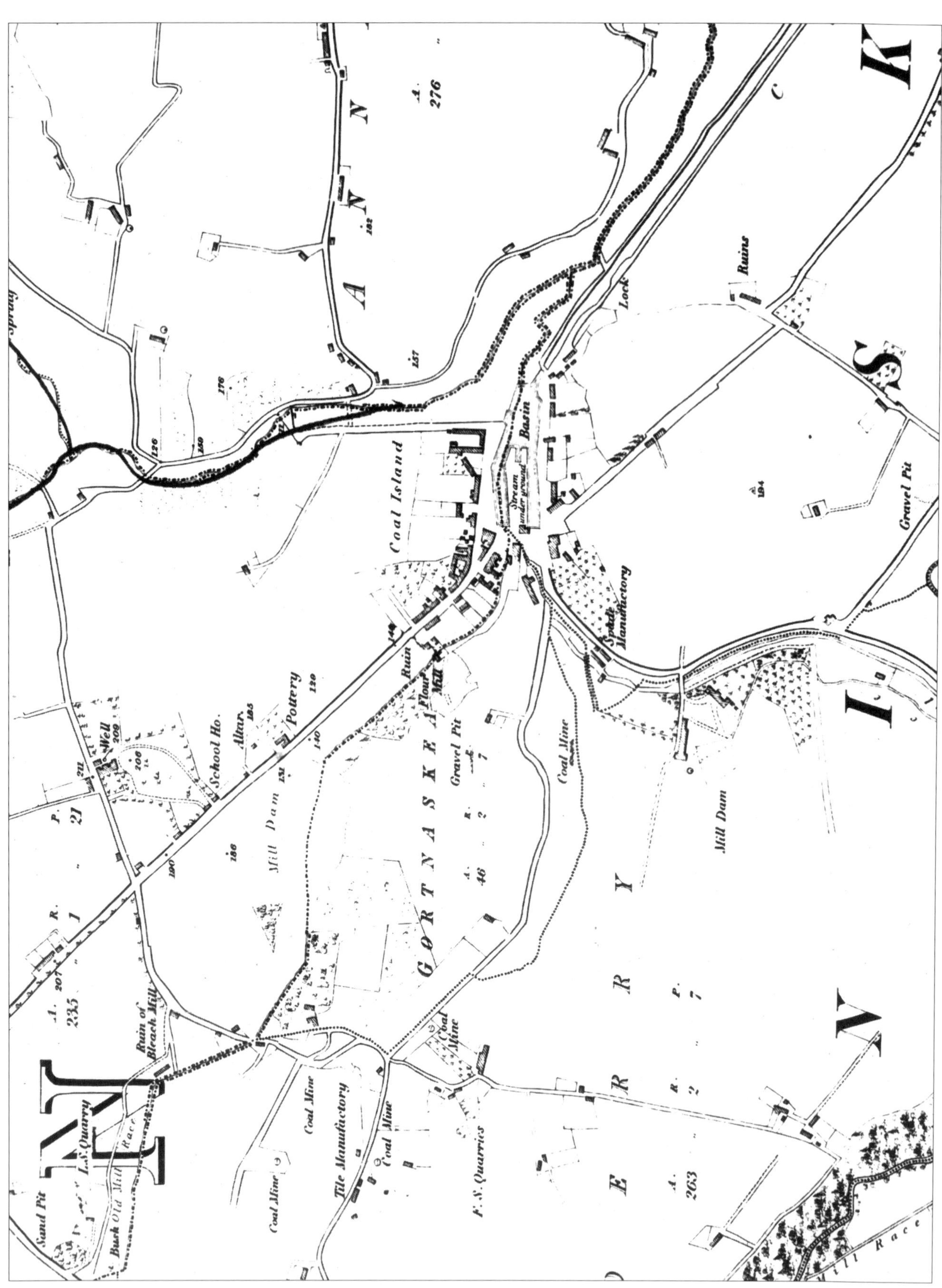

Coalisland. Part of the O.S. map of Co. Tyrone, sheet 47, published 1834 (reproduced at 140%).

Stewart by Jas. I., in 1612, and confirmed by Chas. I. in 1630. A battle took place here at the ford of the river, in 1641, when the chapel of Tamlaght was destroyed by the parliamentarians; and, in 1688, Jas. II. crossed the river at this place, on his march to the siege of Derry. The village, which in 1831 consisted of 76 well-built houses, is pleasantly situated on the road from Magherafelt to Stewartstown, in a fertile vale about two miles from Lough Neagh, and on the river Coagh or Ballinderry, over which is an ancient narrow bridge of stone of six arches. It is the property of William Lenox Conyngham, Esq., in whose family the estate has remained since the year 1663; and was erected about the year 1728, by George Conyngham, Esq., who obtained for it a charter for a market and four fairs. which have been changed to a market held on the first Friday in every month, for the sale of linens and provisions, and to 12 fairs held on the second Friday in every month, for horses, cattle, and agricultural produce. The market-house, a spacious and commodious building. was erected in 1828, by the present proprietor, who also built a good school-house and supports a school for male and female children. The linen market is very considerable; and the fairs, which are toll-free, are numerously attended. It is a constabulary police station and has a penny post to Moneymore. There is a place of worship for Presbyterians in connection with the Synod of Ulster. – See TAMLAGHT.

COAL ISLAND, a post-town, partly in the parishes of DONOGHENRY and CLONOE, but chiefly in that of TULLYNISKAN, barony of DUNGANNON, county of TYRONE, and province of ULSTER, 3 miles (N. E.) from Dungannon: the population is returned with the respective parishes. This flourishing trading village is situated in the centre of the Tyrone coal field, on the roads from Dungannon to Ballinderry, and from Lurgan to Stewartstown: it comprises 184 houses, which are generally well built with stone and covered with slate, and has a sub-post-office to Dungannon. The coal district extends from Mullaghmoyle, on the north, to Dungannon on the south, a distance of six miles, with an average breadth of two. Great difficulty is found in working it, owing to the softness of the bed on which it rests, and the dangerous state of the roof, unless expensively propped. At present the mining operations are confined to Drumglass, in the neighbourhood of Dungannon, and the vicinity of Coal Island: the collieries at the latter place are on a small scale, and principally worked by manual labour, but are moderately profitable. Coal Island originated in the formation of the Tyrone canal, which was begun by Government in 1744, and was intended to intersect the entire coalfield of Tyrone, but was not carried beyond this place. The canal is not more than three miles in length from the river Blackwater, which it joins near Lough Neagh, to Coal Island, but it has been commenced and partially completed in several places westward; bridges have been erected over the line; an aqueduct of three large arches was to have conveyed it over the Terren; and a rail-road was to have connected it with some of the minor collieries, for which purpose a viaduct, here called "the Dry Hurry," was thrown over the Cookstown road, two miles from Dungannon. All these edifices are of hewn freestone, handsomely finished and in good preservation; but in many places the canal is filled up and cultivated, so that in a few years the line will not be traceable.

This is now a place of considerable trade, and has 35 large lighters, or barges, which frequently make coasting voyages to Dublin, and sometimes across the channel to Scotland. Extensive iron-works, forges, and plating-mills were erected here in 1831, and there are others at Oghran and New Mills for the manufacture of spades, edge-tools, &c. Here is also an extensive establishment for the manufacture of fire-bricks and crucibles, commenced in 1834 by two gentlemen from Stourbridge, in Worcestershire. Most of the manufactured articles are sent to London or Liverpool. Near this is a pottery, and there is also a flour-mill, where 2000 tons of wheat are annually ground for the Belfast market. Bleach-greens have been established at Derryvale, Terren Hill, and New Mills, where 20,000 pieces of linen are annually finished for the English market. Several warehouses, granaries, yards, and other conveniences for carrying on an extensive trade are placed round a small but convenient basin, and in the village and its vicinity are the residences of several wealthy merchants. The exports are coal, spades, shovels, fire-bricks, fire-clay, crucibles, earthen-ware, linen cloth, wheat, oats, flour, &c.: the imports are timber, deals, iron, salt, slates, glass, &c. The village being in three parishes, has three churches within two miles of it, and a district church is about to be erected for its use. The R. C. chapel for the parish of Donoghenry is not far distant.

COOKSTOWN, a market and post-town, in that part of the parish of DERRYLORAN which is in the barony of DUNGANNON, county of TYRONE, and province of ULSTER, 20 miles (E. N. E.) from Omagh, and 86$^1/_2$ (N. N. W.) from Dublin, by the mail road, but only 79 by the direct road; containing 2883 inhabitants. This place derives its name from its founder, Allan Cook, who had a lease for years renewable under the see of Armagh, upon whose land the old town was built, about the year 1609. It is situated on the mail coach road from Dungannon to Coleraine, and consists of one wide street more than a mile and a quarter long, with another street intersecting it at right angles, containing 570 houses, many of which are large, well built with stone, and slated. The present town was built about the year 1750, by Mr. Stewart, its then proprietor, and is advantageously situated in a fine and fertile district, which is well wooded and watered, and abundantly supplied with limestone. A patent for a market and fairs was granted to Allan Cook, Aug. 3rd, 1628. The market is on Tuesday for grain, and on Saturday for linen cloth, flax, yarn, cattle, pigs, and provisions. Fairs are held on the first Saturday in every month, for general farming stock. The market-place consists

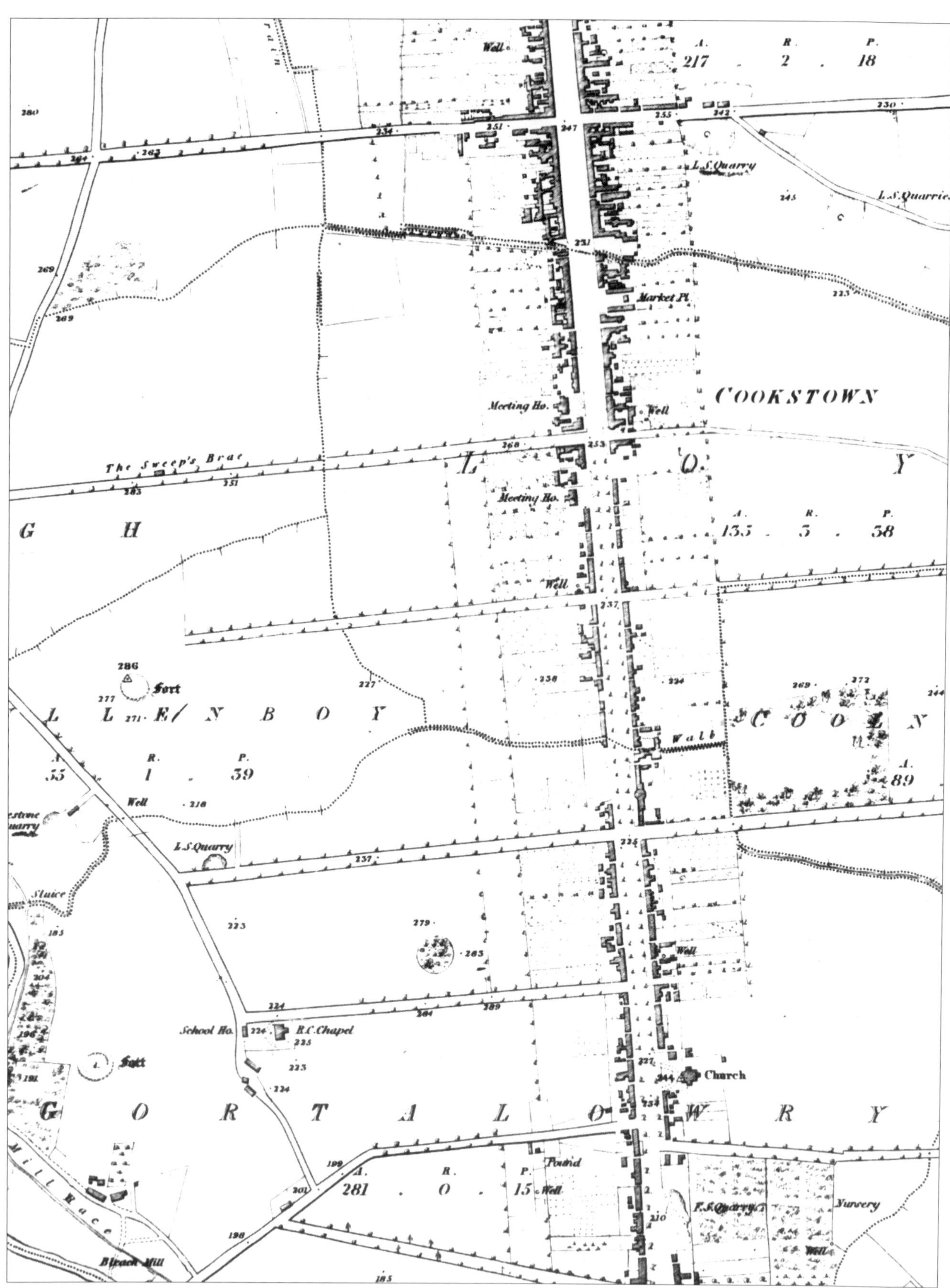

Cookstown. Part of the O.S. map of Co. Tyrone, sheet 29, published 1834 (reproduced at 140%).

chiefly of merchants' stores and shops. At Greenvale is a large establishment for bleaching, dyeing, and finishing linens for the English markets; there are others at Wellbrook and at Ardtrea besides two large ones at Tullylaggan. A constabulary police force has been stationed in the town. A manorial court for the primate's manor of Ardtrea is held here once a month, for the recovery of debts under £5: its jurisdiction extends into the parishes of Lissan, Derryloran, Kildress, Desertcreight, Arboe, Ardtrea, Clonoe, Ballyclog, Tamlaght, Ballinderry, and Donoghenry. Petty sessions are held on alternate Fridays.

Close adjoining the town is Killvmoon, the residence of W. Stewart, Esq., proprietor of the town and of the land immediately adjacent; it was built from a design by Mr. Nash, in the pure Saxon style, and is situated in an extensive demesne, containing some uncommonly fine timber. Not far distant are Loughry, the residence of J. Lindesay, Esq., and Lissan, the seat of Sir T. Staples, Bart. The former is in a demesne of about 200 acres, finely wooded, and watered by the river Loughry: the estate was granted, in 1604, by Jas. I. to Sir Robert Lyndesay, his chief harbinger, and has ever since been the residence of the senior branch of that ancient family, which is among the claimants of the earldom of Craufurd and Lyndesay. The other seats in the vicinity are Oaklands, the residence of Capt. Richardson; the glebe-house, of the Rev. C. Bardin, D. D.; and Greenvale, of T. Adair, Esq.; besides several other handsome houses in and near the town. The parish church of Derryhoran, in the southern part of the town, is a large and handsome cruciform edifice, built of hewn freestone from a design by Mr. Nash, in the early English style of architecture: it has a tower and lofty octagonal spire, and the interior is fitted up in the Saxon style. Near the centre of the town is a large and handsome Presbyterian meeting-house, in connection with the Synod of Ulster, and also one in connection with the Associate Synod, each of which is of the first class and has a manse for the clergyman. A second meeting-house in connection with the Synod of Ulster was built in 1835, and there are places of worship for Wesleyan and Primitive Methodists, and, at a short distance from the town, a large R. C. chapel. An infants' school was established in 1834, by Mrs. Hassard and other ladies,for which a house is now being built; and a parochial school-house is also being erected, on land givenby Mr. Stewart: near the town are several other schools. Here are also a news-room and a dispensary. Close to the town are the ruins of the old church of Derryloran, and not far distant are two large forts, one circular, the other square. In Killymoon demesne are the ruins of an old meeting-house; at Drumcraw is the site of a church, and at Loughry a fine cromlech. – See DERRYLORAN.

CUMBER, UPPER, a parish, partly in the barony of STRABANE, county of TYRONE, but chiefly in that of TIRKEERAN, county of DERRY, and province of ULSTER, $7^1/_2$ miles (N. E.) from Londonderry; containing, with Claudy (which has a daily penny post), 5430 inhabitants. The early history of this parish cannot be satisfactorily traced, further than that St. Patrick, having crossed the Foyle, founded several churches in this district, one of which occupied the site of the present church of Cumber. The original name is variously written by early historians; the present is modern, and acquired since the taxation of Pope Nicholas in 1291. At the Reformation the rectory belonged to the abbey of Derry, and was given by Jas. I. to the bishop, as part of the abbey lands. In 1622, it appears, by the Ulster Visitation book, to have been held with Banagher. The ancient parish of Cumber was the most extensive in the diocese, until 1794, when it was divided into Upper and Lower Cumber, by order in council: the parish of Upper Cumber, according to the Ordnance survey, comprising $26{,}202^1/_4$ statute acres, of which $23{,}072^3/_4$ are in Derry, and $3129^1/_2$ in Tyrone; the latter form a hilly district amid the Mounterloney mountains. In some parts, particularly on the Walworth estate, and on that of Learmout, the land, though hilly, is well cultivated; the extensive bogs are being worked out, and brought into cultivation. The inhabitants combine the weaving of linen cloth, with agricultural pursuits; there are several commodious and excellent bleach-greens on the Faughan water, none of which, however, are now at work. The southern parts of the parish consist chiefly of mountains, the principal of which is Sawel, the highest in the county, being 2236 feet above the level of the sea; its summit, is on the boundary between two counties. These mountains afford excellent pasturage on every side; and the rivers Faughan, Glenrandle, and Dungorthin have their sources in them. There are large woods and much valuable timber in the demesne of Park-Learmont; and the plantations of Cumber, Alla, and Kilcatton greatly embellish the surrounding scenery. There are several large and elegant houses, of which the principal are Learmont, the seat of Barre Beresford, Esq.; Cumber House, of John H. Browne, Esq.; Kilcatton Hall, of Alexander Ogilby, Esq.; and Alla, of the Rev. Francis Brownlow.

The living is a rectory, in the diocese of Derry, and forms the corps of a prebend in the cathedral of Derry, in the patronage of the Bishop: the tithes amount to £740. The glebe, situated in Glenrandle, half a mile from the church, consists of the townlands of Alla, Gilky Hill, and Tullentraim, containing 1508 statute acres. The church is a large modern edifice, with a small bell turret on the western gable, erected in 1757, on the site of an ancient building. In 1831, eight townlands were separated from the parish, to form part of the new district or parish of Learmont, and the rector of Upper Cumber has the alternate presentation to that perpetual cure. In the R. C. divisions the parish is partly included in the union or district of Banagher, and partly forms the head of a district, comprising also a part of that of Lower Cumber; there are chapels at Claudy and Gortscreagan. The Presbyterians have a meeting-house at Claudy, in connection with the Synod of Ulster. The parochial school, situated on the glebe lands of Alla, is well built and convenient; it is supported by the trustees of Erasmus Smith's charity, and is under the management of the rector, who has endowed it with two acres of land. Male and female schools were built and are supported by the Fishmongers' Company; and they have also excellent male and female schools at Gortilca and Killycor. There are also schools at Ballyarton, Craig, Kilcatton, and Claudy. A female school at Claudy is principally supported by Lady Catherine Brownlow, who likewise contributes to some others. A female work school at Cumber was built and is supported by Mrs. Browne and other ladies of the parish. A male and female school at Learmont is principally supported by the Beresford family. There are also Sunday schools and a private day school. At Mulderg is a large dispensary, built and supported by the Fishmongers' Company. There are the remains of a druidical altar at Baltibrecan; and at Altaghoney were discovered, in the summer of 1835, three stone coffins, each covered with three flag stones, and in each an urn containing ashes, calcined bones, &c. The graves were two feet deep in the gravel, where 8 feet of bog had been cut off the surface; and near the coffins were two idols, carved out of solid oak, which, with the urns, are now in good preservation, in the museum of Alex. Ogilby, Esq., of Kilcatton, who has also a good collection of landscapes, groups, &c.. more than 200 of which are from his own pencil.

DERRYGORTREVY, a district parish, in the barony of DUNGANNON, county of TYRONE, and province of ULSTER, 3 miles (S. W. by S.) from Dungannon, on the road to Aughnacloy; containing 5282 inhabitants. This district was formed in 1819, by setting off 36 townlands of the parish of Clonfeacle, or rather from the ancient parish of Eglish, which was united to Clonfeacle in the 15th of Chas. II., and thence the whole was called Clonfeacle. The land is generally good, and in an unimproved state of cultivation. There are rocks of excellent limestone, abundance of freestone, and indications of coal, but none of these have ever been worked. The living is a perpetual curacy, in the diocese of Armagh, and in the patronage of the Rector of Clonfeacle, to whom the entire tithes are paid, and who allows the curate annually £93.9.3. The glebe-house was erected by aid of a gift of £450, and a loan of £50, in 1822, from the late Board of First Fruits; the glebe comprises 20 acres. The church is a small neat edifice, with a lofty square tower, erected in 1815, at a cost of £800 by the same Board; it is situated on an eminence, half a mile west from the ancient church of Eglish. In the R. C. divisions this district is called Eglish, at which place there is a chapel. The parochial school, near the church, was built in 1825, and is aided by an annual donation from Lord Ranfurly. A school at Gort is partly supported by Lord Caledon; and there are others at Clogherney, Cormullan, and Mullicar. About 40 boys and 20 girls are educated in a private school: there is also a Sunday school.

DERRYLORAN, a parish, partly in the barony of LOUGHINSHOLIN, county of LONDONDERRY, but chiefly in that of DUNGANNON, county of TYRONE, and province of ULSTER, on the road from Armagh to Coleraine, and from Omagh to Belfast; containing, with the post-town of Cookstown, 8406 inhabitants. It comprises, according to the Ordnance survey, 12,100¼ statute acres, of which 9656½ are in Tyrone, and 2443¾ in Londonderry. There are 400 acres of woodland and 100 of bog; the remainder is arable and pasture land: the Drapers' Company of London are the chief proprietors. The soil is fertile and well cultivated, and the bog is very valuable as fuel. The parish is well fenced and watered by the river Ballinderry, and ornamented with the plantations of Killymoon and Loughry, which, with the other seats, are more particularly noticed in the article on Cookstown, which see. The living is a rectory, in the diocese of Armagh, and in the patronage of the Lord-Primate the tithes amount to £552.8. The glebe-house was built in 1820, by aid of a gift of £100 and a loan of £1050 from the late Board of First Fruits. The glebe consists of 71 acres. The church, situated in Cookstown, was built in 1822, by aid of a loan of £3000 from the same Board, and the Ecclesiastical Commissioners have recently granted £283 for its repair. In the R. C. divisions the parish is united to that of Desertereight, and contains a chapel at Cookstown, where are also four dissenting meeting-houses. Besides the schools in Cookstown, there are schools for both sexes at Ballygroogan, Tubberlane, Killycurragh, and Derrycrummy, aided by annual donations from Lord Castle-Steuart; two at Cloghoge; and one at Gortolery, aided by collections at the R. C. chapel.

DESERTCREIGHT, a parish, in the barony of DUNGANNON, county of TYRONE, and province of ULSTER, 2¼ miles (S.) from Cookstown, on the road from Dungannon to Coleraine; containing 7516 inhabitants. This parish comprises, according to the Ordnance survey, 14,399½ statute acres, chiefly rich arable and pasture land in a high state of cultivation; in the southern part of it are about 1000 acres of mountain and bog. Here are slate quarries, but they are not now worked; and seams of coal may be distinguished in various parts, but no pits have ever been sunk: freestone and limestone are abundant. At Tullylaggan are two extensive bleach greens, and near Desertcreight is a smaller, which annually bleach and finish upwards of 30,000 pieces for the London market; and a great quantity is woven by the country people in their own houses, the occupation of weaving being followed generally by the inhabitants, in addition to agricultural pursuits. In the upper part of the parish is the village of Rock, where fairs are held on the last Monday in every month, for cattle, sheep, pigs, &c.; and there are four during the year at Tullyhoge. The principal gentlemen's seats are Loughry, the elegant residence of J. Lindesay, Esq.; Desertcreight House, of J. Greer, Esq.; Rockdale, of J. Lowry, Esq.; New Hamburgh, of T. Greer, Esq.; Milton, of W. Greer, Esq.; Turniskea, of the

Misses Bailie; Pomeroy House, of R. W. Lowry, Esq.; Elder Lodge, of Dr. Dickson; Rock Lodge, of Captain Daniell; Lime Park, of the Hon. And. Steuart; and the Glebe-house, of the Rev. A. G. Steuart.

The living is a rectory, in the diocese of Armagh, and in the patronage of the Provost and Fellows of Trinity College, Dublin: the tithes amount to £507.13.10, and the glebe comprises 177 acres. The church is a very ancient edifice, for the repairs of which the Ecclesiastical Commissioners have recently made a grant of £205.14.7: it is situated in a deep and romantic valley. In the R. C. divisions this parish forms part of the union or district of Derryloran; there is a chapel at Tully O'Donnell, also an altar where divine service is performed on alternate Sundays. At Sand-boles is a Presbyterian meeting-house in connection with the Seceding Synod, of the first class; and there is one at Grange for the Covenanters. A commodious school at Tullyhoge was built and is supported by J. Lindesay, Esq.; at Caddy is one built and supported by T. Greer, Esq.; others at Shevy, Sandholes, Drumbellahue, and Grange, are in connection with the Kildare-place Society; and there is one at the slate quarry, in connection with the National Board. There are also three private schools. At Donarisk stood the ancient priory of that name, founded by one of the O'Hagan family, in 1294, of which nothing exists but the cemetery, remarkable as the burial-place of the sept of O'Hagan, and more recently as that of the ancient family of Lyndsay and Crawford, of whom there are several tombs, but the most remarkable is that of Robert Lyndsay, chief harbinger to King James: this Robert obtained the grant of Tullyhoge, &c., from Jas. I., in 1604, where, and at Loughry, the family have ever since resided. Their house and documents were burnt during the civil war of 1641, and this tomb was also mutilated and covered over, in which condition it remained till 1819, when, in sinking a vault, it was discovered. Numerous ornaments of gold, silver, and copper, with various military weapons, have been found here; the latter seem connected with the camp and fortress of Tullyhoge, the chief residence of the sept of O'Haidhagine, or O'Hagan, where the kings of Ulster were inaugurated with the regal title and authority of the O'Nial from the most remote period, Of this important fortress nothing remains but large masses of stone lying scattered around, and the mound, surrounded by deep fosses and ramparts of earthwork.

DONAGHCAVEY, or FINDONAGH, a parish, partly in the barony of OMAGH, but chiefly in that of CLOGHER, county of TYRONE, and province of ULSTER; containing, with the post-town of Fintona, 11,787 inhabitants. At the general plantation, this parish was known as the smaller portion of Fintona, and was granted by Jas. I., partly to Sir F. Willoughby, and afterwards to John Leigh, Esq., under the name of Fentonagh, and partly to Sir. W. Cope, under the name of Derrybard: it is now called the manor of Castlemaine. It is situated on the road from Omagh to Enniskillen, and contains, according to the Ordnance survey, 23,052¼ statute acres, of which 18,342¼ are in the barony of Clogher, and 4710¼ in that of Omagh; 9403 acres are applotted under the tithe act. Much of the mountainous land affords good pasturage for sheep and cattle, and is reclaimable; the bogs afford fuel, but they are fast being worked out. Great benefit has been derived from the improvements of the resident gentlemen in cultivation and planting, and by new lines of road. The country around Fintona is fertile and well planted; and the woods around Eccles are large and flourishing. Limestone is found within the parish, in which are some indications of coal and iron-ore. The inhabitants combine the weaving of linen cloth with their agricultural pursuits: there is a small forge, called a plating mill, for manufacturing spades, shovels, &c. At Fintona a court is held monthly for the manor of Castlemaine. The gentlemen's seats are, Ecclesville, the residence of C. Eccles, Esq.; Derrabard House, of S. Vesey, Esq.; Cavan House, of W. Dickson, Esq.; Cavan Lodge, of C. Lucas, Esq.; and the glebe house, of the Rev. J. McCormick.

The living is a vicarage, in the diocese of Clogher, and in the patronage of the Bishop; the rectory forms the corps of the prebend of Findonagh in the cathedral of Clogher. The tithes amount to £600; there is a glebe-house, and two glebes comprising 400 acres. The gross annual value of the prebend is returned at £865.17.8. The church adjoins the town of Fintona, and was built after the civil war of 1641, during which the old one was destroyed; it is a large and venerable edifice, with a modern square tower, which was erected and the church much improved by aid of a loan of £400, in 1818, from the late Board of First Fruits. The R. C. parish is co-extensive with that of the Established Church; the chapel is near Fintona. There are two large meeting-houses for Presbyterians, and one for Wesleyan Methodists. Here are thirteen schools, in which about 580 boys and 300 girls are taught; and about 400 boys and 200 girls are educated in fifteen private schools: there are also six Sunday schools, On an eminence, in the midst of an extensive cemetery, the ruins of the old church form an interesting object; near the bridge are the remains of a very large cromlech. Nearly adjoining the glebe-house is a valuable sulphureous chalybeate spring. – See FINTONA.

DONAGHEADY, a parish, in the barony of STRABANE, county of TYRONE, and province of ULSTER, on the road from Strabane to Cookstown; containing, with the post-town of Dunamanagh, 10,480 inhabitants. The greater part of this parish was granted by Jas. J. to Sir John Drummond, who founded the town of Dunamanagh, and built a bawn 109 feet square, no part of which remains, as the bawn was removed some years since, and the modern building called the Castle was erected on its site. It comprises, according to the Ordnance survey, 39,398½ statute acres, of which 28,728 are applotted under the tithe act, and valued at £10,271 per annum. There are about 154 acres of water, and 250 of bog; the remainder is arable and pasture land. There is abundance of excellent limestone, both for building and agricultural purposes, but the mountains are chiefly clay-slate. Many of the glens and banks of the rivers are covered with underwood, the remains of the extensive forests of Mounterlony. Formerly there were several bleach-greens in the parish, and a paper-mill near Dunamanagh, all of which are now unemployed; but the inhabitants unite linen-weaving at home with agricultural pursuits. The upper half of the parish, with the exception of the church lands, is in the manor of Eliston, the court for which is held at Gortin; and the lower half is in the manor of Donolonge, which was granted by Jas. I. to the Earl of Abercorn. A court is held at Donolonge monthly, for the recovery of debts under 40s. There are several handsome houses, the principal of which are Earl's Gift, the residence of the Rev. C. Douglas; Loughash, of Capt. Kennedy; Tullarton House, of R. Bond, Esq.; Glenville, of R. McRae, Esq.; Silver Brook, of J. Carey, Esq.; Black Park, of R. Ogilbye, Esq.; Thorn Hill, of A. C. D. L. Edie, Esq.; and the Grange, of T. Hutton, Esq.

The living is a rectory, in the diocese of Derry, and in the patronage of the Marquess of Abercorn: the tithes amount to £1350. The glebe-house was erected in 1792, by aid of a gift of £100 from the late Board of First Fruits: the glebe comprises 1192 acres. The church is a small neat edifice, half a mile west from the ruins of the old church; it is in the Grecian style, with a small cupola and a bell at the western end; and the Ecclesiastical Commissioners have recently granted £202 for its repair. In the R. C. divisions this parish is the head of a union or district, comprising Donagheady and Leckpatrick, and containing one chapel in the former and two in the latter: it is in the benefice of the dean of Derry. There are four Presbyterian meeting-houses, three of which are in connection with the Synod of Ulster, two being of the second class, and one with the Seceding Synod, also of the second class. The male and female parochial schools adjoin the church, and are supported by the Marquess of Abercorn and the incumbent. At Loughash is a large and handsome schoolhouse, erected at an expense of £200: the school is under the National Board, as is another at Lisnarrow. There are also schools at Killeany, Rusky, Tamnaghbrady, Tyboe, Grange, and Ballyneuse; and an agricultural school at Loughash, supported by Capt. Kennedy. At Mount Castle, which gives the title of baron in the Irish peerage to the Marquess of Abercorn, are some fragments of a castle, built in 1619, by Sir Claude Hamilton, on an estate of 2000 acres, called Eden, which was granted to him by Jas. I.: it was the birth-place of Sir George Hamilton, who distinguished himself in the parliamentary war, and of his son, Gen. Hamilton, afterwards sixth Earl of Abercorn, who commanded the Protestant Irish army against Jas. II. at Londonderry and Enniskillen. Extensive ruins of the ancient church of Grange, which belonged to the abbey of Derry, exist on the banks of the Foyle. At Kildollagh are some large artificial caves, formed of loose stones, with flagstones over them covered with earth; they are about a quarter of a mile long, and contain several apartments; there is a less perfect one at Gortmaglen. – See DUNAMANAGH.

DONAGHMORE, or DOONAMOR, a parish, in the barony of DUNGANNON, county of TYRONE, and province of ULSTER, 2 miles (N. N. W.) from Dungannon; containing 12,144 inhabitants. At this place, anciently called Domnach-mor, "the great fortress," St. Patrick founded an abbey, where he placed St. Columb, which soon acquired extensive grants of land and other valuable possessions, and continued to flourish till after the conquest of Ireland by Hen. II. In the taxation of Pope Nicholas, in 1291, it is described as having contained many costly shrines. It appears to have been possessed by the Colidei, or Culdees, of Armagh, as by the inquisition of the 33rd of Hen. VIII. we find the Colidei had its rectory and tithes, which, with many townlands in the adjoining parishes, were granted to the Archbishop of Armagh after the Reformation. Though there are no vestiges, it is ascertained that it stood a little north-east of the present village; within its precincts was a large and elegant cross of freestone, on which were inscribed numerous hieroglyphics representing various passages in the Scriptures; having been thrown down and mutilated in the war of 1641, it remained in that condition till 1776, when Richard Vincent, Esq., caused it to be removed and placed where it now stands, at the head of the village; it consists of a plinth, a shaft, and a cross, and is 16 feet in height. Donaghmore was also an important military station, frequent mention being made of it in the successive wars of Ireland, particularly during the rebellions of the O'Nials and the O'Donnels.

The parish is situated on the road from Dungannon to Omagh, and comprises, according to the Ordnance survey, 18,410½ statute acres, of which, 146 are water; there are about 3000 acres of bog and mountain, but the greater part of the remainder is arable land. The present village has been built since the year 1796, under the direction, and by the spirited exertions, of A. Mackenzie, Esq., and is in a very flourishing state, comprising 88 well built and slated houses, mostly in one street. There is an extensive brewery of the celebrated Donaghmore ale, where upwards of 10,500 barrels of ale and beer are annually brewed; also soap and candle manufactories; much business is transacted in the spirit trade; and there are large brick-works adjoining the village. Near Castle-Caulfield is a small green for bleaching linen cloth, much of which is woven by the farmers and cottiers throughout the parish. A fair is held on the first Tuesday in every month, for cattle, sheep, pigs, &c.; and a manor court on the first Monday in every month in the Primate's manor of Donaghmore, for the recovery of debts under £5. There are some small lakes in the parish; in almost all of them are artificial islands, on which were castles, and where ancient implements of warfare, have been found. Among the principal seats are Fort Edward, that of Capt. Lindsay; Annaquinea, of J. Young, Esq.; Springfield,of R. Forster, Esq.; Beech Valley, of J. Wilcox, Esq.; Donaghmore

Cottage, of J. King, Es9.; Parkanour, of J. Ynyr Burges, Esq.; Mullaghmore, of the Rev. T. Carpendale; Castle Caulfield, of H. King, Esq.; Tullynure Lodge, of the Rev. R. Fraser; and Mullagruen, of A. Mackenzie, Esq., which was built in 1683 by the celebrated Rev. G. Walker, defender of Londonderry, while he was rector of this parish, as appears by a shield bearing his arms and initials.

The living is a rectory and vicarage, in the diocese of Armagh, and in the patronage of the Lord-Primate: the tithes amount to £830.15.4$^1/_2$. There is a glebehouse, with a glebe comprising 459 acres of excellent arable land; and in this parish are also the glebes of Drumglass and Ardtrea. The church is a large plain edifice, situated at Castle-Caulfield: it is in contemplation to erect another church in the village of Donaghmore. In the R. C. divisions the parish forms the head of two unions or districts, being partly united with Pomeroy, and partly with that of Killeshill: there are chapels at Tullyallen and in the village of Donaghmore. There are three meeting-houses for Presbyterians, one in connection with the Synod of Ulster; and a schoolhouse is used as a place of worship by the Independents. The parish school is at Castle-Caulfield: there are seven other schools, in which about 870 children are taught; and Mr. Mackenzie has lately built on his demesne, at the corner of the old churchyard, an infants' school, which is attended daily by more than 70 children, and which he entirely supports, intending to endow it at his death. About 50 boys and girls are educated in two private schools. In 1807, the Rev. George Evans bequeathed £200, two-thirds of the interest to be appropriated to support Sunday schools, of which there are six here, and one-third to the poor of the parish. Thomas Verner, Esq., made a similar bequest for the maintenance of these schools: and there is one supported by the Presbyterian minister. In the burial-ground are an ancient stone font and the pliath of a cross: the ruins of Castle-Caulfield form a beautifully picturesque object. There are several ancient forts in various parts of the parish. – See CASTLE-CAULFIELD.

DONOGHENRY, or DONAGHENDRY, a parish, in the barony of DUNGANNON, county of TYRONE, and province of ULSTER, on the mail coach road from Dublin to Coleraine; containing, with the post-town of Stewartstown, 5364 inhabitants. It comprises, according to the Ordnance survey, 7154$^3/_4$ statute acres, including 50$^3/_4$ in Lough Roughan: 6889 acres are applotted under the tithe act, and valued at £5261 per annum, of which 426 are bog, and 6463 arable. The land is rich and well cultivated, and there are extensive quarries of limestone, freestone, and basalt. Near the glebe-house is an extensive deposit of new red sandstone; and in Anna hone are valuable mines of coal, which, though discontinued in 1825, were formerly worked with great advantage: they are now leased by the owner to a spirited individual, who has recommenced them, with success, upon an extensive scale. Coal, clay, and other valuable deposits exist near Coal Island (see the article on that place). The manufacture of linen and union cloth is carried on to a considerable extent. Mullantean is the handsome residence of Miss Hall; Barahill, of W. Holmes, Esq.; Donaghendry, of the Rev. F. L. Gore; Anketell Lodge, of Roger C. Anketell, Esq.; and Ardpatrick, of the Rev. W. J. Knox, near which are the remains of a Danish fort. The living is a rectory, in the diocese of Armagh, and in the alternate patronage of Sir Thomas Staples, Bart., and E. H. Caulfield, Esq.: the tithes amount to £315. The glebehouse is a large and handsome edifice, built (by aid of a gift of £100, and a loan of £825, in 1811, from the late Board of First Fruits) on a glebe comprising 30 acres of excellent land within the parish; the remainder of the glebe, 210 acres, being in the townland of Tamnavally, in the parish of Arboe. The church is situated in Stewartstown; it was built, in 1694, out of the forfeited impropriations by order of Wm. III., the old building at Donoghenry having been destroyed in the war of 1641; and a lofty square tower and side aisles have been recently added. There is a chapel of ease at Coalisland, lately erected by subscription. In the R. C. divisions the parish is united to that of Ballyclog, and part of Clonoe, forming the union of Stewartstown, in which are two chapels, one at Stewartstown and one at Coalisland. Here are two Presbyterian meeting-houses, one in connection with the Synod of Ulster, and the other with the Seceding Synod, both of the second class. There are nine schools in the parish, including an infants' school lately established, all aided by subscription, and a school for girls supported by Mrs. Gore; about 550 children are taught.

At Roughan are the ruins of an extensive castle, built by the Lord-Deputy Sidney, in the reign of Queen Elizabeth, and afterwards held by the Earl of Tyrone during his rebellion; and in the War of 1641, by Sir Phelim O'Nial, who placed a powerful garrison in it: it was afterwards dismantled, by order of parliament, and is now a picturesque ruin. At Donoghenry is the site of the old church and cemetery, which was the burial-place of the ancient family of Bailie, whose mansion-house adjoining is now in ruins. In a field contiguous is an upright stone, one of the supporters of a cromlech, and near it is another lying on the ground, in the upper side of which is a circular cavity, or artificial basin: about a quarter of a mile westward is a large and perfect cromlech, with a table stone, weighing more than 20 tons, placed within a circle of smaller stones. Near Stewartstown are the remains of a castle built by Sir Andrew Stewart, in the reign of Jas. I., to whom the monarch had granted extensive possessions in this neighbourhood. In 1823, a small cup, or chalice, was discovered in a bog at Dunaghy, full of silver coins of the Danish princes, many of which are preserved in the collection of R. C. Anketell, Esq. In the small lake of Ardpatrick is a floating island, and around its shores human bones, camp-poles, &c., have been discovered: in this lake many persons were drowned in the civil war of 1641; and around its shores the army of Jas. II. encamped on their march to Denny in 1689. – See STEWARTSTOWN.

DROMORE, a parish, in the barony of OMAGH, county of TYRONE, and province of ULSTER, 8 miles (S. W.) from Omagh, on the road from that place to Enniskillen; containing 10,422 inhabitants. In the war of 1641 the insurgents were defeated in some skirmishes near this place, but revenged themselves by burning the church and killing many of the inhabitants, when the English were obliged to retire. According to the Ordnance survey, it contains $25{,}492\frac{1}{2}$ statute acres, the greater part of which is productive, but there are more than 4000 acres of bog and mountain land. The canal, by which it is intended to connect Loughs Foyle and Erne, will pass through this parish. The village, which comprises about 100 thatched houses, is a constabulary police station, and has a penny post to Omagh, and a dispensary. Fairs are held for farming stock on Feb. 1st, March 17th, Easter-Monday, Whit-Monday, May 1st, June 24th, Aug. 1st, Sept. 29th, Nov. 1st and 26th, and Dec. 26th. The principal seats are Lakemount, the residence of J. Hamilton, Esq.; Fairy Hill, of A. Sproule, Esq.; and the Glebe-house, of the Rev. H. Lucas St. George. The living is a rectory and vicarage, in the diocese of Clogher, and in the patronage of the Bishop: the tithes amount to £694.1.4. The glebe-house has been lately erected, and the glebe comprises 589 acres. The church is a small plain building, erected in 1694. The R. C. parish is coextensive with that of the Established Church, and has a chapel in the village. At Gardrum is a Presbyterian meeting-house in connection with the Synod of Ulster, of the first class; and at Toghardoo is a place of worship for Methodists. There are four public schools, in which about 450 children are educated; and sixteen private schools, in which are about 850 children; also a Sunday school. Here are some large and perfect forts; and it is stated that St. Patrick founded a nunnery here for St. Certumbria, the first Irish female who received the veil from his hands. At Kildrum was a religious house or church, which is supposed to have been the parochial church; but no vestige of the building can be traced, and the burial-ground is partially cultivated. The townlands of Shamragh and Agherdurlagh are called abbey lands, and are tithe-free.

DRUMGLASS, a parish, in the barony of DUNGANNON, county of TYRONE, and province of ULSTER, on the road from Armagh to Coleraine; containing, with the market and post-town of Dungannon (described under its own head), 5926 inhabitants. According to the Ordnance survey it comprises $3503\frac{3}{4}$ statute acres, of which 30 are waste land and the remainder arable and pasture, the greater part of which is fertile and well cultivated, particularly near the town. The surrounding country is ornamented with several gentlemen's seats, the principal of which are Northland Lodge, the residence of the Earl of Ranfurly, proprietor of the town and manor; Dungannon House, of E. Evans, Esq.; Millton, of J. Falls, Esq.; the Castle, of T. K. Hannington, Esq.; Killymeel, of J. Shiel, Esq.; and the seat of J. W. S. Murray, Esq. Here are extensive collieries worked by the Hibernian Mining Company under lease from the Lord-Primate. The upper and best seam is about a foot thick; under it is a thin stratum of iron-stone, and then a seam of coal two feet thick. About 180 persons are employed, who raise 500 tons weekly. A drift is being made from these works to coal beds on the Earl of Ranfurly's estate, about a mile distant; and a line of railway has been marked out from the collieries to the Tyrone canal at Coal Island. The living is a rectory, in the diocese of Armagh, and in the patronage of the Lord-Primate: the tithes amount to £200, and there is a glebe-house with a glebe of 59 acres near it, and one of 347 acres in the parish of Donaghmore. The church, which is in Dungannon, is a large and handsome edifice, for the repair of which the Ecclesiastical Commissioners have recently granted £307. In the R. C. divisions it is the head of a union or district, called Dungannon, comprising the parishes of Drumglass, Tullaniskin, and Killyman, and containing four chapels, one of which is at Dungannon. There are meeting-houses for Presbyterians, connected with the Synod of Ulster and the Seceding Synod, both of the second class, and one for Wesleyan Methodists. A royal free school was founded by Charles I. at Dungannon, at which place is the parochial school, endowed with £10 per ann. by the rector; and an infants' school was established in 1833. In these and two other public schools about 400 children are educated, besides about 280 in eleven private schools.

DRUMQUIN, a market-town, in the parish of EAST LONGFIELD, barony of OMAGH, county of TYRONE, and province of ULSTER, 7 miles (W. N. W.) from Omagh, on the river Roe, and on the nearest road from Londonderry to Enniskillen; containing 406 inhabitants. It consists of one street and some detached houses, which, with the exception of a few of recent erection, are indifferently built and thatched; and was founded by Sir John Davis, about 1617, on a tract of 2000 acres of land granted to him by Jas. I. in 1611, under the name of Clonaghmore, on which he located 16 British families. He also built castles at Kerlis and at Gavelagh, on the Derg, at which latter place he had another grant of 2000 acres; and between the two castles constructed an excellent road, seven miles in a straight line over mountains and bogs, which in several places still remains perfect. There is a daily penny post to Omagh. The market, on Thursday, is well supplied with provisions and yarn; and fairs are held on Jan. 17th, March 21st, May 2nd, June 9th, Aug. 15th, Sept. 17th, Nov. 9th, and Dec. 12th, for general farming stock: those held in March and June are large and well attended. Here are a meeting-house for Presbyterians, in connection with the Synod of Ulster, a large male and female school, and a dispensary.

DRUMRAGH, a parish, in the barony of OMAGH, county of TYRONE, and province of ULSTER, on the mail coach road from Dublin to Londonderry; containing, with the post-town of Omagh, 11,289 inhabitants. It comprises, according to the Ordnance survey, 20,164 statute acres, of which $161^3/_4$ are under water, and 15,630 are applotted under the tithe act. About seven-eighths of the land are arable and pasture, and one-eighth waste and bog: the land in the middle portion of the parish is very good, and under a tolerable system of cultivation; but the higher grounds, approaching the mountains, are wet and cold, though capable of great improvement by draining. The inhabitants unite the spinning of linen yarn and the weaving of cloth with their agricultural pursuits. There are several large and handsome houses in and around Omagh: the principal in the rural portion of the parish are New Grove, the residence of Sam. Galbraith, Esq.; and Riverland, of the Rev. Robert Burrowes, D.D. A court baron is held at Ballynahatty, every third Wednesday, for the manor of Touchet (anciently called Fintonagh), for the recovery of debts under 40s. The living is a rectory, in the diocese of Derry, and in the patronage of the Provost and Fellows of Trinity College, Dublin. The tithes amount to £600. The glebe-house is situated five miles from the church, upon a glebe comprising 550 acres. The church, situated in Omagh, a large handsome edifice, with a tower and spire, which were added at the expense of Dr. Knox, Bishop of Derry, was erected in 1777 by the Mervyn family, and was greatly enlarged in 1820. The R. C. parish is co-extensive with that of the Established Church: there is a chapel at Omagh, and another at Drumragh. There are places of worship for Presbyterians, in connection with the Synod of Ulster, of the first and third classes, and of the second class, in connection with the Seceding Synod; also for Wesleyan and Primitive Methodists. About 400 children are taught in the seven public schools of the parish, of which one is endowed with a house and 2 acres of land, and one for girls is supported by Mrs. Spiller; there are also eleven private schools, in which are about 450 children, and eight Sunday schools. The old parish church is now a fine ruin, having the side walls and gables entire. – See OMAGH.

DUNAMANAGH, a village and post-town, in the parish of DONAGHEADY, barony of STRABANE, county of TYRONE, and province of ULSTER, on the road from Strabane to Cookstown, 6 miles (N. E. by E.) from Strabane, and 113 (N. N. W.) from Dublin: the population is returned with the parish. This village, which situated in a deed and retired glen amidst the Mounterloney mountains, was founded by Sir John Drummond in 1619. It has a station of the constabulary police, and a sub-post-office to Strabane. Fairs are held on Jan. 13th, Feb. 28th, April 14th, May 27th, July 14th, Aug. 27th, Oct. 13th, and Nov. 28th. In and around the village are extensive deposits of limestone. Here is a meeting-house for Presbyterians, in connection with the synod of Ulster, a large and handsome building: that which formerly belonged to the covenanters is in ruins. At a short distance from the village are the parochial church, and male and female schools. On the site of the bawn built by Sir John Drummond is a building which, from that circumstance, is called the Castle.

DUNGANNON, a borough, market and post-town, in the parish of DRUMGLASS, barony of DUNGANNON, county of TYRONE, and province of ULSTER, 10 miles (N. by W.) from Armagh, and 76 (N. N. W.) from Dublin, on the road from Armagh to Coleraine; containing 3515 inhabitants. This place appears to have been the chief seat of the O'Nials from the earliest period of Irish history; but the first direct notice of it, under its present name, is in a spirited letter addressed in 1329 to Pope John, from Dungannon, by Donald O'Nial, in which he styles himself "King of Ulster and true heir of the whole dominion of Ireland." He declares that, previously to the coming of St. Patrick, 130 of his royal ancestors had been kings of Ireland; and that from that period till the landing of Hen. II., in 1172, "sixty monarchs of the same princely family had swayed the Hibernian sceptre." In 1364, O'Nial, in his letters to Edw. III., styles himself "Prince of the Irishry in Ulster," and dated from this place, whence, in 1394, he went to make his submission to Rich. II. at Drogheda. Henry O'Nial gave a splendid entertainment here to the Primate Bole, and assigned to the church of Armagh all his lands in Moydoyn; and in 1489 Con O'Nial founded a Franciscan monastery, which he amply endowed. This establishment continued to flourish till the Reformation, when it was granted by Queen Elizabeth to the Earl of Westmeath, and it was subsequently assigned to Sir Arthur Chichester in the reign of Jas. I. In 1492, Con O'Nial, the founder, being murdered by his brother Henry, was buried in this monastery with great pomp; and Neal McArt O'Nial rising in arms to avenge his death, the Earl of Kildare marched into Ulster to oppose him, took the fortress of Dungannon by storm, and soon reduced O'Nial to obedience. In 1501, the Albanian Scots attacked the fortress on St. Patrick's day, but were driven back with great slaughter by O'Nial, who then held it for the English government. In 1517, O'Nial was found again in rebellion against the English, but the Earl of Kildare having reduced Dundrum and taken Maginnis prisoner, marched against Dungannon, stormed the fort and burnt the town, both of which were restored by O'Nial after his submission. Con O'Nial, in 1538, took up arms against Henry VIII., in favour of the see of Rome, marched from this place with a powerful army into the English pale, and laid waste the country as far as Meath, where he was met by the Lord-Deputy Grey, who defeated him at Bellahoe, and compelled him again to retreat to his strong hold of Dungannon; he soon after submitted to the English authority, and in 1542 took the oaths of allegiance. After this battle Henry assumed the title of King, instead of Lord of Ireland; and O'Nial covenanted to renounce the name of O'Nial, to adopt the English habit and language, and to build houses and farm the lands after the English mode. For this submission he was created Earl of Tyrone, and his illegitimate son Matthew was made Baron of Dungannon, and received the estate of the O'Nials by patent.

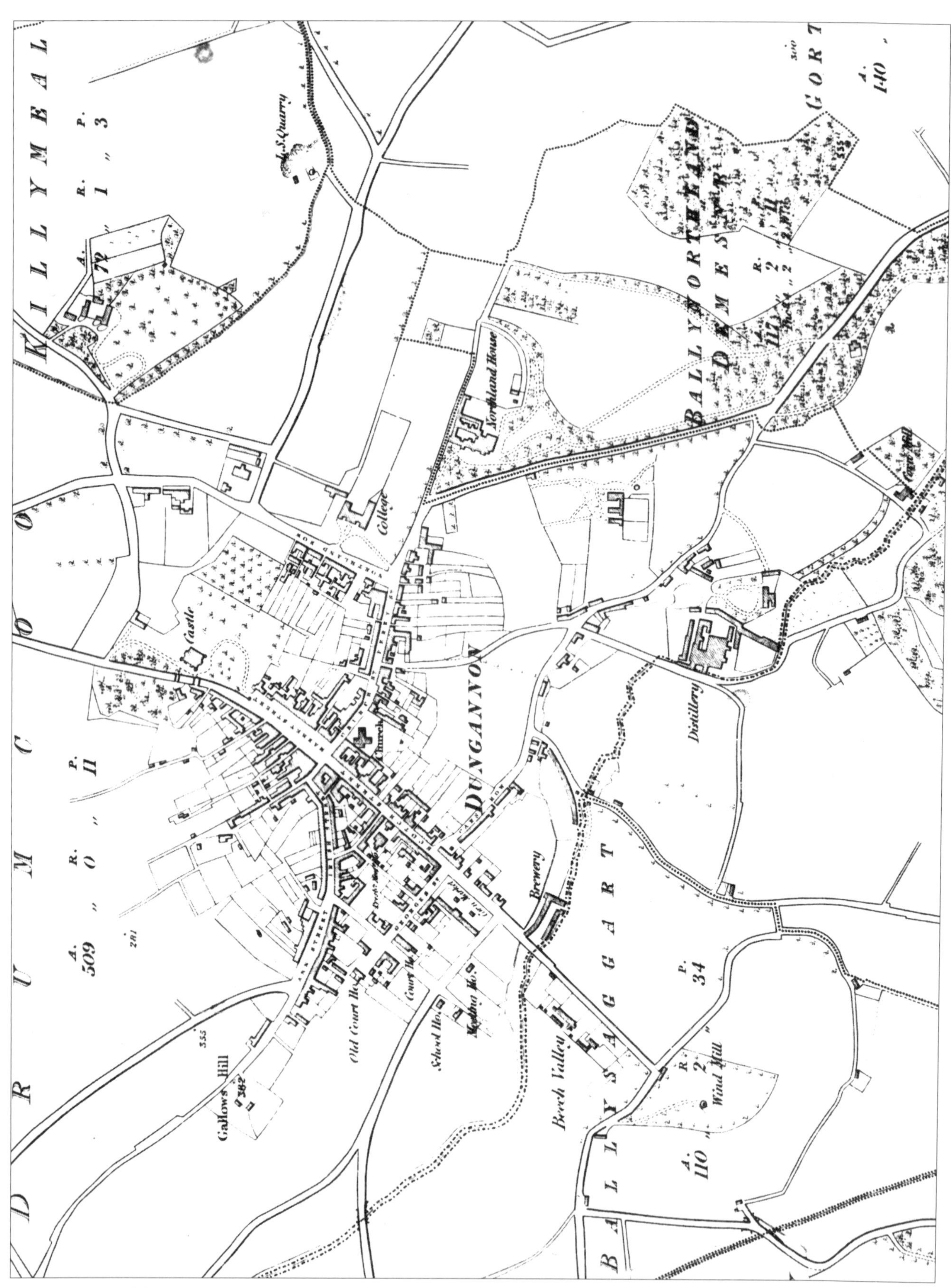

Dungannon. Part of the O.S. map of Co. Tyrone, sheet 54, published 1834 (reproduced at 140%).

In 1552, Shane O'Nial, son of the Earl of Tyrone, appeared in arms against his father, and destroyed the fortress of Dungannon, and committed other depredations; but in 1556, Fitzwalter, then lord-deputy, marched against him, expelled him from the territory, and replaced the Earl in his possessions. Shane again revolted in 1559, and in the following year burst into the English pale, but was reduced to submission by the Lord-Deputy Sussex. From Dungannon he proceeded to England, accompanied by his body-guard, consisting of 600 soldiers, who marched through the streets of London, armed with their battle-axes, and dressed in the costume of their country. He was graciously received by Elizabeth, pardoned, and loaded with favours; but shortly after his return to Dungannon, he again appeared in arms, destroyed the city of Armagh with its venerable cathedral and monasteries, and left only a few mud cabins remaining: he also destroyed the city of Derry and laid waste the whole county; but in 1567 he was treacherously murdered in the Scottish camp. Hugh O'Nial, who by the favour of Elizabeth had been raised to the earldom of Tyrone, commenced building a magnificent castle at Dungannon, and imported large quantities of lead for its roof; in 1587 he obtained from Elizabeth the grant of a weekly market and fairs, and in 1591 the lordship of Tyrone was formed into a county, subdivided into eight baronies, and this place made the county town and a gaol built in it accordingly.

In 1595, the Earl of Tyrone rebelled against the English government, and, placing himself at the head of 14,000 men, took and destroyed several forts, burnt Portmore bridge, laid siege to Monaghan, and having melted into bullets the lead which he had imported under pretence of roofing his castle, ultimately made himself master of the whole of that county. Having defeated the English in many engagements, particularly at Benburb, he was universally hailed as the champion of Ireland, and received in his fortress here the envoy of the Pope, who brought him valuable presents. The Lord-Deputy Mountjoy marched against this powerful chieftain and defeated him in several battles; and in June 1602, having secured Armagh and Charlemont, advanced towards Dungannon. Tyrone, aware of his approach, set fire to the place and retreated northward; but being thus driven from the venerable seat of his ancestors, he never regained his lost power. In the following year he made his submission at Mellifont and was pardoned; he was restored to his earldom, and obtained a grant of his lands by letters patent; but meditating new designs against the state, he was discovered, and dreading the power of Jas. I., fled to the Continent in 1607, leaving the whole of his extensive possessions to the king, who, in 1610, granted the castle and manor of Dungannon, with all their dependencies, to Sir Arthur Chichester. In 1612, Sir Arthur obtained from the king a charter of incorporation for the town which he was about to build, a grant of 1140 acres of land, and of 500 acres more for the site of the intended town; upon the former he built a bawn of limestone, 120 feet square, with bulwarks and a deep fosse; and upon the latter, previously to 1619, six large stone houses, six strong houses of frame-work timber, and a spacious church, which, with the exception of the roof, was completed at that time, whence may be dated the origin of the present town.

On the breaking out of the war in 1641, Sir Phelim O'Nial, having taken the fort of Charlemont by stratagem, and made the governor prisoner, seized the castle, town, and fort of Dungannon on the same night; and having put many of the inhabitants to death, kept possession of it till after the battle of Benburb, in 1646, after which the town and church were burnt, and soon after the castle was dismantled by order of the parliament. The castle was rebuilt soon after the Restoration, and in 1688 the Rev. George Walker, rector of Donaghmore, raised a regiment in his parish and marched with it to Dungannon, to secure that garrison for the Protestants; it was entrusted to the care of Col. Lundy, who deserted his post on the 13th of March, and the inhabitants fled to Strabane. It was garrisoned in 1689 by the troops of Jas. II., who, on the 13th of April, in that year, visited this town and inspected the garrison, whence he marched to Omagh and Strabane; but his forces occupied the town and neighbourhood during the whole of that important struggle. From this period the only event of historical importance connected with the place is the meeting of delegates from 269 corps of Ulster volunteers, who, in 1782, assembled at Dungannon, and passed 20 resolutions, declaratory of the independence of the parliament of Ireland.

The town, situated about three miles from the south shore of Lough Neagh, is spacious, handsome, and well built; and consists of a square, and four principal and several smaller streets. Improvements upon a very extensive scale have been recently made, and are still in progress; handsome houses have been built within and around the town, several lines of road have been constructed, and gas-works are now being erected for lighting it. The surrounding country is richly diversified, and the situation of the town on a lofty hill of limestone, commanding interesting and extensive prospects on every side, renders it both a healthy and a pleasant place of residence. It is second only to Omagh in extent, and is rapidly increasing in opulence and importance. News-rooms are supported by subscription, and assemblies are held occasionally. At a short distance to the east is Northland Lodge, the seat of the Earl of Ranfurley, and in the immediate neighbourhood are many gentlemen's seats, which are noticed in the account of the parish. The principal trade of the town and neighbourhood is the manufacture and bleaching of linen, for which it has long been celebrated; there are several bleach-greens on a large scale, all in full operation; the manufacture of earthenware and fire-bricks, for which there are large potteries within three miles of the town, is extensive: there is a large distillery, which annually consumes 29,000 barrels of grain, and not far from it are some extensive flour-mills. A flourishing trade is also carried on in wheat, flax, oats, and barley.

The Drumglass collieries, one mile distant, are the most extensive, in the North of Ireland; they were formerly worked without much success, but are now conducted by the Hibernian Mining Company aiid have been rendered productive of great benefit to the town and neighbourhood; the coal is of good quality and is procured in great abundance; the demand is ample, and the prices moderate from the competition of English and Scottish coal, which are brought hither by the Lagan and Newry navigations and by Lough Neagh. There are also ironworks, and some extensive lime-works near the town. The markets, originally granted in 1587, by Queen Elizabeth, to Hugh O'Nial, Earl of Tyrone, and in 1612 by Jas. I., to Sir Arthur Chichester, are held on Tuesday and Thursday; the former for grain, and the latter for brown linen, yarn, cattle, pigs, and provisions of all kinds, with all of which it is very extensively supplied. Fairs, granted in 1611 by Jas. I. to Sir Arthur Chichester, and in 1705 to T. Knox, Esq., are held on the first Thursday in every month. The market-house, shambles, grain stores, and provision sheds are commodious and well adapted to their use. A chief constabulary police station has been established in the town, which is the headquarters of the constabulary police force of Ulster, for whose accommodation a police barrack has been built.

The inhabitants under the title of the "Provost, Free Burgesses, and Commons of the borough of Dungannon," received a charter of incorporation from Jas. I., in 1612, by which the site of the town, with three parcels of land called Crosse, Brough, and Ferneskeile, (with the exception of the castle, and a space of 500 feet around it, in every direction, from its walls), was created a free borough, and the corporation made to consist of a portreeve, twelve free burgesses, and commonalty. The portreeve is chosen annually, and has power to hold a court every Friday for the recovery of debts not exceeding five marks, but this court has not been established. The charter also conferred the right of returning two members to the Irish parliament, which was exercised till the Union, since which period it has returned one member to the Imperial parliament. The right of election, formerly in the portreeve and burgesses, has, by the 2nd of Wm. IV., cap. 88, been vested in the resident freemen and £10 householders. The liberties of the borough comprised the whole of the townlands of Drumcoo and Ranaghan, a considerable portion of the townland of Gortmenon, and three small pieces in three other townlands, comprising together about 836 statute acres; but not being connected with the elective franchise, a narrower boundary has been drawn round the town, containing 224 statute acres. In 1836 the number of registered voters was 197, consisting of 11 free burgesses and 186 £10 householders: the portreeve is the returning officer. A court for the manor of Dungannon, granted in 1621 by Jas. I. to Arthur, Lord Chichester, and now the property of the Earl of Ranfurley, is held once in three weeks, and has jurisdiction to the amount of £20 extending over 40 townlands. General sessions of the peace for the division of Dungannon, which comprises the baronies of Dungannon and Clogher, are held here and at Clogher, alternately, twice in the year; and petty sessions are also held once a fortnight before the county magistrates. The court-house is a spacious and handsome building, erected in 1830; under it is the bridewell, containing a day-room and four large cells for male prisoners, with a yard, day-room, and cells for female prisoners; the same accommodation for debtors, and apartments for the keeper.

The church of the parish of Drumglass having been destroyed in the wars during the reign of Elizabeth, a new church was erected by Sir Arthur Chichester in the town of Dungannon, in 1619. This building, which was nearly destroyed in the war of 1641, was restored in 1672, and was rebuilt in 1699, since which time it has been considerably enlarged, and is now a handsome edifice with a lofty octagonal spire. There is a R. C. chapel in the town, also places of worship for Presbyterians in connection with the Synod of Ulster and the Seceding Synod, and for Wesleyan Methodists. The free grammar school, or Royal College, was founded by letters patent of Chas. I., in 1628, which gave in trust to the Primate of Armagh and his successors six townlands in the parish of Clonoe, for the support of a school at Mountjoy, in that parish; but this place being only a garrison, the school was, after many years, removed to Dungannon, and the first account we find of it is in 1726, nearly a century after its foundation, when it was held in a lane near High-street, where it continued till 1786, when the present college was erected by order of Primate Robinson, who a few years before had erected the college of Armagh. The building comprises a centre and two deeply receding wings, erected at an expense of £4626.8.2, of which £2000 was given from the Primate's private purse. It is situated on a gentle eminence on the east side of the town, on grounds comprising 9 acres purchased by Primate Robinson and given to the school. The establishment is conducted by a principal and three classical assistants, two English masters, and drawing, French, and music masters, and is adapted for 100 pupils; the masters take private boarders and day scholars; at present there are no scholars on the foundation. The lands with which it is endowed comprise 3900 acres, producing a rental of £1430, and are under the management of the Commissioners of Education, who, in their report for 1834, state that "considerable improvement has been effected in the condition of the tenantry and appearance of their farms;" and there is every prospect that the rental will be nearly doubled in a few years. The principal, who is appointed by the Lord-Primate, has a salary of £500 per annum and £100 for assistants; £400 per ann. was appropriated, in 1834, to the founding of ten exhibitions in Trinity College, Dublin, 5 of £50 and 5 of £30 per annum, tenable for 5 years by boys from this school, under the appellation of King's scholars. A school for boys and girls has also been established here by the trustees of Erasmus Smith's charity; it is situated near the courthouse, and is capacious and handsome. There are also two other schools, and an infants' school, supported by subscription. There is a dispensary; and a Mendicity Society is supported by subscription, Of the castle and fortress of the Earl of Tyrone not a vestige is remaining; nor are there any traces of the castle and bawn erected by Sir Arthur Chichester. The monastery, founded by Con O'Nial, was situated near the site of the present distillery; some fragments were remaining a few years since, but every vestige has now disappeared. Dungannon gives the title of Viscount to the family of Trevor, of Brynkinalt, near Chirk, in the county of Denbigh.

ERRIGAL-KEROGUE, a parish, in the barony of CLOGHER, county of TYRONE, and province of ULSTER, on the river Blackwater and on the road from Aughnacloy to Omagh; containing, with the greater part of the district parish and post-town of Ballygawley, 9782 inhabitants. This parish, which is also called Errigal-Kieran, from the supposed dedication of its ancient church to St. Kieran, comprises, according to the Ordnance survey, 21,139$^3/_4$ statute acres, including 18 townlands, which now form part of the district parish of Ballygawley. The greater portion is rich arable, meadow, and pasture land, with a large extent of profitable mountain, and a considerable tract of waste. The hills towards the south are low and fertile, but towards the north they rise into mountains, the flat summits of which are bog and heath; the mountain of Shantavny rises, according to the Ordnance survey, 1035 feet above the level of the sea. The valleys are watered by streams which, in their descent from the mountains, form numerous picturesque cascades; and in one of them are found fossils and shells, washed down from the beds of limestone. There are extensive quarries of limestone and freestone, from the latter of which was taken the stone for building several of the churches and gentlemen's seats in the neighbourhood; and thin veins of coal have been found near Lismore, but though lying very near the surface, they have not been worked. The scenery is strikingly diversified; the glen called "Todd's Leap" abounds with romantic features, and at the southern extremity of the parish is a very handsome bridge of one arch over the Blackwater, which river is also crossed by two other bridges. The principal gentlemen's seats are Ballygawley House, the residence of Sir H. Stewart, Bart., situated on a rising ground, sheltered in the rear by the conspicuous precipice called the "Craigs;" Cleanally, of G. Spier, Esq.; Bloom Hill, of T. Simpson, Esq.; and Ballygawley Castle, of R. Armstrong, Esq. There are several large corn-mills and a tuck-mill for finishing the woollen cloths made in the various farm-houses. The manors of Donoughmore, Favour Royal, Cecil, and Ballygawley, are in this parish; in the first a court is held monthly, in which debts to any amount may be recovered; and in the three others are held similar courts every three weeks, with jurisdiction limited to £2.

The living is a rectory, in the diocese of Armagh, and in the patronage of J. C. Moutray, Esq.: the tithes amount to £380. The glebe-house is at Richmount, near Ballygawley, on a glebe of 266 acres, and there is another glebe of 297 acres, constituting the townland of Gort. The church, a handsome edifice in the later English style, with an embattled tower, was erected in 1831, near the site of the ancient structure at Balhinasaggard, at an expense of £1300, of which £1100 was a loan from the late Board of First Fruits. The R. C. parish is co-extensive with that of the Established Church; the chapel is a small plain edifice, and there are two stations or altars, where service is occasionally performed. There are places of worship for Presbyterians in connection with the Synod of Ulster of the third class, Independents, and two for Wesleyan Methodists. About 700 children are taught in the public schools, of which the parochial school is chiefly supported by the incumbent, one by Miss Montgomery, and another by Mr. Leslie; and there are three private schools, in which are about 180 children. There are some remains of the old church, in which are several of the carved stones of an ancient friary, founded by Con O'Nial; in the churchyard is a large stone cross, and near it a holy well. The friary was of the third order of Franciscans, and near it was an ancient round tower. There are many conical raths in the parish, of which the most remarkable is that on the steep height called the Craigs; it is supposed that the native chiefs of Eirgal, or Uriel, had their seat in this parish, near which a monastery was founded by St. Macartin. In the townland of Sess-Kilgreen is a carved stone, part of a kistvaen, and in that of Lismore are the ruins of a square bawn, with round towers at the angles.

FINTONA, a post-town, in the parish of DONAGHCAVEY, barony of CLOGHER, county of TYRONE, and province of ULSTER, 7 miles (S.) from Omagh, and 97$^3/_4$ (N. by W.) from Dublin, on the road from Omagh to Enniskillen; containing 1714 inhabitants. At the plantation of Ulster, by Jas. I., this district was placed in the lesser proportion of Fentonagh, and was granted, in 1611, to Sir Francis Willoughby, who neglecting to comply with the terms of the grant, the lands reverted to the Crown. In 1614, 2000 acres were granted to John Leigh, Esq., who, prior to 1619, had built a bawn and house, in which he resided, and then commenced building the town. It now consists of one main and several smaller streets, very irregularly formed, comprising 354 houses, some of which are well built; and is situated in a fertile vale, on both sides of the Fintona water, occupying an advantageous position for trade, in a fine and improving country. The only manufactures are the weaving of linen and the making of spades. The market is on Friday, and is well supplied with all kinds of provisions; and large quantities of brown linens are sold every alternate Friday to the bleachers, who attend from a great distance. A fair is held on the 22nd of every month, which is large and well attended. Petty sessions are held on the second Tuesday in each month; and a court leet and baron for the Manor of

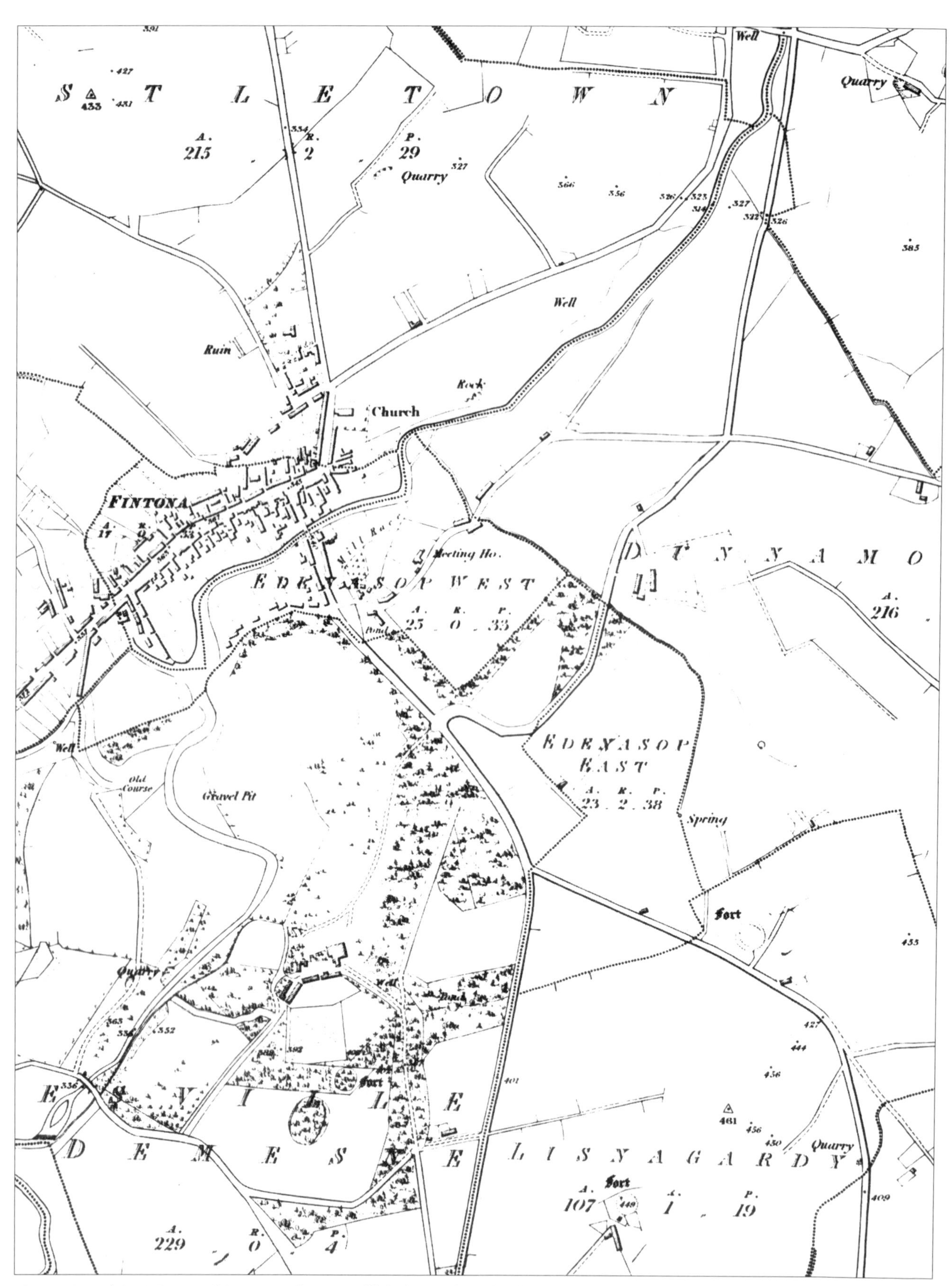

Fintona. Part of the O.S. map of Co. Tyrone, sheet 51, published 1834 (reproduced at 140%).

Castlemaine once a month, for the recovery of debts under 40s, by a senesehal appointed by C. Eccles, Esq., the lord of the manor. Here is a constabulary police station, for which most convenient barracks have been recently built, and another at Barr. The gentlemen's seats in the neighbourhood are Ecclesville, that of C. Eccles, Esq.; Derrabard House, of S. Vesey, Esq.; Cavan House, of W. Dickson, Esq.; Cavan Lodge, of C. R. Lucas, Esq.; and Dundiven glebe-house, of the Rev. Jos. McCormick. The parochial church, and a Presbyterian, and a Wesleyan Methodist meeting-house are in the town, within a short distance of which is the R. C. chapel.

FIVE-MILE-TOWN, or BLESSINGBOURN, a post town, in the parish and barony of CLOGHER, county of ANTRIM, and province of ULSTER, 6 miles (W. by S.) from Clogher, and 79$^3/_4$ (N. W.) from Dublin, on the road from Lisnaskea to Clogher, and on the confines of the county of Fermanagh; containing 758 inhabitants. This place has been sometimes called Mount-Stewart, from the name of its founder, Sir Wm. Stewart, to whom Jas. I. granted 2000 acres of land, called Ballynacoole. Prior to 1619, Sir William had built the castle of Aghentine, and commenced the village, which was occupied by British tenants. He afterwards obtained a charter for markets and fairs; the latter are now held on the third Monday in every month. The town is gradually improving: it consists of one principal and two smaller streets, and comprises about 140 houses, several of which are modern and well built. A constabulary police force is stationed here, and petty sessions are held on alternate Thursdays. A neat chapel of ease, with a spire, was built in 1750, at the expense of Mr. Armor. A public school is supported by Col. Montgomery, who built the school-house; and there are two other public schools. Near the town is Blessingbourn Cottage, the neat residence of Col. Montgomery. The ruins of Aghantine castle, in the neighbourhood, are boldly situated on elevated ground: it was destroyed by Sir Phelim O'Nial, in 1641.

GORTIN, a village, in the parish of LOWER BADONY barony of STRABANE, county of TYRONE, and province of ULSTER, 5 miles (E.) from Newtown-Stewart, on the road to Cookstown; containing 441 inhabitants. This place is situated in a deep valley watered by the river Nagle, and in the district of the Mounterloney mountains, of which it may be considered the chief town. It consists of one irregular street, containing 82 houses indifferently built; the surrounding scenery, though boldly picturesque, is destitute of embellishment from the want of wood, which is found only in the demesne of Beltrim, the handsome residence of A. W. C. Hamilton, Esq., which is surrounded by young and thriving plantations. There is a small distillery in the village; and fairs are held on the first Wednesday in every month, for cattle, sheep, and pigs, and a pleasure fair on Easter-Monday. It has a penny post to Omagh, and is a constabulary police station; a court baron for the manor of Eliston, in which debts to the amount of 40s. are recoverable, is held here on the first Tuesday in every month; and petty sessions every second Friday. The parish church, a neat small edifice, is situated here, also the parochial school, and a dispensary.

GRANGE, a village, in the parish of DESERTCREIGHT, barony of DUNGANNON, county of TYRONE, and province of ULSTER, 2$^1/_2$ miles (E) from Cookstown, on the road from Stewartstown to Moneymore; containing 147 inhabitants. It comprises 32 houses, generally well built, and has a fair on Nov. 12th. Here is a meeting-house for Covenanters of the third class, and a school; and near the village is Killymoon, the elegant residence of Col. Stewart.

KILDRESS, a parish, in the barony of DUNGANNON, county of TYRONE, and province of ULSTER, 3 miles (W. by N.) from Cookstown, on the road from Omagh to Belfast; containing 7062 inhabitants. This parish anciently formed part of the O'Hagans' country, and subsequently belonged to the Earls of Tyrone, by whose rebellion it was forfeited, and in 1638 was granted by Chas. I. to R. Richardson, Esq., whose descendant, Capt. W. Stewart Richardson, is the present proprietor. According to the Ordnance survey it comprises 26,251$^1/_2$ statute acres, of which 3212 are mountain and bog, the remainder being under an excellent system of cultivation. The mountain tracts consist of sienite, granite, quartz, and basalt, and in the valleys are found clay-slate, limestone, coal, and valuable freestone. The principal seats are Oaklands, the residence of Capt. W. S. Richardson; Drumshambo, of the Rev. R. Stewart; and Wellbrook, of J. Gunning, Esq. A manorial court for Manor-Richardson is held at Legnacash the second Monday in every month, for the recovery of debts under 40s. At Wellbrook is a large bleach-green. The living is a rectory, in the diocese of Armagh, and in the patronage of the Lord-Primate: the tithes amount to £354. The church is a large and handsome building with a lofty square tower, erected in 1818, for which the late Board of First Fruits granted a loan of £1600, and recently repaired by aid of a grant of £151 from the Ecclesiastical Commissioners. The glebe-house was built by aid of a gift of £100, in 1791, from the late Board of First Fruits: the glebe consists of the townland of Drumshambo, containing 871 acres, of which 225 are unprofitable land. The R. C. parish is co-extensive with that of the Established Church, and has a small plain chapel at Killanan and another at Dunamore. At Oritor is a Presbyterian meeting-house of the third class, in connection with the Synod of Ulster. About 450 children are educated in five public schools, to one of which the Rev. R. Stewart gave £50 and two acres of land, and about 120 in two private schools. The ruins of the old church are about a mile eastward from the present church; it was burnt in the war of 1641, but restored in 1698, and was used for divine service till 1818. Here are also the ruins of Maheraglass priory, which was founded by Terence O'Hagan in 1242, and fortified by the O'Hagans in the rebellion against Queen Elizabeth, from which it is sometimes called Maheraglass Castle. – See ORITOR.

KILLESHILL, KILLISHIL, or KILLESHAL, a parish, in the barony of DUNGANNON, county of TYRONE, and province of ULSTER, 6 miles (S. W.) from Dungannon, on the road from that place to Ballygawley; containing 4615 inhabitants. This parish was formed by order of council in 1732, by separating 27 townlands from the parish of Carrenteel, and Archbishop Robinson endowed the living with the townland of Glencal for a glebe, which was exchanged for the present glebe adjoining the church. According to the Ordnance survey it comprises 9839$^{1}/_{4}$ statute acres (including a detached portion of 241$^{1}/_{4}$ acres), of which 8879 are applotted under the tithe act, and valued at £4817 per annum. About half the land is arable, one-fourth pasture, and the remainder bog and waste land; limestone is abundant and is burnt for manure. The soil is cold and thin, but is well cultivated: the inhabitants combine weaving with their agricultural pursuits. The principal seat is Anahue, the residence of H. Crosslee, Esq. The living is a rectory, in the diocese of Armagh, and in the gift of the Lord Primate; the tithes amount to £300. The church is a small neat edifice, built in 1776 by aid of a gift of £481 from the late Board of First Fruits. The glebe-house was erected by aid of a gift of £100, in 1817, from the same Board: the glebe comprises 514a. 3r. 26p. In the R. C. divisions this parish forms part of the union or district of Donaghmore; it has no chapel, but an altar in the open air. There are places of worship for Presbyterians in connexion with the Synod of Ulster and the Seceding Synod. The parochial school, in which are about 140 children, is on Erasmus Smiths foundation, and is aided by the rector the late Rev. D. Kelly contributed £50 towards the erection of the school-house: there are five other public schools, two of which are aided by a donation of £7 per annum from Col. Verner, and two by £8 per annum from J. Gough, Esq.; they afford instruction to about 440 children.

KILLYMAN, a parish, partly in the barony of O'NEILLAND WEST, county of ARMAGH, but chiefly in that of DUNGANNON, county of TYRONE, and province of ULSTER, 2 miles (N.) from Moy, on the river Blackwater and the road from Belfast to Dungannon; containing 7579 inhabitants. According to the Ordnance survey it comprises 10,559$^{1}/_{4}$ statute acres, of which 3154$^{3}/_{4}$ are in Armagh, and 7404$^{1}/_{2}$ in Tyrone, and of which 7729 are applotted under the tithe act and valued at £8534 per annum. The land is exceedingly fertile, and the system of agriculture improved; there is abundance of bog, and on the lands of Dungorman a quarry of red sandstone, which is chiefly used for building and for flags. The river Blackwater for nearly two miles forms here a boundary between the counties, and after separating those parts of the parish which are in opposite baronies, falls into Lough Neagh; it is crossed by Verner's bridge, a handsome structure of one arch, with others on each side, forming a continued causeway, which is frequently overflowed, leaving only the central arch visible above the river. The surface is marked by numerous elevations, the highest of which are Drumina, Roan hill, and Lowestown, the valleys between which are good meadow land. There are extensive meadows along the banks of the Blackwater and the Roan, and at Bernagh is an extensive wood of full-grown oaks, which, with the plantations of Roan hill and the other woods and plantations in the parish, has a very fine effect. Limestone, freestone, basalt, quartz, clay, and clay-slate are found in abundance; there are also indications of coal. In the sandstone near Roan hill are interesting specimens of fossil fish entirely perfect, with the fins minutely distinct. The gentlemen's seats are Bernagh, the residence of the Hon. Mrs. Knox, a handsome mansion on the great line of road; Church Hill, the seat of Col. Verner, a spacious and elegant residence, situated in an extensive and improved demesne, and commanding a fine view of the river Blackwater; the Grange, of Miss Thompson; Grange Park, of H. H. Handcock, Esq.; Brookfleld, of H. Atkinson, Esq.; Rhone Hill, of T. Greer, Esq.; Tamnamore, of Jackson Lloyd, Esq.; and Crane-brook, of 3. Cranston, Esq. The manufacture of linen and cotton is extensively carried on throughout this neighbourhood; and there are three large bleach-greens. At Twyford is a paper-mill, and at Lower Corr, a large manufactory for coarse earthenware, of which there are also others on a smaller scale in various parts of the parish. A manorial court is held monthly by the seneschal of the Lord-Primate, in which debts to the amount of £5 are recoverable. The living is a rectory, in the diocese of Armagh, and in the patronage of the Lord-Primate; the tithes amount to £484.12.4. The church, a neat structure, was erected in 1823. The glebe-house is a handsome edifice, and the glebe comprises 226 acres. In the R. C. divisions the parish forms part of the union or district of Dungannon: the chapel is a neat stone building, roofed with slate. There is a place of worship for Wesleyan Methodists. About 250 children are taught in four public schools, of which the parochial school is aided by £10 annually from the incumbent, and another is wholly supported by Col. Verner; there are also four private schools, in which are about 200 children, and a Sunday school. At Mullinakill is an ancient cemetery, which is still used.

KILSKERRY, a parish, in the barony of OMAGH, county of TYRONE, and province of ULSTER, 7 miles (N. by E.) from Enniskillen, on the road to Omagh; containing, with the market-town of Trillick, 8790 inhabitants. This place, during the war of 1641, was attacked by the Irish forces under Sir Phelim O'Nial, whom the inhabitants succeeded in driving back to the mountains; but they suffered severely in a subsequent attack, in which the assailants were successful. Near Corkhill Lodge are the remains of a fortress, which was garrisoned by the inhabitants, who resolutely defended the ford of the river, where a handsome bridge was subsequently erected. The army of Jas. II. encamped twice in this parish during his contest with Win. III., and marched hence against Enniskillen. The parish, which is six miles long and as many broad, comprises, according to the

Ordnance survey, 20,439 statute acres, of which 14,650 are applotted under the tithe act; the surface is boldly undulating and tine soil generally fertile. The system of agriculture is rapidly improving; more than 1000 acres of waste land have been already brought into cultivation, principally under the encouragement of the rector. The principal seats are Trillick Lodge, the property of Gen. Archdall, near which are the remains of Castle Mervyn, built by a person of the name of Mervyn, from whom Gen. Archdall derives his title to his estate in this county; Relagh, of J. H. Story, Esq.; Corkhill Lodge, of J. Lendrum, Esq.; Corkhill, of the Rev. A. H. Irvine; and the glebe-house, of the Rev. J. Grey Porter. There are two other seats almost dilapidated, which were formerly the residences of the Barton and Bryan families. There are several mountains in the parish, and several lakes, from which small streams descend to Lough Erne, between which and Lough Foyle it is in contemplation to form a communication by a canal. There is a small establishment for milling blankets. A manorial court, petty sessions, and fairs are held at Trillick, which see.

The living is a rectory and vicarage, in the diocese of Clogher, constituting the corps of the prebend of Kilskerry in the cathedral of Clogher, in the patronage of the Bishop: the tithes amount to £675.9.4. The glebe-house, a spacious and handsome residence, surrounded by old plantations, was built in 1774 at an expense of £1200, of which £92.6 was a gift from the late Board of First Fruits. The glebe comprises 380 acres of profitable land, valued at £1 per acre, besides which there are 636¾ acres of mountain glebe, which is annually in process of being reclaimed and rising in value. The church, an elegant structure in the early English style, with a square tower surmounted by an octagonal spire, was built in 1790, at an expense of £1060, defrayed by the Rev. Dr. Hastings; the original spire was taken down and the present one erected in 1830, at the expense of the parish. Divine service is performed by the clergymen of the Establishment in the Wesleyan meeting-houses at Trillick, monthly in winter, and once a fortnight in summer. The R. C. parish is co-extensive with that of the Established Church; the chapel, a spacious building, is at Maralough. There are places of worship for Wesleyan and Primitive Methodists at Trillick. The parochial school is supported by the rector and the Association for Discountenancing Vice, and a school-house at Magheralough was built by the Rev. A. H. Irvine, curate, on land given by Col. Perceval, who allows a salary to the master; one by J. H. Story, Esq., a female school on the glebe by Mrs. Porter, and there are four other public schools, 12 private, and six Sunday schools, and a dispensary. Here was a monastery in the 7th century, of which no vestiges can be traced, nor are any particulars of its history recorded.

LANGFIELD (EAST or UPPER), a parish, in the barony of OMAGH, county of TYRONE, and province of ULSTER, 6 miles (W.) from Omagh; containing, with the market-town of Drumquin (which is separately described), 2919 inhabitants. The old parish of Langfield was, in 1800, divided by act of council into the two parishes of East and West Langfield; the former portion comprises, according to the Ordnance survey, 9716¼ statute acres, of which 22¼ are water. The land in some parts is good, but the soil is generally light, particularly near the mountains, which, though lofty, afford good pasturage for cattle; the system of agriculture is slowly improving, and there is an extensive tract of bog. Excellent freestone is found at Claremore, and in several parts of the parish are indications of coal. The principal seats are Drumrane Lodge, the residence of J. Boyle, Esq.; Burle's Folly, of E. Sproule, Esq.; and the glebe-house, of the Rev. J. Pilkington. The manufacture of linen is carried on in the farm-houses to a considerable extent. The townland of Magheraney, on which is the church, is the property of the Bishop of Derry. The living is a rectory, in the diocese of Derry, and in the patronage of the Bishop; the tithes amount to £245. The glebe-house, towards which the late Board of First Fruits gave £100, in 1804, is a good residence; the glebe comprises 26 Cunningham acres. The church, which was erected soon after the separation of the parish, is a small neat edifice with a square tower; the late Board of First Fruits gave £500, in 1800, towards its erection, and the Ecclesiastical Commissioners have recently granted £254 towards its repair. In the R. C. divisions the parish, with that of West Langfield, forms the union or district of Langfield; there is a place of worship for Presbyterians in connection with the Synod of Ulster, of the third class. About 180 children are taught in three public schools, of which the parochial school, situated on the glebe, is supported by the rector; there are also four private schools, in which are about 150 children. About a quarter of a mile from the parish church are the remains of an ancient church with a burial-ground.

LANGFIELD (WEST or LOWER), a parish, in the barony of OMAGH, county of TYRONE, and province of ULSTER, 8 miles (W.) from Omagh, on the road from Londonderry to Enniskillen; containing 4865 inhabitants. The parish comprises, according to the Ordnance survey, 23,906¾ statute acres, of which 176 are water, and about 6700 are mountain and bog. The mountains afford good pasturage for cattle and sheep, and their declivities are in a state of progressive cultivation; a great portion of the bog is also being rapidly reclaimed, and the system of agriculture is fast improving. In Dunwest are extensive beds of coal in three strata, all easy of access; and though at every flood large masses are detached by the river Poe, and carried down the stream, no attempt has yet been made to work them: coal of very good quality is also found in other parts of the parish. In Kerlis are extensive and valuable quarries of freestone, from which was raised the stone for the portico of the court-house of Omagh and for other public edifices; the higher mountains, of which Dooish rises, according to the Ordnance survey, 1119 feet above the level of the sea, are of mica slate. The river Poe rises in these mountains, and after passing through Drumquin falls into the river Foyle, about two miles below Omagh; there are several lakes in the parish, of which the largest is 58 acres in extent. The inhabitants combine with their agricultural pursuits the weaving of linen, and many of the females are employed in spinning linen and cotton yarn; there is also a small tuck-mill for dressing home-made woollen cloth, and there are several corn-mills.

The parish is partly within the bishop's manor of Derg, and partly in that of Hastings, which was granted to Sir J. Davies by Jas. I., under the name of Clonaghmore; and for which a court is held at Drumquin monthly, for the recovery of debts under 40s. The living is a rectory, in the diocese of Derry, and in the patronage of the Bishop; the tithes amount to £295.17. The glebe-house is a good and comfortable residence, situated near the church on a glebe of 108 acres, and embosomed in thriving plantations; there are also belonging to the rectory 10 townlands at Gortinasoal, about three miles distant, comprising together 2589 acres, of which 1426 are under cultivation, and the remainder mountain and bog. The church is a small ancient edifice surmounted by a cupola. In the R. C. divisions the parish, together with that of East Langfield, constitutes the union or district of Langfield; there is a large chapel at Drumquin, which serves for both parishes. About 460 children are taught in six public schools, of which the parochial school is principally supported by the rector, who in 1820 erected a good house for the master on the glehe, with an excellent garden; he also erected a school-house for another on the glebe at Loughmulharn, which he also supports. There are three private schools, in which are about 80 children, and five Sunday schools. There are some extensive remains of the spacious and handsome castle of Kerlis, or Curlews, built by Sir John Davies, prior to 1619, upon the manor of Clonaghmore, with freestone found on the spot, and with which he constructed a road eight feet wide and seven miles in length, leading over mountains and morasses, to his other castle on the Derg; much of the road may still be traced near the castle, paved with large blocks of stone. There are numerous forts in various parts of the parish, some of which are very large and tolerably perfect.

LECKPATRICK, a parish, in the barony of STRABANE, county of TYRONE, and province of ULSTER; containing, with part of the post-town of Strabane, 6030 inhabitants This parish, which is also called Leghpatrick, comprises, according to the Ordnance survey, 13,451 statute acres, of which 10,087 are applotted under the tithe act, and valued at £5806 per annum; and 104 are in the tideway of the Foyle. The soil is generally cold and wet, but part of the land is well cultivated and fertile. There are considerable tracts of mountain pasture and valuable bog. Here is an extensive bleach-green, not used at present; also two manufactories for spades and edged-tools. The Strabane canal passes through this parish from its lower lock on the Foyle to the quay of Strabane. The principal seats are Holy Hill the residence of J. Sinclair, Esq.; the glebe-house, of the Rev. G. Smithwick; and Mount Pleasant, of F. O'Neill, Esq. The living is a rectory, in the diocese of Derry, and in the gift of the Bishop; the tithes amount to £646.3.1. There is a glebe-house, with a glebe of 148a. 3r. 12p, Cunningham measure, of which 112a. 1r. 32p are cultivated land. The church, a plain edifice without tower or spire, was built by a loan of £600 from the late Board of First Fruits, in 1816, and much enlarged in 1834. In the R. C. divisions the parish forms part of the union or district of Donagheady, and has chapels at Cloghcor and Glenmornan. A Presbyterian meeting-house is in course of erection at Artigarran. There is a parochial school, to which the Marquess of Abercorn, who is proprietor of nearly all the parish, subscribes £10, and the rector £5 annually; and three other public schools, to two of which the Marquess of Abercorn contributes £5 each: about 520 children are educated in these schools, and about 160 in five private schools; there are also five Sunday schools. Near the glebe-house is an ancient rocking-stone.

LISSAN, or LISANE, a parish, partly in the barony of DUNGANNON, county of TYRONE, and partly in that of LOUGHINSHOLIN, county of LONDONDERRY, and province of ULSTER, 3 miles (N. by E.) from Cookstown, on the road to Moneymore and on that from Omagh to Belfast; containing 6163 inhabitants. This parish, which is bounded on the north by the mountain of Slieve Gallion, comprises, according to the Ordnance survey, 24,684½ statute acres, including 147¾ in Lough Fea, and of which 12,917½ are in the county of Tyrone. The greater portion is in the manor of Ardtrea, belonging to the see of Armagh, and part is in the manor of Moneymore and the property of the Drapers' Company of London. In the war of 1641, the castle, which at that time was the property of the Staples family, to whom it was granted on the plantation of Ulster, was seized by Nial O'Quin for Sir Phelim O'Nial, who plundered the house of Sir Thomas Staples while rendezvousing at Moneymore castle, and compelled the men employed in his iron-works on the Lissan water to make pikes and pike-heads from the stores of their master. The land is mountainous and boggy; about one-third is under tillage and produces excellent crops, and the remainder affords good pasture; the system of agriculture is improved, and much of the bog is of valuable quality; limestone abounds and is extensively quarried for agricultural uses. The mountain of Slieve Gallion has an elevation of 1730 feet above the level of the sea; the surrounding scenery is strongly diversified and in some parts very picturesque. The principal seats are Lissan Park, the residence of Sir Thos. Staples, Bart., a noble mansion in an extensive demesne embellished with thriving plantations, an artificial sheet of water with cascades, and a picturesque bridge, built by the celebrated Ducart; Muff House, of the Rev. J. Molesworth Staples; and Crieve, of W. Maygill, Esq. The linen manufacture is carried on to a great extent by the whole of the population, who combine it with agricultural pursuits. The living is a rectory, in the diocese of Armagh, and in the patronage of the Lord-Primate: the tithes amount to £500. The glebe-house was built at an expense of £1313.14.5, of which £100 was a gift and £650 a loan from the late Board of First Fruits, in 1807, and the remainder was paid by the incumbent; the glebe comprises 87¼ statute acres, valued at £67.10 per annum. The church is a plain and very ancient structure, with an east window of stained glass. In the R. C. divisions the parish is the head of a union or district, comprising also part of the parish of Desertlyn; the chapel is a neat edifice. About 400 children are taught in five public schools, of which the parochial school, for which a house was built by the Rev. J. M. Staples, at an expense of £500, and a school at Grouse Lodge, for which a house was built by Mrs. Wright, who endowed it with an acre of land, are supported under the trustees of Erasmus Smith's charity; a school at Crevagh was built and is supported by Sir T. Staples, Bart., and one at Donaghbreaghy is aided by the Drapers' Company. There are also a private school, in which are about 30 children, and four Sunday schools.

MAGHERACROSS, a parish, partly in the barony of OMAGH, county of TYRONE, and partly in the barony of LURG, but chiefly in that of TYRKENNEDY, county of FERMANAGH, and province of ULSTER, 5½ miles (N. by E.) from Enniskillen, on the road to Omagh; containing 5313 inhabitants. It comprises, according to the Ordnance survey, 10,452¼ statute acres, of which 343¾ are in the barony of Omagh, 170¼ in Lurg, 71 water, and 7505 are applotted under the tithe act, and valued at £6015.2.9 per annum. About 50 acres are woodland, 1500 waste and bog, and the remainder good arable and pasture land; the soil is fertile, the system of agriculture improved, and there is a good supply of peat for fuel. The principal seats are Jamestown, the residence of G. Lendrum, Esq.; Crocknacrieve, of H. M. Richardson, Esq.; and Barn, of the Rev. J. Irwin. A large fair, chiefly for horses, is held on Feb. 12th at Ballinamallard. The living is a rectory and vicarage, in the diocese of Clogher, and in the patronage of the Bishop: the tithes amount to £328.4.2. There is no glebe-house; the glebe comprises 300 acres, valued at £176 per annum. The church is a plain neat edifice in good repair, and was erected about 50 years since. In the R. C. divisions the parish forms part of the union or district of Whitehall, or Derryvullen; the chapel is a small thatched building. There are places of worship for Wesleyan and Primitive Wesleyan Methodists in connection with the Established Church. About 400 children are taught in the parochial and six other public schools, of which a female school is supported by G. Lendrum, Esq.; and there are five private schools, in which are about 200 children; two Sunday schools, and a dispensary.

MOUNT-FIELD, an ecclesiastical district, in the barony of STRABANE, county of TYRONE, and province of ULSTER, 5 miles (E. N. E.) from Omagh, to which it has a penny-post, and on the river Shrule; containing 2634 inhabitants. It comprises 10,366¾ statute acres, chiefly in tillage. The late Sir William McMahon, Bart., made some progress in the erection of a town here, where fairs are to be established; and a new road has been opened through this district direct from Omagh to Belfast. The living is a perpetual curacy, in the diocese of Derry, and in the patronage of the Rector of Cappagh, of which parish it forms part. The curate receives a stipend of £75, of which £50 is paid by the rector, and £25 from Primate Boulter's augmentation fund. The church is a small but neat edifice with a lofty spire, erected in 1826 on the side of a mountain, at an expense of £830.15.4½, defrayed by the late Board of First Fruits. In the parochial and another public school, both aided by Lady McMahon, about 150 children are educated; about 70 children are taught in a private school; and there are three Sunday schools.

MOY, a market and post-town, and an ecclesiastical district, partly in the barony of O'NEILLAND WEST, county of ARMAGH, but chiefly in that of DUNGANNON, county of TYRONE, and province of ULSTER, 5¼ miles (N.) from Armagh, and 71¼ (N. by W.) from Dublin, on the mail coach road from Armagh to Dungannon; containing 6646 inhabitants, of which number, 902 are in the town. This place, commanding the chief pass of the river Blackwater, was a post of considerable importance during the wars in the reign of Elizabeth, and its intimate connection with Charlemont rendered it in succeeding reigns a station of much interest to the contending parties. The town is situated on the western bank of the Blackwater, over which is a bridge connecting it with the ancient borough of Charlemont; it consists principally of a square, or market-place, and one steep street, containing 172 houses, several of which are neatly built, and most are of modern character. A considerable trade in corn, timber, coal, slate, iron, and salt is carried on by means of the river Blackwater, which is navigable for vessels of 100 tons burden; and there are extensive bleach-greens near the town, where great quantities of linen are annually finished for the English market. The weaving of linen is also carried on to some extent, and there are several small potteries for earthenware of the coarser kind; but the inhabitants are chiefly employed in the trade of the river, and in agriculture. The Ulster canal, now in progress, passes through the parish and falls into the Blackwater a little below the town. The market, which has been recently established, is on Friday, and is well supplied with grain and provisions of all kinds; and fairs for live stock are held on the first Friday in every month, and are numerously attended, especially by horse-dealers. A very commodious market-house and a spacious market-place have been constructed by the Earl of Charlemont, who is the proprietor of the town. A constabulary police force has been stationed here; petty sessions are held on alternate Mondays; and a court for the manor of Charlemont and Moy, which has extensive jurisdiction in the counties of Armagh and Tyrone, is held occasionally by the seneschal.

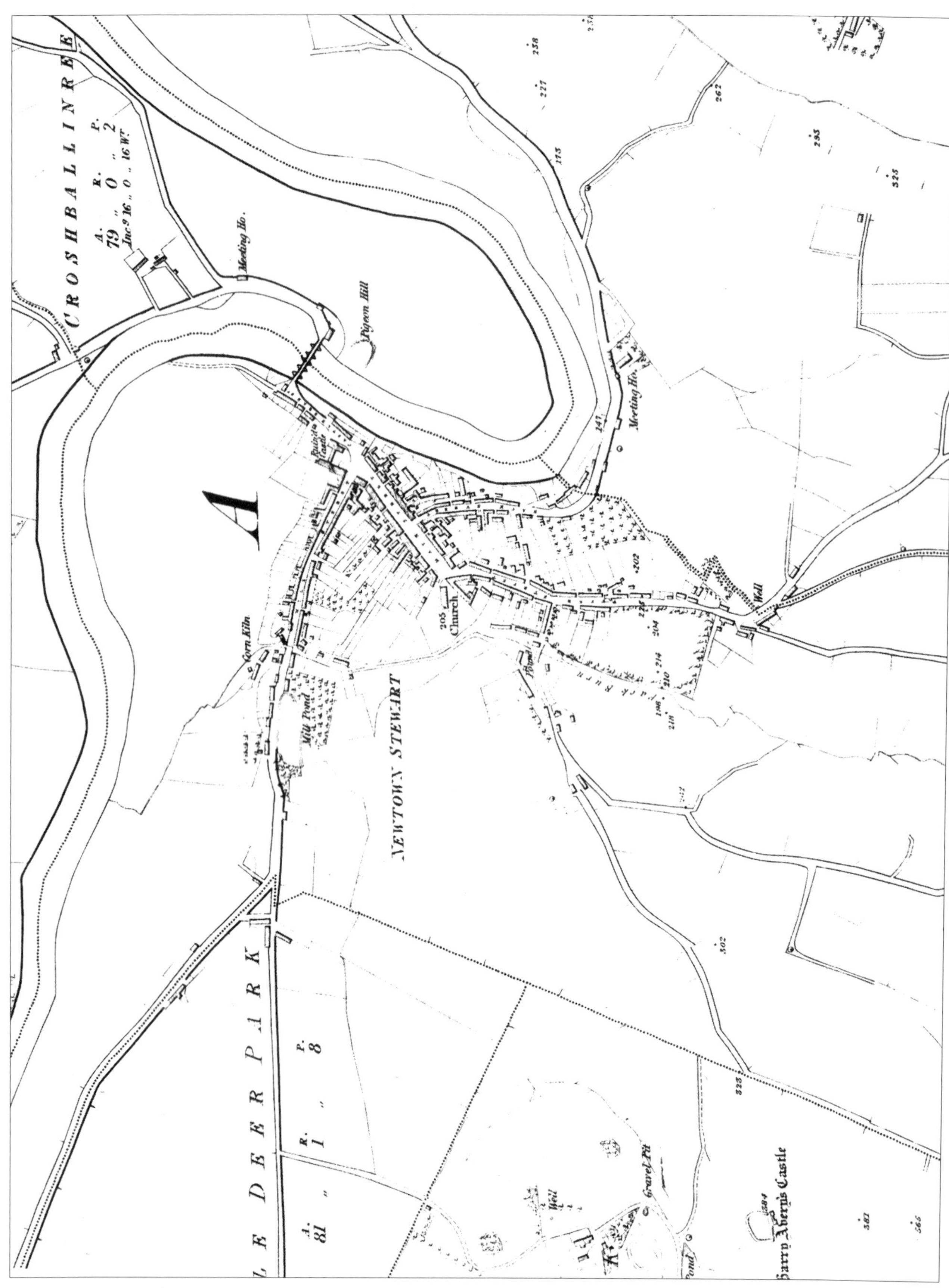

Newtownstewart. Part of the O.S. map of Co. Tyrone, sheet 17, published 1834 (reproduced at 140%).

The district parish was constituted in 1819, by separating 33 townlands from the parish of Clonfeacle, of which 27 are in the county of Tyrone, and 6 in the county of Armagh. The land, though of a light and gravelly nature, is productive under a good system of agriculture. Limestone is found in abundance and quarried for manure; sandstone, basalt and whinstone are found here alternating; and there are indications of coal in several places. In the vicinity of Grange fossil fish have been found in red sandstone, a fine specimen of one of which has been deposited in the museum of the Geological Society, London. The lands westward of the Blackwater are extremely fertile. There are several handsome seats, of which the principal are Argory, the residence of W. McGeough Bond, Esq.; the Grange, of Miss Thompson; and Grange Park, of H. Handcock, Esq. The living is a perpetual curacy, in the diocese of Armagh, and in the patronage of the Rector of Clonfeacle; the stipend is £100 per ann., of which £75 is paid by the rector, and £25 from Primate Boulter's augmentation fund. The glebe-house, towards which the late Board of First Fruits contributed a gift of £450 and a loan of £50, was built in 1820; and there are about 2 roods of glebe. The church, a small neat edifice in the early English style, with a square tower, was built in 1819, at an expense of £1569, of which £900 was a gift and £500 a loan from the same Board. In the R. C. divisions the parish forms part of the union of Clonfeacle; the chapel is a large and handsome edifice, recently erected. There are places of worship for the Society of Friends, Independents, and Wesleyan Methodists. About 300 children are taught in eight public schools, of which an infants' and a female school at Roxborough House are wholly supported by Lady Charlemont; an infants' and a female school at Argory were built and are supported by Mrs. McGeough Bond; a school for girls at Grange by Miss Thompson, and two at Goretown and Drummond by funds bequeathed by the late Lord Powerscourt.

NEWMILLS, a village, in the parish of TULLANISKIN, barony of DUNGANNON, county of TYRONE, and province of ULSTER, 3 miles (N. N. E.) from Dungannon, on the road to Cookstown; containing 105 inhabitants. It derives its name (formerly Tullaniskin) from two corn-mills erected here, in 1758, by the proprietor of the adjoining lands; and in 1831 comprised 20 houses, most of which are indifferently built. Here is the parochial church, a large and handsome edifice, in the later English style, with a square embattled tower; and nearly adjoining it is the parochial school, with a residence for the master, endowed with a portion of the glebe land, comprising one acre. The ruins of the ancient church adjoin the present edifice. – See TULLANISKEN.

NEWTOWN-SAVILLE, an ecclesiastical district, in the barony of CLOGHER, county of TYRONE, and province of ULSTER, 4½ miles (N.) from Clogher, on the new road from Dublin to Omagh; the population is returned with Clogher. The lands were part of those granted by Jas. I., in 1610, to Sir W. Cope, then called Derrybard; and, in 1619, a bawn was built thereon. It comprises 13,768½ statute acres, and was formed, in 1820, by disuniting 29 townlands from the parish of Clogher, in the manors of Cecil and Cope, at which time the district was an entire waste of unenclosed and uncultivated common, having been since reclaimed by the judicious management of the proprietor. The land varies in quality, some being light, some indifferent, and some good, but there is none of the best description; a small portion is mountain: yet, in consequence of its judicious management, where nothing but bog and heath was to be found 20 years since, crops of corn, flax, and potatoes, and the richest verdure, are now general. The inhabitants combine spinning and weaving with agricultural pursuits. There are indications of coal, and pure specimens of carbonate of lead have been discovered: excellent freestone is found in several parts. Numerous escars run entirely through the district, curiously undulating, and rising into gentle swells consisting of sand and water-worn pebbles, principally of trap, greenstone, hornblende, quartz, porphyry and agate. The village is small, comprising only 17 poorly built houses: a court is held here, once a month, for the manor of Cecil and Cope, for the recovery of debts under 40s. Fairs were formerly held, but have been discontinued owing to the numerous quarrels to which they led. Cecil is the handsome residence of the Rev. F. Gervais, the spirited proprietor of the district; Raveagh, of Captain Edwards; and the glebe-house, of the Rev. H. A. Burke, around which are beautiful plantations.

The living is a perpetual cure, in the diocese of Clogher, and in the patronage of the Dean, who appropriates £60 per ann. towards the income of the curate. The glebe-house was erected in 1824, by aid of a gift of £450, and a loan of £50, from the late Board of First Fruits: the glebe comprises 15 acres, valued at £15 per annum. The church was built in 1815, at an expense of £895, of which the same Board gave £738, and the proprietor of the estate the residue: it is a neat edifice, in the Gothic style, with a lofty square tower. At Escragh is a R. C. chapel, and there is a meeting-house for Presbyterians in connection with the Associate Synod at Longridge. A school-house at Beltony, with a residence for the master and mistress, was built partly by the Rev. F. Gervais and partly by the trustees of Erasmus Smith's charity; the school is endowed with two acres of land by the Rev. F. Gervais. Escragh male and female school is principally supported by the perpetual curate; Lislee school is supported by R. W. Maxwell, Esq.; Tullyvernon school was built and is supported by the Rev. F. Gervais; and there is one at Escragh Bridge in connection with the National Board, in which divine service is every Sunday performed by the curate, as it is 3½ miles from the church.

NEWTOWN-STEWART, a market and post-town, in the parish of ARDSTRAW, barony of STRABANE, county of TYRONE, and province of ULSTER, 7¼ miles (N. W.) from Omagh, and 99¼ (N. N. W.) from Dublin, on the road to

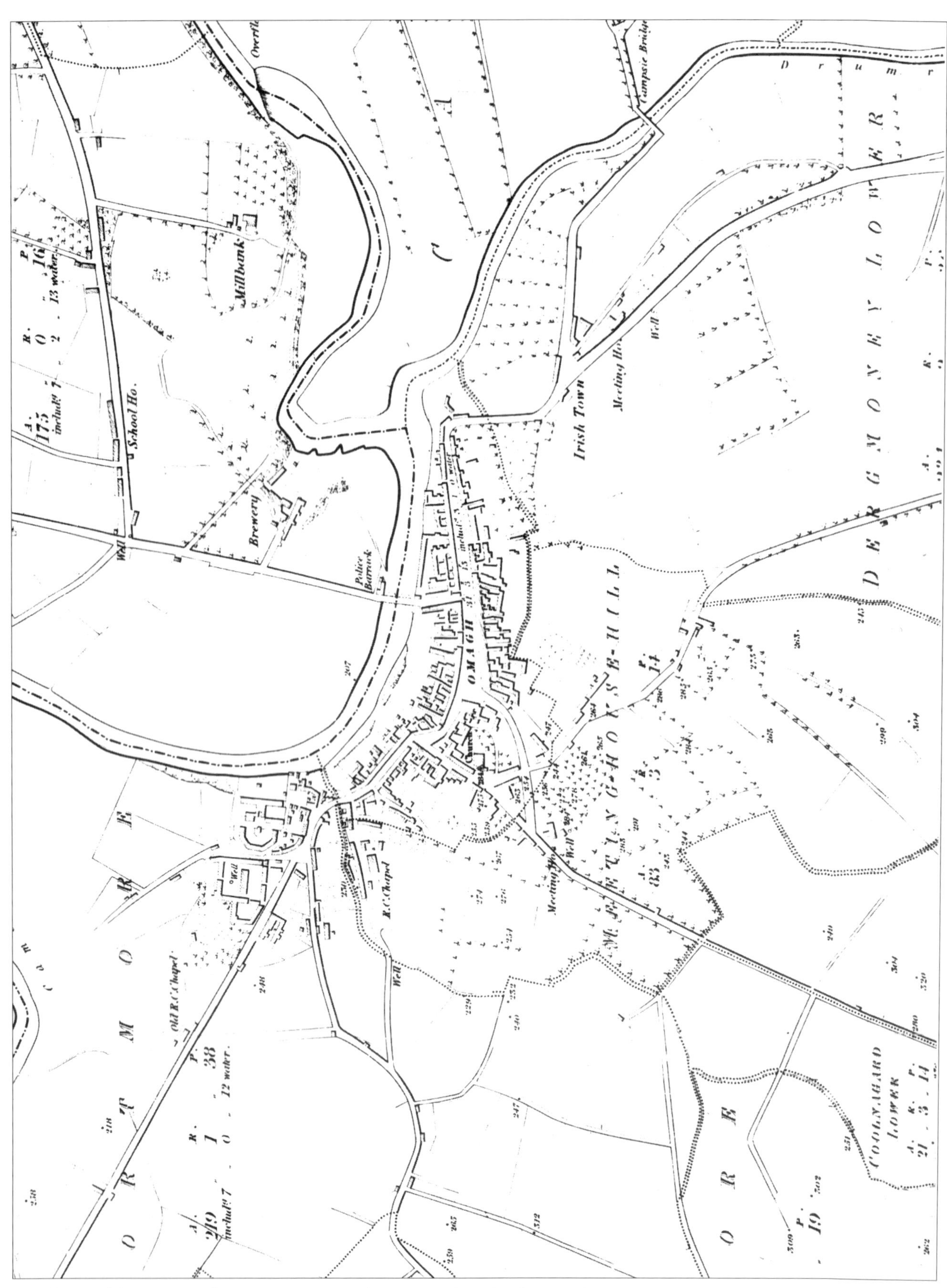

Omagh. Part of the O.S. map of Co. Tyrone, sheet 35, published 1834 (reproduced at 140%).

Londonderry; containing 1737 inhabitants. This town, which is beautifully situated on the western bank of the river Mourne, about halfway between Omagh and Strabane, and surrounded by the lofty mountains of Munterloney, was anciently called Lislas, and appears to have been a place of early importance, commanding the only pass through this extensive and mountainous district. The adjacent lands were granted by Jas. I., on the settlement of Ulster, to Sir J. Clapham, who not having complied with the conditions of the grant, the property became forfeited to the Crown, and was granted by Chas. I. to Sir W. Stewart, from whom the present town takes its name. Sir Phelim O'Nial, having obtained possession of the castle in 1641, cut off all communication with this part of Tyrone, and compelled the King's forces to retreat from every post they occupied in this part of the country. In the war of the Revolution, Jas. II. lodged for one night in the castle on his way to Londonderry, and also on his return from Lifford, and on leaving it the following morning, ordered it to be dismantled and the town to be burned, which orders were carried into effect, and the town continued in ruins till it was restored by one of the Stewart family in 1722. After its restoration it soon became a place of considerable trade, from its situation in the centre of the great linen district; and in 1727, Dr. John Hall, rector of Ardstraw, built a handsome church here at his own expense, which has ever since continued to be the parish church.

The town, which is the property of C. J. Gardiner, Esq., at present consists of three principal and three smaller streets, and contains 346 houses, which are neat and well built; the principal streets are well paved, and the inhabitants are amply supplied with water from a spring at the south-western end of the town, conveyed by pipes to the more respectable houses, and into public reservoirs in several parts of the town for the supply of the poorer inhabitants' in the main street are two good hotels. A considerable trade is derived from its situation on a great public thoroughfare, and many of the inhabitants are employed in the numerous limestone and freestone quarries in the neighbourhood, which are extensively worked. The limestone found on the lands of Baronscourt is of remarkably fine quality for building. The market, on Monday, is amply supplied with every kind of agricultural produce, and with unbleached linen. Fairs, which are numerously attended, are held on the last Monday in every month, and are chiefly for cattle, sheep, and pigs. A small constabulary police force is stationed in the town, and petty sessions are held monthly. The church is a large and handsome structure on a gentle eminence, and has a lofty and well-proportioned octagonal spire, which was added to it in 1803, in the time of the Rev. G. Hall, then rector, and afterwards Bishop of Dromore. There are also a R. C. chapel, two places of worship for Presbyterians and two for Wesleyan Methodists and a dispensary. In the town are the remains of the castle, which, with the exception of the roof, is nearly entire, forming a noble and highly interesting ruin. In the vicinity is Baronscourt, the seat of the Marquess of Abercorn, a stately mansion, situated in a widely extended demesne, combining much romantic and beautiful scenery, embellished with three spacious lakes, and enriched with fine timber. Moyle House, the residence of the Rev. R. H. Nash, D.D.; Newtown-Stewart Castle, of Major Crawford; and Cross House, of A. W. Colhoun, Esq., are also in the neighbourhood. Adjoining one end of the bridge is an ancient fort thrown up to defend the ford of the river; there is a similar one at Ardstraw bridge, and also at Moyle, to guard the ford of the river Glenally. There are also numerous other forts in the neighbourhood, and various cairns, which are more particularly noticed in the article on ARDSTRAW.

OMAGH, an assize, market and post-town, partly in the parish of CAPPAGH, but chiefly in that of DRUMRAGH, barony of OMAGH, county of TYRONE, and province of ULSTER, 26¼ miles (S. E.) from Londonderry, and 86 (N. N. W) from Dublin, on the mail road between these two cities; containing 2211 inhabitants. This place, which was anciently called Gigh-Magh and Oigh-Rath, signifying "the seat of the chiefs," is supposed to have owed its origin as a town to an abbey founded here in 792, which was converted into a house for the third order of Franciscans in 1464, and continued to flourish as such until the dissolution, when its site and possessions were granted to Sir Henry Piers. No notice is taken of the town as a fortress or place of defence until 1498, when Mac Art O'Nial, having taken up arms against the English government, fortified himself in the castles of Omy and Kinnard, upon which the Earl of Kildare, then Lord-Deputy, marched against the former, took it, razed it to the ground and compelled Mac Art to submit to the King's authority. In 1602, Lord Mountjoy, Lord-Deputy, placed a strong garrison in Omy, under the command of Sir Henry Docwra, whence he marched with all his forces against the Earl of Tyrone and succeeded in taking the whole of his magazines, military chest and other valuables; and after driving the discomfited Earl to Castle Roe, on the Bann, penetrated as far as Enniskillen. Tyrone never recovered after this defeat, and soon after made his final submission at Mellifont. On the plantation of Ulster in 1609, the town, with its surrounding district, was granted to Lord Castlehaven in the following divisions; 2000 acres at Addergoole, being Omagh and the adjoining townlands: 2000 acres at Fintona; 2000 at Brade and 3000 at Ravone. But this nobleman having neglected to erect castles and settle British subjects on the land, according to the articles of plantation, the grant reverted to the Crown; and the district of Addergoole was granted by Chas. I., in 1631, to James Mervyn, Esq., under the name of the manor of Arleston or Audleston; and the greater part of Fintona or Ballynahatty, to the same person, under the name of the manor of Touchet. Gen. Archdall, the descendant of the grantee, is now lord of the manor. In 1641, Sir Phelim O'Nial, shortly after the commencement of the war, marched against the castle of Omagh, which by an immediate surrender escaped the sufferings inflicted on those places in the county that made a more vigorous resistance. Jas. II. passed through the town in the spring of 1689, on his march northward to Strabane. The garrison which he placed here was soon afterwards driven out with great slaughter, but before they evacuated it the soldiers set it on fire and destroyed it, with the church and the castle built by Mervyn. In 1743, the town, having been rebuilt in the intermediate period, was again destroyed by fire, two houses only having escaped the flames. It was soon after rebuilt on a new plan, and has become a thriving and rapidly improving place.

It is situated on a gentle eminence on the southern bank of the river Stroule, here known by the name of the Drumragh water, a branch of the Foyle, and consists of three principal streets with several smaller branching from them: many of the houses are large and well built; the streets are paved, but not lighted; and the inhabitants have but a scanty supply of water, as there are no public fountains or wells. It is now the county town, a distinction formerly enjoyed by Dungannon, but at what time the change took place has not been ascertained, farther than that it occurred previously to 1768. It contains 715 houses, of which 585 are of respectable appearance and slated. The communication between the parts of the town in the parishes of Drumragh and Cappagh is maintained by.a fine bridge over the Stroule. A reading-room is furnished with newspapers, but not with periodicals or other literary works. The trade is very limited; the only manufactures are those of tobacco and of ale and beer, of which latter there is an extensive brewery, the produce of which has acquired some celebrity. The land in the vicinity is tolerably cultivated and well planted; the seats not noticed under the head of either of the parishes of which the town forms part, are New Grove, the residence of Sam. Galbraith, Esq.; and Mount-Pleasant, of the Rev. C. Cregan. The market, held on Saturday, is well supplied with provisions, and on alternate Saturdays brown linens are exposed for sale: a market-house was built in 1830, in which grain and vegetables are sold, and a very convenient range of shambles was opened in 1834. Fairs are held on the first Saturday of every month for all kinds of cattle.

The assizes for the county are held here; as are the quarter sessions for the baronies of Omagh and Strabane, alternately with the town of Strabane. A court baron is also held every third Thursday for the manor of Audleston, at which the seneschal of the lord of the manor presides: debts to the amount of £4 are recoverable in it. The court-house is a large and handsome edifice, erected on the highest ground in the town: it has in front a fine portico of four Doric columns, with the royal arms in the tympanum: the stone of which the front is formed was raised from the quarries of Kirlis, eight miles distant. On the northern side of the town is the county prison, built in 1804, and enlarged in 1822, according to a plan adapted to the better classification of the prisoners: it has a tread-mill, which is not applied to any profitable use. To the north of the gaol are the barracks, originally intended for artillery, but now enlarged and fitted up for infantry, being the depot and headquarters of the north-west military district; they contain accommodations for a field officer, 7 other commissioned officers, 110 privates and 60 horses, with an hospital for 12 patients. Here is a chief constabulary police station, with a barrack. The county infirmary was established here in 1796, and though considerably enlarged in 1810, its arrangements being still considered imperfect, further additions are now being made to it; a building for a fever hospital is also in progress. A dispensary, established in 1831, is supported in the usual manner. The parochial church of Drumragh, in the town, is a large and handsome edifice, erected in 1777, by the Mervyn family, and enlarged in 1820 with a north aisle and galleries, at the expense of the parish: it is in the Grecian style, with a lofty tower and spire, built at the expense of' Dr. Knox, late Bishop of Derry. In the town is a large and handsome R. C. chapel for the union or district of Drumragh and Omagh; there are also two meeting-houses for Presbyterians in connection with the Synod of Ulster, and two others belonging respectively to the Wesleyan and Primitive Methodists. The male and female parochial schools, near the church, were built and are supported by the rector and parishioners: there is also a school in connection with the Board of National Education. No trace of the ancient abbey is now in existence, and even time locality of its site is matter of doubt: a small fragment of the ruins of Castle Mervyn is still visible on the side of a brook near the pound. Dr. John Lawson, author of "Lectures on Oratory," was born in this town, in 1712.

ORITOR, a village, in the parish of KILDRESS, barony of DUNGANNON, county of TYRONE, and province of ULSTER, 3 miles (W.) from Cookstown, on the road from Omagh to Belfast; the population is returned with the parish. The village comprises 22 houses; fairs are held here on the second Wednesday in July, Aug. 3rd, Oct. 10th, and the third Wednesday in Nov., for cattle, sheep and pigs. A court for the manor of Oritor is held on the first Monday in each month, for the recovery of debts under 40s: its jurisdiction extends over 12 townlands in the parish of Kildress, which were granted by Jas. I. to the Annesley family, and are now the property of Lord Castle-Steuart. Here is a large Presbyterian meeting-house, erected in 1825.

POMEROY, a parish, in the barony of DUNGANNON, county of TYRONE, and province of ULSTER, 7¼ miles (N. W.) from Dungannon, on the road to Omagh; containing 7182 inhabitants, and comprising, according to the Ordnance survey, 15,951 statute acres. The district was granted by Jas. I. to Sir Arthur Chichester, then lord-deputy, and soon after was created a manor under the name of Manor Chichester. It was then altogether an extensive forest, some of the oaks of which, when cut down several years since, measured 29 feet in circumference. During the unsettled period of 1641 it was nearly stripped of its timber, and for many years after remained in a neglected state, until 1770, when the Rev. James Lowry undertook its management: he planted a great portion of the demesne, which now exhibits some very fine timber, and bequeathed a sum to erect the present mansion. In the demesne, which consists of 556 acres, is a small lake, the borders of which resemble in shape the coast of Ireland, on a scale of about one foot to a mile. Near it is a very abundant spring of water, strongly impregnated with carbonic acid gas. The village, which is small and meanly built, on the summit of a hill, consists of a square and a long street, the roadway of which having been cut down in order to diminish the ascent, has placed the houses on each side in an unsightly and even dangerous situation. A court leet and baron for the manor is held here every three weeks, in which debts to the amount of 40s. are recoverable: petty sessions are held on the third Wednesday in every month. It is a constabulary police station, and has a penny post to Dungannon and Omagh. Fairs are held on the second Tuesday of every month, for the sale of cattle; and two annual fairs on June 1st and Oct. 31st. The eastern and southern parts of the parish are fertile and well cultivated; the western, which forms part of the Altmore mountain, and comprises nearly 3000 acres, is uncultivated mountain and bog. Granite, basalt, quartz, limestone, freestone, clayslate, ironstone and coal have been found within its limits. The principal seats are Pomeroy House, the fine residence of R. W. Lowry, Esq., already noticed; Mulnagore Lodge, of Mrs. Stafford; Drummond Lodge, of J. Suter, Esq.; and the glebe, of the Rev. Thos. Twigg.

The parish was erected in 1775, by an order of council, at the application of Primate Robinson, by severing 41 townlands from that of Donaghmore: it is a rectory and vicarage, in the diocese of Armagh, and in the patronage of the Lord-Primate; the tithes amount to £389. The glebe-house, built in 1786 at an expense of £414, supplied by Primate Robinson, and enlarged in 1793 at a cost of £322 by the then incumbent, has a glebe of 560 statute acres (of which 145 are irreclaimable), valued at £198 per annum, also purchased by the same Primate: the gross value of the benefice, tithe and glebe included, is £586.17.1½ per ann. The townland of Gortfad, in this parish, forms part of the glebe of the rectory of Desertcreight. The church, built in 1775 on a site three miles from the village, is a handsome edifice, yet, though spacious, it does not afford sufficient accommodation for the congregation during the summer months. In the R. C. divisions the parish forms part of the union or district of Donaghmore, and has a chapel in the village of Pomeroy; where also there is a meeting-house for Seceders. The parochial school, situated near the church, was built and endowed with six acres of land by Primate Robinson, and is supported by the rector: there are schools at Pomeroy and Lisnaglees, in connection with the Board of National Education, in all of which are about 280 boys and 100 girls; also three private schools, in which are 100 boys and 70 girls, besides two Sunday schools, one supported by the rector, the other by R. W. Lowry, Esq. In the higher chain of the Aitmore mountains are the ruins of the castle erected by Sir Thos. Norris, in the reign of Elizabeth, to protect the mountain pass; and not far distant are the remains of two barracks, erected during the last century for stations for troops placed here to put down the bands of robbers that then infested the country.

PORTCLARE, a manor, in that part of the parish of ERRIGALTROUGH which is in the barony of CLOGHER, county of TYRONE, and province of ULSTER: the population is returned with the parish. This ancient district, which comprises 3000 acres of arable land and extends over the present towns of Aughnacloy and Augher, including the districts of Lismore and Garvey, with all the intermediate country, was granted, in 1613, by Jas. I. to Sir Thomas Ridgwaie, Knt., and confirmed in 1665 by Chas. II., who changed the name of the manor from Portclare to Favour Royal, by which it is at present known. A spacious and handsome mansion, called, after the estate, Favour Royal, was erected here by the proprietor, in 1670, but being destroyed in 1823 by an accidental fire, a larger and more magnificent structure was erected in 1825, by John Corry Moutray, Esq., its present resident proprietor. This mansion is situated on the bank of the river Blackwater, and is built of' freestone found on the estate, in the Elizabethan style, highly embellished with a noble portico, and with elegant architectural details; the demesne comprises 740 acres of fertile and highly cultivated land, and is finely diversified and richly wooded. Within it Mr. Moutray has erected a handsome cruciform church, in the later English style, with a square tower rising from the north-eastern angle, forming an interesting and beautiful object in the grounds, and corresponding in character with the house. It is built of the freestone procured on the estate, and was completed at an expense of £1000, for the accommodation of the inhabitants of the neighbourhood, who have no other church within a distance of three miles. The living is a donative, in the patronage of the founder, who has endowed it with £50 per ann. charged on his estate, to which the Ecclesiastical Commissioners have added £30, making the stipend of the minister £80 per annum. The church was consecrated on the 3rd of July, 1835, and is designated St. Mary's, Portclare.

SIX-MILE-CROSS, a village, in the parish of TERMONMAGUIRK, barony of OMAGH, county of TYRONE, and province of ULSTER, 8 miles (S. E.) from Omagh, on the road to Dungannon; containing 275 inhabitants. The parish church of Termon was erected here on establishing the village in 1634; it remained until the parish was divided, and the two churches of Termon and Clogherney were built. The village contains 65 meanly built houses, mostly thatched, in one small street, though some good houses have been lately built: it has a penny post to Omagh and Dungannon. A court for the manor of Fena is held here once a month, for the recovery of debts under 40s.

The village, manor, and lands around are the property of the Earl of Belmore. A very handsome church has recently been erected, by aid of a grant of £900 from the late Board of First Fruits; it is a district church, embracing several townlands of the parish and some of Errigal contiguous. Here is a meeting-house for Presbyterians in connection with the Associate Synod; and a male and female school. The Lords Glenawley had formerly their chief residence here, a small fragment of the castle being still in existence.

SKIRTS, or SKIRTS of URNEY, also called DERG, a parish, in the barony of OMAGH, county of TYRONE, and province of ULSTER, 8 miles (W.) from Newtown-Stewart, on the river Derg; containing, with the post-town of Castlederg, 3113 inhabitants. This parish, which in the ecclesiastical divisions is generally known as Derg, Derg-bridge, or Castlederg, was formerly considered to be included in the parishes of Urney and Ardstraw, but in 1812 the portion of the latter parish was claimed by its rector, and since that period the parish has been called the Skirts of Urney. It comprises 17 townlands, containing (together with the portion of Ardstraw before mentioned), according to the Ordnance survey, 14,286 statute acres. Petty sessions are held every second, and a court for the manor of Hastings every third, Saturday, at Castlederg, where also are held a monthly court for the manor of Ardstraw and a monthly fair. The living is a perpetual cure, in the diocese of Derry, and in the patronage of the Rector of Urney: the tithes of the 17 townlands, over which the cure extends, amount to £258.9.3. The glebe-house is a neat building, erected in 1795, at an expense of £200, of which £150 was a gift from the late Board of First Fruits; and there is a glebe of 30 Cunningham acres. The church is situated at Castlederg, which see. In the R. C. divisions the parish forms part of the union or district of Urney: the chapel is at Castlederg; and there is a place of worship for Presbyterians in connection with the Seceding Synod. About 270 children are educated in the national schools at Castlederg, Ganvaghan, Kilelean, and Mount Bernard, of which the first and last are patronised by Sir R. Ferguson, Bart.: there are also three private schools, in which are about 130 children; and three Sunday schools.

STEWARTSTOWN, a market and post-town, in the parish of DONAGHENRY, barony of DUNGANNON, county of TYRONE, and province of ULSTER, 16 miles (N.W.) from Armagh, and 82 (N. by W.) from Dublin, on the mail coach road to Coleraine; containing 1010 inhabitants. This place, also called Steuartstown, derives its name from its founder, Sir Andrew Steuart, to whom Jas. I. granted the surrounding district; in 1608 he erected here a strong bawn of limestone, which afterwards was converted into a castle, and laid the foundation of a village according to the conditions of the grant. The present town consists of a spacious square and three principal streets, and contains 204 houses, well built of stone and roofed with slate; many of the houses are large and handsome, several of modern erection, and the whole place has an appearance of cheerfulness and prosperity. The manufacture of linen cloth and a fabric called unions (a mixture of linen and cotton) is carried on to a considerable extent; and the town derives a good inland trade for the supply of the neighbourhood, and considerable traffic, from its situation on a great public thoroughfare. The market is on Wednesday; and fairs for cattle, sheep, and pigs are held on the first Wednesday in every month (O. S.). The market-house is a handsome building in the centre of the town. A constabulary police force is stationed here; a court is held monthly for the manor of Castlestewart, at which debts to the amount of 40s. are recoverable; and petty sessions on alternate Tuesdays. The parish church is situated in the town, in which are also a R. C. chapel, two places of worship for Presbyterians, some large school-houses, and a dispensary. There are some remains of the old castle, but they have long been in a neglected state, and retain scarcely any traces of their original character. The country around exhibits much picturesque scenery, and is embellished with several handsome seats. About two miles from the town, in an extensive and improved demesne, with a fine park, is Stewart Hall, the seat of the Earl of Castle-Steuart, who derives his titles of baron and earl from this place.

STRABANE, an incorporated market and post-town (formerly a parliamentary borough), partly in the parishes of LECKPATRICK and URNEY, but chiefly in that of CAMUS-JUXTA-MORNE, barony of STRABANE, county of TYRONE, and province of ULSTER, 12 miles (S. S. W.) from Londonderry, 14¼ (N. W. by N.) from Omagh, and 107 (N. N. W.) from Dublin, on the mail coach road, and at its junction with that from Sligo, to Londonderry; containing 4700 inhabitants. Little notice of this place occurs prior to the 14th century, when a Franciscan monastery of the third order was founded here, which flourished only for a short time and ultimately merged into the abbey of Scarvaherin. This place was formerly in the district of Munterlony, but on the formation of part of the territory of Tir-Owen into the county of Tyrone, in 1591, it was made the head of the barony of Strabane. It appears, however, to have been merely an inconsiderable village till the plantation of Ulster by Jas. I., who, in 1611, granted the surrounding district to the Earl of Abercorn, who, previously to the year 1619, had erected a strong castle, around which he built a town of 80 houses, and settled 120 families, mustering together 200 armed men, for whom, in 1612, he obtained a charter of incorporation and other valuable privileges. He also erected three water-mills for grinding corn, and began to build a church. The town now ranks the third in the county, and promises to rival Omagh and even Dungannon. In 1641 it was besieged by Sir Phelim O'Nial, who took the castle and carried off the Countess of Abercorn and detained her as a prisoner till ransomed by the payment of a large sum of money. The Irish forces of O'Nial remained for a long time in possession of the castle, till it was at length retaken by the troops under the command of Col. Sir G. Hamilton, brother

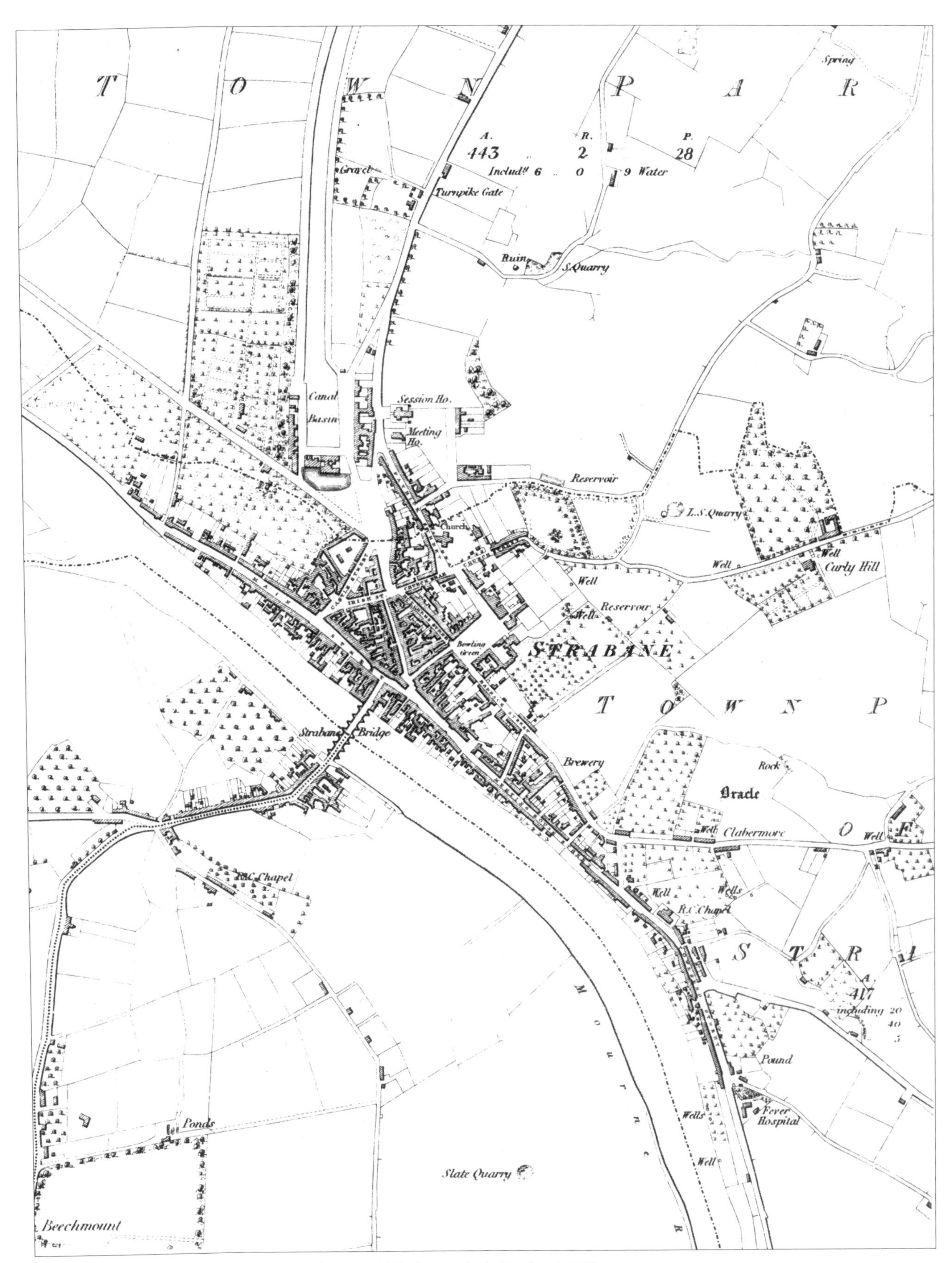

Strabane. Part of the O.S. map of Co. Tyrone, sheet 5, published 1834 (reproduced at 140%).

of the Earl of Abercorn. In the war of the Revolution it was garrisoned for the Protestants, and on the 14th of March, 1688, afforded an asylum to the inhabitants of Dungannon and its neighbourhood, when abandoned by Col. Lundy; but in the following month it fell into the hands of the enemy, and on the 18th of April, Jas. II. arrived in person at this place and passed the ford to Lifford. From Lifford he proceeded to Londonderry, but finding that city in a state much more opposed to his views than he had anticipated, he returned to the castle of Strabane on the 20th, and received a deputation who surrendered to him the fort of Culmore.

The town is situated on the river Morne, near its confluence with the Fin, and consists of ten principal and several smaller streets; it contained 836 houses in 1831, since which time several more have been built and great improvements made, among which are the newly constructed roads to Londonderry, Newtown-Stewart, and Castlefin. The houses generally are well built and many of them are spacious and handsome, especially in such of the principal streets as are of more recent formation. Over the river Morne is a bridge, which has been recently widened; and over the Foyle, by which name the united rivers Morne and Fin are called, is another, to which three arches have been added. The appearance of the town is strikingly prepossessing, and the effect is further increased by the thriving orchards attached to the houses and in the immediate neighbourhood, producing apples, pears, and cherries in abundance. The manufacture of corduroys and other cotton fabrics was formerly carried on here to a limited extent; and in the neighbourhood are several bleach-greens, none of which at present are in operation. The principal trade is in grain, of which more is sold in this market than in any other in the county; great quantities are annually shipped for Liverpool, Glasgow, and other ports. The provision trade is also very extensive; more than 1000 tierces of beef and 2000 barrels of pork are annually cured here for the English market. There is a large ale and beer brewery of some celebrity, chiefly for the supply of the town and neighbourhood, yet considerable quantities are sent to Londonderry, Coleraine, Lifford, Donegal, and other places.

The chief exports are wheat, oats, barley, flax, pork, beef, butter, eggs, and poultry; and the imports, timber, iron, staves, groceries, and articles of general merchandise. The trade of the place is much facilitated by the Strabane canal, which meets the river Foyle at Leck, about three miles below the town, and is navigable for vessels of 40 tons' burden. It was constructed in 1793, at an expense of £12,000, defrayed by a grant from the Commissioners of Inland Navigation, aided by the Marquess of Abercorn, and brought into the town by two locks. On its banks are large ranges of warehouses and stores for grain, with wharfs and commodious quays, well adapted to the carrying on of an extensive trade. Near the town, on the river Foyle, is a salmon fishery, which belonged formerly to the corporation of Lifford, but is now the property of the Earl of Erne; great quantities of fish are annually taken. The market is on Tuesday, and is largely supplied with corn, provisions, and brown linen; and fairs are held on the first Thursday in every month, and on the 12th of May and November (O. S.), for horses, cattle, sheep, and pigs. The market-house is a commodious and handsome building; and the grain and meal markets, built by the corporation in 1823, are large and well arranged; over the principal gateway are the arms of Strabane.

Jas. I., in the 10th of his reign, made the town a free borough, and granted the inhabitants a charter of incorporation, by the title of the "Provost, Free Burgesses and Commonalty of the borough of Strabane", with a weekly market, two annual fairs, and the power of rcturning two members to the Irish parliament, holding a court of record and other privileges. By this charter the corporation consists of a provost, twelve free burgesses, and an indefinite number of freemen, assisted by a recorder, chamberlain, two serjeants-at-mace, and other officers. The provost, who is also clerk of the market and judge of the borough court, is annually elected on the 29th of Sept. from the free burgesses, by a majority of that body; if no election takes place, he continues in office till the next appointment. The free burgesses fill up vacancies as they occur, from the freemen, by the provost and a majority of their own body, and also admit freemen by favour only. The corporation continued to return two members to the Irish parliament till the union, when the borough was disfranchised. The court of record held before the provost had jurisdiction to the amount of 5 marks, but after the abolition of arrest for small sums, the business of the court declined, and it has since fallen into disuse. The corporation has no property but the tolls of the fairs and market, which are under their regulation. There is a chief constabulary police station; the quarter sessions for the county are held here in April and October; petty sessions on alternate Tuesdays, and a court for the manor of Strabane, every month, at which debts to the amount of 40s. are recoverable. The church built here in 1619, by the Earl of Abercorn, has, since the parliamentary war of 1641, been the parish church of Camus-juxta-Morne: it has been enlarged from time to time and is now a handsome cruciform structure in the Grecian style, with a cupola, and the arms of the founder over the principal entrance. There are a spacious R. C. chapel, and two places of worship for Presbyterians and two for Wesleyan and Primitive Methodists. A handsome school-house, with apartments for the master and mistress, was erected in 1826 by the Marquess of Abercorn, who endowed it with £40 per ann.; and there is a fever hospital, with a dispensary attached. About one mile from the town, on the road to Londonderry, is a chalybeate spring, containing iron, magnesia, and sulphur, held in solution by carbonic acid gas. Of the castle built by the Earl of Abercorn, nothing now remains; the site is occupied by a dwelling-house and merchant's stores. Strabane gives the inferior titles of Baron and Viscount to the Marquess of Abercorn.

TAMLAGHT, a parish, partly in the barony of LOUGHINSHOLIN, county of LONDONDERRY, but chiefly in that of DUNGANNON, county of TYRONE, and province of ULSTER, 3¼ miles (S. by E.) from Moneymore, on the roads from Toome to Moneymore and from Cookstown to Magherafelt and on the river Ballinderry; containing 2854 inhabitants. The river here forms the southern boundary of the county of Londonderry, and on its south bank, close to its junction with Lough Neagh, stands the village of Coagh, which is described under its own head. According to the Ordnance survey, the parish comprises 4954¾ statute acres, 2447¾ acres being in the barony of Dungannon, and 2507 in that of Loughinsholin, all fertile land, except about 300 acres of waste and bog: about two-thirds of the surface are arable and the rest meadow and pasture; there is no mountain land. The inhabitants combine with agriculture the weaving of linen cloth, here carried on to a great extent. There are several quarries of good limestone, much of which is burned for manure. A little westward of the church are seen strata of white limestone, which enter from Seagoe and Maralin, in the county of Down, pass under Lough Neagh, nearly due east and west, and here emerging from their subterranean bed, continue to the neighbourhood of Moneymore, and so on to the Magilligan strand. Here were formerly two extensive bleach-greens in full operation, neither of which is now worked.

Tamlaght was created a parish in 1783, by Primate Robinson, by separating 6 townlands from the parish of Ballyclog, in the barony of Dungannon, and 5½ from that of Ballinderry, in the barony of Loughinsholin: the Primate also built the church and purchased the glebe, with which he endowed it, together with the tithes of the 11½ townlands. The living is a rectory, in the diocese of Armagh, and in the patronage of the Lord-Primate; the tithes amount to £200. The glebe-house was built in 1781, at an expense of £496, of which £92 was a gift from the late Board of First Fruits, the residue having been supplied by the then incumbent. The church is a small plain edifice in the Londonderry portion of the parish. In Coagh is a meeting-house for Presbyterians in connection with the Synod of Ulster, of the second class; within the parish is a meeting-house for those in connection with the Associate Synod; and there are places of worship for Baptists and Wesleyan Methodists, the latter in the market-place of Coagh. The parochial schools at Tamlaght are supported by the rector, who also contributes to the support of a school at Aghery; and there is a school at Coagh, supported by W. L. Cunningham, Esq.; in these schools are about 280 children. There are also three private schools in which about 90 children are educated; and four Sunday schools. On the glebe stands a cromlech called Cloughtogel, composed of a stupendous table stone of granite, weighing 22 tons, raised 13 feet above the ground on six uprights of basalt, and under it there is a chamber or vault of considerable extent: there were formerly several other cromlechs connected with this, extending in a line due east and west, the whole surrounded by a circle of upright stones; but, in the process of fencing and other alterations, all have been removed except the first-named. In a field called the "Honey Mug," not far distant, is a large upright pillar of marble of a singular kind, beneath which is an artificial cave: and there are other remarkable stones in the neighbourhood.

TERMONAMUNGAN, a parish, in the barony of OMAGH, county of TYRONE, and province of ULSTER, 11 miles (S. W.) from Strabane, on the road from Pettigoe to Newtownstewart; containing 7253 inhabitants. This parish, which is situated on the river Derg, and bounded on the south by the Longfield mountains, comprises, according to the Ordnance survey, 45,399 statute acres, of which 288 are water, and 28,435 are applotted under the tithe act. The surface is mountainous and interspersed with several small lakes; not more than one-fourth of the land is in cultivation, but the mountains afford good pasturage for cattle. Limestone, freestone, whinstone and grauwacke are found in the valleys, and in some parts are indications of coal. The scenery is beautifully diversified; but the whole parish is deeply secluded, and there are but few gentlemen's seats: the principal are Derg Lodge, the residence of Sir R. A. Ferguson, Bart.; Lisnacloon, of J. Anderson, Esq.; and Woodside, of the Rev. George Nesbit, the rector. Several new lines of road have been opened, and others are in progress, which will greatly improve the district. Fairs are held in the small village of Killeter, on the 21st of May, July, September, and Nov.; and a constabulary police force is stationed there. The living is a rectory, in the diocese of Derry, and in the patronage of the Bishop: the tithes amount to £438.9, and the glebe comprises 20 acres, valued at £161 per annum. The church, for the erection of which the late Board of First Fruits granted a loan of £600, is a neat small edifice with a bell turret; it was built in 1822 on a site near the village, and on the south bank of the river Derg. The R. C. parish is co-extensive with that of the Established Church; the chapel is at Aughryarn, and there is also an altar in the open air. There is a place of worship for Presbyterians in connection with the Synod of Ulster. About 400 children are taught in six public schools; and there are three private schools, in which are 130 children, and two Sunday schools.

TERMONMAGUIRK, or TARMON-McGUIRK a parish, partly in the barony of STRABANE, but chiefly in that of OMAGH, county of TYRONE, and province of ULSTER, 9 miles (S. E.) from Omagh, on the road to Dungannon and on the new line of road to Belfast; containing, with the village of Six-mile-cross (which is separately described), 10,307 inhabitants. The parish, which is situated in a mountainous district, comprises, according to the Ordnance survey, 4675¾ statute acres, of which 1352¾ are in the barony of Strabane, and the remainder in that of Omagh; of these 291¼ are water, and 31,817 are applotted under the tithe act. The land is in general of good quality, but there are some extensive tracts of mountain and bog that cannot be brought into cultivation. The system of agriculture is rapidly improving under the auspices of the rector and Sir Hugh Stewart, Bart.; the cultivation of wheat has been lately introduced and attended with success in sheltered situations. There is abundance of good freestone, with indications of coal in several parts; also an extensive range of quartz rock, in which have been found lead and copper ore. There are several very good houses in the parish, but the only seat is Loughmacrory, the handsome residence of Sir Hugh Stewart, Bart.; the principal lakes are Loughmacrory and Loughfinnee. Of the mountains, few have any great elevation; the highest is Carrickmore, on which the village, called by the country people the Rock, is built. Fairs are held there on the last Friday in every month. A portion of the parish, called the Eighteen Townlands, belongs to the Primate of Armagh, who by his seneschal holds a monthly court for his manor of Tonnen, at Nine-mile-house, for the recovery of debts under £10; and a court for the manor of Fena is held at Six-mile-cross, for debts under 40s.

The living is a rectory and vicarage, in the diocese of Armagh, and in the patronage of the Marquess of Waterford: the tithes amount to £803.1.6$^1/_2$. The glebe-house was built in 1815, at an expense of £3293.1.7$^1/_4$, British, of which £100 was a gift and £1500 a loan from the late Board of First Fruits, and the remainder was defrayed by the incumbent; the glebe comprises 1459 acres, valued at £680.13.4 per annum. The church, for the repair of which the Ecclesiastical Commissioners have lately granted £198, is a spacious edifice with a square tower, towards the erection of which, in 1786, the late Board of First Fruits contributed a gift of £500. A large church is now in progress of erection at Six-mile-cross, to which will be attached a district comprising several townlands of this parish and the parish of Errigal-keroge, the church of which is 9 miles distant; in the meantime divine service is performed in the Presbyterian chapel every Sunday before the Presbyterian congregation assembles. The R. C. parish is co-extensive with that of the Established Church: there are three chapels, situated respectively at Creggan, Loughmacrory, and Rocktown, and an altar at which the R. C. clergy of the parish of Cloghany officiate. There is a place of worship for Seceders of the first class at Six-mile-cross. About 1200 children are taught in ten public schools, of which the parochial school is supported by the rector, a school at Loughmacrory by Sir Hugh Stewart, and a school at Cloghfin by Col. Verner; there are also four private schools, in which are about 200 children, and 13 Sunday schools, and a dispensary.

In the townland of Sluggan, on a mountain close to the road from Dungannon to Pomeroy, is preserved an ancient bell, called the Clogh or Termon, much corroded by time, which is said to have been found among the ruins of a church by one of the McGuirks; there are many traditionary records concerning it, and it is still occasionally used in cases of solemn asseveration. About a mile to the south of the church is the isolated hill of Drummisk, on which Jas. II. encamped on his return from Strabane, in 1689, and whence he marched towards Armagh. Adjoining the village are the picturesque remains of the old church of Termon, the side walls and eastern gable of which are nearly perfect; the windows are of beautiful design, and the building appears to have been an elegant specimen of the decorated English style; the cemetery is still used as a favourite burial-place by the R. C. parishioners; near it is a separate burial-place for children, and within a quarter of a mile is one exclusively for women. On the glebe are the remains of a fallen cromlech, the table stone of which is entire and of very large dimensions; and there are several forts in various parts of the parish.

TRILLICK, a market-town, in the parish of KILSKERRY, barony of OMAGH, county of TYRONE, and province of ULSTER, 9 miles (N. by E.) from Enniskillen, on the road to Omagh, to both which places it has a penny post: the population is returned with the parish. It owes its origin to the family of Mervyn, who settled at the neighbouring castle of Mervyn in the reign of Jas. I., and is a small but very improving town, being a convenient stage from Enniskillen, and having an excellent hotel. The surrounding district is undulating and hilly and is embellished with several lakes: the land in cultivation is generally fertile, and a large tract of wasteland has lately been reclaimed. Here is a good market-house, recently repaired by Gen. Mervyn Archdall, of Trillick Lodge, the proprietor of the town and adjacent lands, in which a market is held every Tuesday, chiefly for butter and provisions; and there is a fair on the 14th of every month. This is a constabulary police station; petty sessions are held on alternate Mondays; and courts leet and baron every three weeks, for the recovery of debts under 50s. Here are meeting-houses for Wesleyan and Primitive Methodists, in the former of which also divine service is performed by the clergyman of the Established Church, monthly in winter and once a fortnight in summer. No vestiges are discernible of the abbey said to have been founded here in the 7th century; but near the town are the ruins of Castle Mervyn.

TULLAGHOG, a village, in the parish of DESERTCREIGHT, barony of DUNGANNON, county of TYRONE, and province of ULSTER, 2$^1/_4$ miles (S. E.) from Cookstown, on the road from Stewartstown to Coleraine; containing 137 inhabitants. This place, though now an insignificant village, was of regal importance at an early period: on the summit of a gentle eminence, a little westward from the village, is a large circular encampment, surrounded by deep fosses and earthworks, on which stood the princely residence of the ancient clan of O'Haedhagain, or O'Hagan; in this fortress the kings of Ulster were solemnly inaugurated into the style and authority of "The O'Nial." The Earl of Tyrone retired into this stronghold when retreating before the victorious army of Elizabeth; and here, in 1602, the Lord-Deputy Mountjoy remained for some time, and broke in pieces the strong chair of stone in which the kings of Ulster had been crowned. On June 27th, 1603, Sir Garrett More had here the first audience with the Earl of Tyrone, the last prince of the O'Nial race; and two days afterwards Tyrone left this fortress, and on the 30th, at Mellifont abbey, submitted to the English government; on the same day he received a pardon, and was shortly afterwards restored to his earldom and possessions. All that remains of this regal city is the fortress before noticed: a great number of unhewn blocks of limestone lie scattered around, but the last vestige of the regal chair has been carried away, though there were pieces of it in the orchard belonging to the glebe-house so lately as 1776. The fortress is covered with brambles and full-grown forest trees: it forms part of the glebe of Desertereight. The village comprises 29 houses, among which are handsome male and female schools, with residences for the master and mistress, built and supported by John Lindesay, Esq. Four fairs are held during the year. Close adjoining it is the site of the ancient priory of Donarisk, founded by one of the O'Hagans in 1294, of which nothing remains but the cemetery, the ancient burial-place of the clan of O'Hagan, and more recently of the family of Lindesay: a remarkable tomb is erected to the memory of "Robert Lyndsay, Chiefe Harbeger to y King James."

TULLANISKEN, a parish, in the barony of DUNGANNON, county of TYRONE, and province of ULSTER, on the road from Dungannon to Stewartstown, and on the Tyrone canal; containing, with the post-town of Coal-Island (which see), 4102 inhabitants. This parish comprises, according to the Ordnance survey, 446 1¼ Statute acres, of which 26 are under water; the surface is remarkably undulating and the soil various; that part which is under tillage is generally productive of good corn crops and flax. At Derryvale, Torren Hill, and New Mills, are large greens for bleaching linen cloth, where about 20,000 pieces are annually finished, chiefly for the English markets. At Coal Island, Oghran, and New Mills, are also extensive iron-works, forges, and plating-mills, for the manufacture of spades, shovels, edge-tools, &c. At Coal Island also is a very large establishment for the manufacture of fire-bricks, pots for glass-houses, and crucibles, which was established in 1834 by two English gentlemen from Stourbridge: the greater part of the goods manufactured here, are for London, Liverpool and other principal manufacturing towns in Lancashire. Here are also extensive coal-works, earth-enware manufactories, and many other trades dependent on the above, all in full operation and productive of great benefit to this part of the country. The surrounding scenery is interesting and the land is well planted. Among the principal seats are Lisdhue, the residence of the Hon. A. G. Steuart; Bloomhill, of Jas. Scott, Esq.; Drumreagh, of W. Lowry, Esq.; Torren Hill, of J. S. Murray, Esq.; Beech Grove, of J. Pike, Esq.; Derryvale, of J. Davis, Esq.; and Tullanisken glebe, of the Rev. Robert Kingsmore.

The living is a rectory, in the diocese of Armagh, and in the patronage of the Lord-Primate; the tithes amount to £200. The glebe-house was built about 1791, at a cost of £813 British, of which £100 was a gift from the late Board of First Fruits. The old church was destroyed in the war of 1641; and in the 15th of Chas. II. this parish was united to that of Drumglass, and Tullanisken church remained in ruins until 1792, when Primate Robinson dissolved the union and erected the present church at New Mills, near the ancient one; it is in the later English style, with an embattled square tower, and was built at a cost of £553 British, of which £461 was a gift from the before-mentioned Board, £35 was raised by parochial assessment, and the residue by private subscription. In 1823 a gallery was added at an expense of £73, of which £40 was subscribed by individuals, the residue being raised by parochial assessment. In the R. C. divisions the parish is one of three forming the union or district of Drumglass, and has one small chapel. The parochial schools, at New Mills, near the church, are aided by the rector; the school-house was built in 1821, with a residence for the master, and is endowed with an acre of land from the glebe. A school at Creenagh is aided by an annual donation from Lord Castlesteuart: in these schools are about 180 children. There are also a school at Edendork and a private school. Near Lake Farlough is an ancient mansion named after it, distinguished as occupying the site of Tyrone's favourite camp; and a little westward from Tullanisken church, on the northern bank of the Torren, is a large and well-fortified encampment thrown up by Turlogh O'Nial. In the churchyard is a venerable ash tree, measuring 29 feet in circumference; and near Drumrea is a valuable sulphureous spring, much resorted to and highly beneficial in scorbutic cases. Ducart, the celebrated engineer, resided for some years in this parish, and under his direction the aqueducts, bridges, &c., were constructed, by the Board of Inland Navigation.

URNEY, a parish, partly in the barony of RAPHOE, county of DONEGAL, but chiefly in that of STRABANE, county of TYRONE, and province of ULSTER, 2 miles (S. S. W.) from Strabane; containing, with the village of Claudy and part of the town of Strabane (each separately described), 7277 inhabitants. This parish, comprising 14,489½ statute acres, according to the Ordnance survey, is bounded on the north-west by the county of Donegal, and is situated for the most part between the rivers Finn and Mourne, which, uniting at its northern extremity, form the Foyle. The greater portion of the land is remarkably fertile, and under its present improved treatment produces abundant crops of allkinds of grain: there is abundance of excellent limestone, which is extensively used both for building and agriculture; the bogs are greatly increasing in value, and the mountains afford excellent pasturage. The inhabitants combine with their rural employments, to which most attention is given, the manufacture of linen cloth: a large mill is now in progress of erection at Seeir, upon the Mourne river, for the spinning of linen yarn. The produce of the soil and of the manufactories finds a ready market at Strabane, and much of the grain is sent to Derry by the river Finn, in barks of from 60 to 80 tons burden. At the northern extremity of the parish is a bridge of twelve arches over the Foyle, leading to Lifford; another near the church, over the same river, leads to Donegal; and at Bridgetown a third of eight arches over the Mourne connects the parish with the thriving and commercial town of Strabane. It is partly within the manor of Strabane, and partly within that of Ardstraw, for the latter of which a court is held once a month at Castle-Derg. The vale of Urney is among the most fertile and highly cultivated parts of the county: the houses are in general well built, and have gardens and orchards attached to them; those of the higher classes are embellished with flourishing plantations. The principal seats are Urney Park, the residence of Lady Galbraith; Urney House, of the Rev. R. Hume; Fyfinn Lodge, of Conolly Gage, Esq.; Galany, of J. Smith, Esq.; Ballyfatton, of M. C. Hamilton, Esq.; and Castletown, of Major Semple.

The living is a rectory in the diocese of Derry, and in the patronage of the Bishop: the tithes amount to £700. The old glebe-house having been accidentally burnt, a new one was erected in 1798, during the incumbency and at the sole expense of Dr. Fowler, the present bishop of Ossory, who did not charge his successor with any portion of the outlay. The glebe of 286 Cunningham acres is in two portions; one, on which the glebe-house stands, contains 83 acres on the banks of the Finn, from the inundations of which river it is protected by an embankment 12 feet high and nearly a mile long; the other, called Rabstown, is let to tenants; the entire glebe is valued in the Commissioners' books at about £300 per ann. The church, in the vale of Urney, a handsome edifice in the Grecian style, built in 1734, underwent a thorough repair in 1809. The right of nomination to the perpetual cure of Skirts, or Derg, belongs to the incumbent of this benefce. In the R. C. divisions the parish is the head of a union or district, comprising this parish and that of Skirts. There are places of worship for Presbyterians at Somerville and Alt, the former in connection with the Synod of Ulster and the latter with the Associate or Seceding Synod. The male and female parochial schools, built on the glebe at the joint expense of the rector and parishioners, are wholly supported by the former, who also maintains a school at Alt; a female work school, also on the glebe, is supported by the rector's lady, and two schools at Sion and Tullywisker are aided by the Marquess of Abercorn: about 300 boys and 260 girls are taught in these schools. There are also two private schools, in which are 60 boys and 30 girls; and four Sunday schools. Andrew Sproule, Esq., in 1801, bequeathed £1000 to the rector and churchwardens for ever, in trust for the poor of the parish, the interest of which is annually distributed in winter clothing. The Hon. and most Rev. Dr. Beresford, late Archbishop of Tuam; the Rt. Rev. Dr. Forster, late Bishop of Kilmore; and the Rt. Rev. Dr. Fowler, the present Bishop of Ferns and Ossory, were successively rectors of Urney.

Acknowledgements

Grateful acknowledgement is due to the following for the use of illustrations in their possession: the Linen Hall Library for the two Lewis maps and the O.S. maps of Co. Fermanagh; the map library of the school of geography at QUB for the O.S. maps of Co. Tyrone; Fermanagh County Museum for the two Burgess views of Enniskillen and Devenish.

For their valuable assistance thanks must be expressed to Mr John Killen, Mrs Norah Essie, Mrs Margaret McNulty, Ms Maura Pringle, Mrs Angelique Bell , Mr Patrick McWilliams, Dr Helen Lanigan Wood, Mr Jack Johnston, and Dr W.E. Vaughan.